HANGING BRIDGE

HANGING BRIDGE

RACIAL VIOLENCE AND AMERICA'S CIVIL RIGHTS CENTURY

JASON MORGAN WARD

OXFORD
UNIVERSITY PRESS

OXFORD

UNIVERSITY PRESS

Oxford University Press is a department of the University of Oxford.
It furthers the University's objective of excellence in research, scholarship,
and education by publishing worldwide. Oxford is a registered trade mark of
Oxford University Press in the UK and certain other countries.

Published in the United States of America by Oxford University Press
198 Madison Avenue, New York, NY 10016, United States of America

Library of Congress Cataloging-in-Publication Data
Names: Ward, Jason Morgan.
Title: Hanging bridge : racial violence and America's civil rights century /
Jason Morgan Ward.
Description: Oxford : Oxford University Press, 2016. | Includes
bibliographical references and index.
Identifiers: LCCN 2015036630 | ISBN 9780199376568 (hardback : acid-free paper)
Subjects: LCSH: Lynching—Mississippi—Clarke County—History—20th century.
| African Americans—Violence against—Mississippi—Clarke
County—History—20th century. | Racism—Mississippi—Clarke
County—History—20th century. | African Americans—Civil
rights—Mississippi—Clarke County—History—20th century. | Civil rights
movements—Mississippi—Clarke County—History—20th century. | Clarke
County (Miss.)—Race relations—History—20th century. | Shubuta
(Miss.)—Race relations—History—20th century. | Shubuta
(Miss.)—Biography. | BISAC: HISTORY / North America. | HISTORY / United
States / State & Local / South (AL, AR, FL, GA, KY, LA, MS, NC, SC, TN, VA, WV).
Classification: LCC HV6465.M7 W27 2016 | DDC 364.1/34—dc23 LC record
available at http://lccn.loc.gov/2015036630

1 3 5 7 9 8 6 4 2
Printed by Sheridan, USA

For Mom and Dad

CONTENTS

ILLUSTRATIONS

ACKNOWLEDGMENTS

Glenda Gilmore first told me that I could, and should, write this book. Despite the fact that the Hanging Bridge had already distracted me from my dissertation for a couple of years, she believed in book 2 well before I finished book 1. Jonathan Holloway and Beverly Gage enabled my multitasking as well, and David Blight, John Demos, Jon Butler, and Stephen Pitti have never stopped cheering me on. Plenty of great teachers before graduate school, including Paul Ortiz, Wayne Lee, Sydney Nathans, Kristin Neuschel, John Herd Thompson, Melvin Peters, Charles Payne, Larry Goodwyn, and Peter Jocys, set me on the path.

Mississippi State University has stood behind this project. The personal interest and encouragement of my provost, Jerry Gilbert, is appreciated, as is the financial and logistical support provided by the College of Arts and Sciences. Deans Gary Myers and Greg Dunaway, and Associate Dean for Research Walter Diehl, provided timely and crucial assistance. A grant from the college's Humanities and Arts Research Program funded archival trips, and college staff—especially Carly Cummings—pulled off a minor miracle that allowed me to spend a year completing the manuscript in Philadelphia. My department head, Alan Marcus, has never wavered in his support of my research and writing, and Pam Wasson and Patsy Humphrey help keep my head screwed on straight. Colleagues within and beyond the department, especially Jim Giesen, Anne Marshall, Mark Hersey, Michael Williams, Alix Hui, Matt Lavine, Shalyn Claggett, Amanda Clay Powers, Donald Shaffer, K. C. Morrison, Shirley Hanshaw, Cade and Becky Smith, Chris Snyder, and Tommy Anderson, have provided encouragement and welcome distractions.

The generous and timely support of the University of Pennsylvania's Penn Humanities Forum allowed me to complete this project. Director Jim English called me with the good news. Interim Director Karen Beckman ably led a remarkable and diverse group and, most important, paired me up with Eric Schneider. Associate Director Jennifer Conway and Administrative Coordinator Sara Varney provided expert assistance and good cheer in equal measure, and my fellow Fellows—Bea Jauregui, Jessica Goethals, Shayna Silverstein, and office neighbor Lisa Homann—helped make the archives wing of the Penn Museum more than a writing cave.

Several institutions and colleagues provided opportunities to hone my skills and share my research. The Advanced Oral History Summer Institute, sponsored by the Regional Oral History Office at the University of California at Berkeley, helped to broaden my vision for the project. One of my first presentations took place at Shubuta's New Mt. Zion United Methodist Church, at a racial reconciliation event sponsored by the Mississippi Conference and the denomination's General Commission on Religion and Race. Margaret Burnham not only invited me to Boston to share my research with the Northeastern University School of Law's Civil Rights and Restorative Justice Project but also connected me with Samuel Kennedy-Smith, whose research into the 1942 lynchings uncovered sources that I had not found in years of research. Craig Friend convened a symposium on death in the American South at North Carolina State University, which resulted in an excellent collection, coedited with Lorri Glover, and provided a new lens for viewing this project. For their hospitality and support, I also thank the Millsaps College Friday Forum, Drew University's Colloquium in History and Culture, Elizabeth Herbin-Triant and the St. John's University Academic Lecture Series, Rob Riser and the University of West Alabama's Black Belt Symposium, and the Triangle African American History Colloquium.

When I set out to tell the story of a lynching bridge in rural Mississippi, I did not expect my research to span a dozen states and twice as many archives. Wherever I went, I encountered able assistance. I owe a special thanks to my home base, Mississippi State University's

Mitchell Memorial Library, which houses multiple archives and exceptionally helpful faculty and staff. Ryan Semmes in the Congressional and Political Research Center, and Mattie Abraham and Neil Guilbeau in Special Collections, provided guidance and helped track down permissions, while Randall McMillen digitized approximately a third of the photographs for this book in one fell swoop. The Mississippi Department of Archives and History, including the treasures housed in the Historic Preservation Division, proved once again to be a gold mine. Caroline Gray Primer, an MDAH employee who grew up near Shubuta, pointed me to local contacts and even hit the trail herself and shared some remarkable finds. Cindy Lawler at the University of Southern Mississippi's McCain Library and Archives went above and beyond to help me with photo reproductions and permissions. More distant archives, in particular Stanford's University Archives and Swarthmore College's Peace Collection, provided expert assistance long before I was able to visit in person.

Numerous people with direct connections to this story generously gave of their time through interviews, correspondence, and leads on sources. The Reverend James F. McRee provided my only living link to the 1942 lynchings as well as some remarkable insights from his years as a civil rights activist. Yahya Ibn Shabazz (formerly John Otis Sumrall) sat through multiple interviews and arranged an interview tour during a trip home. Gayle Graham Yates, a distinguished scholar and Shubuta native, generously shared sources from her own book on her hometown. She also led me to John Cumbler, who shared memories, correspondence, and photographs. Betty Chapman at Ced's Rib Shack pointed me to knowledgeable guides and revealing interviews. For sharing their time and their memories, I am indebted to Caroline Buxton Thomas, Charles Killingsworth, Patricia Killingsworth, Charles Hill, Gail Falk, Gregory Kaslo, Joseph Gelb, Jonathan Shapiro, Joseph Morse, Gerald Stern, Warren Black, MacArthur Gray, Wendy Mills Cassidy, Carrie Davis, Ruby Howze Ducksworth, and the staff of the Manuel-Goff Center—Clarke County's lone remaining Friends of Children of Mississippi Head Start program.

The expert advice and encouragement I received from fellow scholars never failed to astound. Joe Crespino and John Dittmer went to bat for the project at a crucial stage. Chris Waldrep mailed me a stack of FBI documents—the backbone of chapter 3—that I had had no luck finding on my own. William Sturkey whipped the first full draft into shape. Françoise Hamlin, Chris Myers Asch, Curtis Austin, and Stewart Tolnay read later drafts front to back. Stephen Berrey, Stephanie Rolph, Steve Prince, Sam Schaffer, Steve Kantrowitz, Crystal Sanders, Aram Goudsouzian, Kathleen Belew, Kidada Williams, Kenneth Janken, Annelise Orleck, Bruce Baker, and my first PhD student, Kevin Boland Johnson, provided crucial feedback along the way. Clarke County's own Kasey Mosley provided expert last-minute map advice.

While I still cannot explain exactly how or why Wendy Strothman decided to represent me, I am so glad that she did. Her guidance, along with Lauren MacLeod's encouragement and assistance, has been invaluable. I thank Daniel Sharfstein for facilitating the introduction—despite having never met me—and for his ongoing interest in my work. Brandon Proia at the University of North Carolina Press briefly inherited me from my former editor, David Perry, and both provided advice and support well beyond any professional obligation. At Oxford University Press, Susan Ferber did the same. My editor, Tim Bent, has maintained an unshakable confidence in this book and its author from jump, and offered his peerless counsel at every turn. Alyssa O'Connell will take the publishing world by storm, and I regret that I slowed her ascent with far too many e-mails. Gwen Colvin guided the book through production without a hitch. Christian Purdy patiently marked up and shopped a steady stream of op-eds on my behalf. Alice Thiede makes beautiful maps. Andrew Lichtenstein tromped through the outskirts of Shubuta with me and generously shared his photographs—including the one that graces the book's cover.

This project started years ago, long before I knew that it would become a book. Along the way, plenty of friends and colleagues helped me to get to this point. Because of Kat Charron, Adriane Lentz-Smith, Tammy Ingram, Julie Weise, Julia Irwin, Grace Leslie-Waksman, Eden Knudsen McLean, Dana Schaffer, Kirsten Weld, David Huyssen, Caitlin

Casey, Kathryn Gin Lum, Robin Morris, Brenda Santos, Rebecca McKenna Lundberg, Bill Rando, and Yvette Barnard, I miss New Haven every day. Kevin McKenna and Aaron Knight remind me of where we come from and how far we have come, and Matt Allen always answers the knock at the door. Matt Kull knows how deep it gets, in Mississippi and beyond. My students, from Ruleville Central Elementary School to Mississippi State University, remind me why this book matters.

My family—Greenes, Morgans, and Wards—make this thing I call a job possible. Larry and Margaret Greene always show up at the right time, and their love and support makes life and work easier and more meaningful. Miranda and Tom Callis provide a home away from home. From the top—Sam and Doris Perry Morgan, Max and Evelyn Strickland Ward—on down, my extended family has provided love and lodging along the way. Tim Tyson read every word, yet again, and Phil Morgan's perspective and advice is always appreciated. My sister, Brooke, has packed several lifetimes into this book's lifespan, yet she always has time to talk. The only native Mississippians in the family, Amos and Theo, showed up during the first chapter draft and final edits, respectively. They and their mother, Alison Collis Greene, put this project in perspective and, more important, gave me the best reasons to put it down. Alison has gone above and beyond not just because she believes in me but because she believes in this book. Finally, my parents have poured themselves out, both for my two home states and for me. I dedicate this book to them with gratitude and love.

"Mr. Ward, when are we going to learn black history?"
—Kadarius Maurice Cannon (1992–2002)

Mississippi Map by Alice Thiede

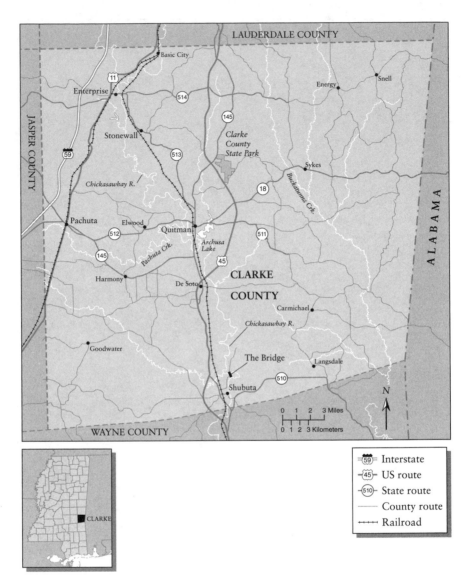

LAUDERDALE COUNTY

JASPER COUNTY

ALABAMA

Basic City

11

Enterprise

514

145

Snell

Energy

Clarke
County
State Park

Stonewall

513

Sykes

59

18

Chickasawhay R.

Buckatunna Crk.

Pachuta

Elwood

512

Quitman

145

Harmony

Pachuta Crk.

Archusa
Lake

511

45

CLARKE

COUNTY

Carmichael

De Soto

Chickasawhay R.

Goodwater

The Bridge

Langsdale

Shubuta

510

N

0 1 2   3 Miles
0 1 2 3 Kilometers

WAYNE COUNTY

CLARKE

Interstate
59

US route
45

State route
510

County route

Railroad

Clarke County Map by Alice Thiede

HANGING BRIDGE

INTRODUCTION

In June 1966, a black civil rights worker in Clarke County, Mississippi, met a fresh recruit at the local bus station. He loaded up John Cumbler, a white college student from Wisconsin, and took him for a ride. He drove south toward Shubuta, a small town of seven hundred located at the southern end of the county. Just north of town, John Otis Sumrall turned left onto a dirt road. Pocked with puddles, the route wound past a few clusters of cabins before narrowing into a densely wooded corridor. It seemed a road to nowhere, or at least nowhere one might want to go. A fork in the road revealed the Chickasawhay River, and a rusty bridge.[1]

The steel-framed span loomed thirty feet above the muddy water. At the far end of the hundred-foot deck, the forest swallowed up a dirt road that used to lead somewhere. Years of traffic rumbling across the bridge had worn parallel streaks into the deck, and heavy runner boards covered holes in rotted planks. Metal rails sagged in spots. Still, the reddish-brown truss beams on either side stood stiff and straight, and overhead braces cast shadows on the deck below. On that rusty frame, between lines of vertical rivets, someone had painted a skull and crossbones and scribbled: "Danger, This Is You" (fig. I.1).[2]

"This," Sumrall announced to Cumbler, his new recruit, "is where they hang the Negroes."

"The way he said it," Cumbler remembered, "it could have happened a hundred years ago, or last week."[3]

Now closed to traffic, the Hanging Bridge still stands. In 1918, nearly a century ago and just five weeks after Armistice Day, a white mob hanged four young blacks—two brothers and two sisters, both pregnant—from its rails. This was several days after their white boss

3

FIGURE 1.1
In the mid-1960s, local civil rights workers drove summer volunteers
out to Shubuta's upper river bridge "where they
hang the Negroes." Shubuta, Mississippi, 1966. Photograph by
John Cumbler. Courtesy of John Cumbler.

turned up dead. "People says they went down there to look at the bodies," a local woman recalled fifty years later, "and they still *see* those babies wiggling around in the bellies after those mothers was dead." When the National Association for the Advancement of Colored People (NAACP)—an organization less than ten years old at the time—demanded an investigation, Mississippi governor Theodore Bilbo told them to go to hell.[4]

Twenty-four years later, white vigilantes hanged Ernest Green and Charlie Lang—fourteen and fifteen respectively—after a white girl accused them of attempted rape. Newspapers nationwide ran photographs of the two boys' corpses and that same river bridge. "Shubuta Bridge's Toll Stands at Six Lynch Victims," the *Chicago Defender* announced. "Some place the figure at eight," the prominent black newspaper continued, "counting two unborn babies." In the wake of the latest atrocity, the *Defender* dispatched a black journalist to the nation's new

lynching capital. In Meridian, a small city forty miles north, the undercover reporter asked a black taxi driver for a ride to Shubuta. "No sir,"
the cabbie replied. "I'd just as soon go to hell as to go there."[5]

Local whites proved just as blunt. A white undercover investigator
sent to Clarke County in November 1942 spoke with a local farmer
who bragged of his town's most infamous landmark. "It's not in use
anymore as a bridge," he boasted. "We just keep it for stringing up niggers." Whites had to "mob" blacks from time to time, he explained, to
keep them in line. "We had a case of that here just recently," he added,
"two fourteen-year-old boys....We put four up during the last war."[6]

From Jim Crow's heyday to the earliest hints of its demise, the Shubuta
bridge cast its shadow on Mississippi's white supremacist regime and
the movement that ultimately overthrew it. In the World War I era, on
the heels of a three-decade campaign to disenfranchise and segregate
African Americans across the South, vigilantes used brutal violence to
deter challenges to white supremacy. A generation later, during World
War II, local whites again relied on racial terrorism to prop up an order
they claimed was under unprecedented attack. In both of these pivotal
moments, national attention and protest politics collided at a lonely
river bridge, where the pervasive violence of the twentieth-century
South rose sharply and tellingly to the surface.

The bridge boasted a history as gory as any lynching site in America,
but its symbolic power outlasted the atrocities that occurred there. While
local whites emphasized its usefulness in shoring up white supremacy,
civil rights supporters recognized its potential to galvanize protest. After
the 1942 lynchings, a black journalist branded the bridge a "monument to 'Judge Lynch.'" The "rickety old span," Walter Atkins argued,
"is a symbol of the South as much as magnolia blossoms or mint julep
colonels." With its grim history, as well as with the myths and legends
it inspired, the bridge reinforced white control and deterred black resistance. The structure was not just a monument but also an "altar" to
white supremacy, as the journalist put it, a place "to offer as sacrifices"
anyone who threatened that power. The river below the bridge flowed
gently, yet Atkins predicted "a long overdue flood that will smash and
sweep away Shubuta bridge and all it stands for."[7]

A generation after the 1942 lynchings, that flood finally hit. Civil rights workers, federal agents, and television reporters poured into the state in the mid-1960s, though the rising tide of protests and marches did not reach everywhere. Despite massive demonstrations in nearby places such as Meridian and Hattiesburg, Clarke County seemed left high and dry. Even as local activists and allies across the state challenged segregation and disenfranchisement, the Hanging Bridge still stood as a reminder of Jim Crow's past and violent potential. Few civil rights workers ever set foot in Clarke County. The Mississippi movement's high-water mark—1964's Freedom Summer—came and went with no Freedom Schools and no marches in Shubuta; only a handful of the county's black residents registered to vote.

Local people had a ready answer for anyone who wondered why the movement seemed to have passed them by. Old-timers across the county still spoke of a bottomless "blue hole" in the snaking Chickasawhay River, where whites had dumped black bodies. Far more mentioned the bridge that spanned the murky water. The myths could be just as muddy, the details dependent on the storyteller. However the events were mythologized, a fundamental truth remained. "Down in Clarke County," a Meridian movement leader recalled, "they lynched so many blacks." A white northern journalist who visited in the wake of the 1942 lynchings predicted that the mob impulse would die hard. "The lynching spirit means more than mob law," he warned. "It means the inability of so many white Southerners to keep their fists, their clubs, or their guns in their pockets when a colored person stands up for his legal rights."[8]

When black activists in Clarke County defied mobs and memory in pursuit of political power and economic opportunity, they provoked a new round of violent reprisals. In the process, they fixed outside attention on problems that persisted in the wake of the soaring speeches and legislative victories of the civil rights era. In this rural corner of Mississippi previously known for lynchings, those activists used that infamous reputation to focus national attention on ongoing battles against racial terrorism, grinding poverty, and government repression. Their story reaches back into generations when the rural South seemed all but cut off from national campaigns against discrimination and abuse, but grassroots activism in Clarke County also extends the story deep into the 1960s and beyond. Racial violence—both in bursts of savagery that sent tremors far beyond Mississippi's borders and in the everyday brutalities that sustained and outlived Jim Crow—connects the generations and geographies of America's civil rights century. In reclaiming these stories, we bridge the gap between ourselves and a past less distant than many care to admit. To acknowledge the role of violence in shaping our racial past is no guarantee that we can face honestly the ways in which it informs our racial present, but it is a place to start. In the history of lynching, *place* is often difficult to pin down with precision—hanging trees long since felled, killing fields reclaimed by nature, rivers and bayous that hide the dead. Yet one of America's most evocative and bloodstained lynching sites still spans a muddy river, and it still casts a shadow.

———

The Chickasawhay cuts through the center of Clarke County as it snakes south toward the Gulf of Mexico. Like the earliest local bridges, built before railroads and highways, Shubuta's upper river bridge connected the town to the prairie that stretches eastward to the Alabama line. Squeezed between the Red Clay Hills to the north and the Piney Woods to the south, this strip of land had been carved up by slaveholding pioneers seeking their fortune in the "old Southwest." As a series of Indian treaties opened up Mississippi to white settlers, Carolina migrants spilled over the Alabama line seeking to build a cotton kingdom from the ground up. In 1833, three years after the Choctaws ceded fifteen million acres in the Treaty of Dancing Rabbit Creek, white elites carved Clarke County out of the southern tip of this newly opened tract of land.[9]

Unlike the agricultural empire that sprouted along the Mississippi River, Clarke County was never destined to be a cotton kingdom—though not for lack of effort. Mississippi's southeastern counties were never as prosperous or politically powerful as the river counties to the west. Nevertheless, the rapid expansion of slavery along the southern frontier drove the young county's development. Clarke's population tripled between 1840 and 1860, and the proportion of enslaved residents increased from a third to nearly half of the total. While only four locals owned more than one hundred slaves each on the eve of the Civil War, the 1860 census counted one slaveholder for every two white families in the county.[10]

Antebellum plantation dreams lured migrants like Clement Lang, who inherited an estate near Shubuta when his sister married into another wealthy settler family. His "Prairie Palace," a six-columned Greek Revival mansion, could have held its own in the more prosperous ports along the Mississippi River. Such showy homes were rare in southeastern Mississippi. Yet the wistful lore surrounding Lang's impressive estate revealed how badly some whites pined for a glimmer of a glorious plantation past. The legends they passed down in later years—that the bachelor planter imported the columns from Europe, lorded over as many as five hundred slaves, and summoned them daily with a bell cast from six hundred silver dollars—fed this nostalgia for the "old easy life of plantation days."[11]

The relics around the Lang estate revealed less glamorous truths. A branding iron—"not for cattle," as a history buff conceded in a local newspaper feature—still hung by the doorframe. Beside the silver-dollar bell stood a stout little jailhouse "for unruly slaves." Brick cabins, each fitted with barred windows and doors that bolted from the outside, prevented overnight escapes. Nevertheless, a local historian maintained that Clarke County slaves, at Langsdale and elsewhere, "proved to be faithful to the end."[12]

Despite these paeans to "benevolent feudalism" and loyal slaves, evidence suggests that many local blacks seized their first chance at freedom. The Shubuta bridge, which linked Langsdale and other rural communities to town, lies just a few miles south of the diagonal swath that General William T. Sherman blazed across the state in early 1864. As legend has it, slaves on Clement Lang's plantation "saw the smoke of Quitman burning" after soldiers set fire to the county seat's mills and military hospital. Outside town, a slave led Union troops to a swampy thicket where his master hid with his human chattel and the family silver. Other slaveholders had fled already to escape the advancing armies that followed in their wake. A local Baptist preacher lit out for Louisiana and Texas with enslaved African Americans, including a young Allen Manning, in tow. "He been taught that they was jest like his work hosses...that it was all right to have slaves and treat them like he want to," Manning recalled. "He lived up to what he been taught."[13]

While some slave owners were prepared to travel to the ends of the earth to avoid emancipation, others parted bitterly with the enslaved and looked for new places to live. Shubuta, the largest local town spared from the destruction of Sherman's march, became a refuge for former slaveholders. Cradled between an easterly curve in the Chickasawhay River and a murky creek that branches off to the southwest, the town took its name from a Choctaw word for *smoky* or *dusky* water. River and rail were the lifeblood of Shubuta, at one point the most populous town on the line (fig. I.2) that connected the Alabama port city of Mobile to Meridian, Mississippi's largest city well into the twentieth century.[14]

Eucutta Street, Shubuta, Miss.

FIGURE I.2

Shubuta's prosperity peaked in the two decades before World War I. The largest town between Mobile, Alabama, and Meridian, Mississippi, Shubuta boasted a bustling commercial district. "Eucutta Street, Shubuta, Miss.," n.d., item 2422, Forrest L. Cooper Postcard Collection. Courtesy of the Mississippi Department of Archives and History.

Unlike the small-farmer dominated hill country and pinelands that surrounded it, Shubuta retained a majority of formerly enslaved African Americans. The town's ruling clique of merchants and mill owners were loath to embrace black freedom. "The whites find it very hard to labor for themselves, and do not care to pay the Freedmen for work" a northern white missionary and schoolteacher reported in 1868. Yet their former slaves, she added, "take pride in working and providing for *themselves*." Where government funds fell short, and when whites shut them out, local African Americans organized schools—in some cases year-round—to prepare their children for life as citizens. A century before Freedom Summer, the Freedmen's Bureau reported an "eminently successful" summer school session in Shubuta.[15]

The formerly enslaved embraced the privileges and the politics of freedom. Clarke County freedmen backed the state's Reconstruction government, an interracial political coalition that enraged the area's white supremacist Democrats. Local enthusiasm for the pro-Republican, pro-Reconstruction Loyal Leagues unsettled many ex-Confederates. In early 1868, Shubuta lawmen jailed a white Republican organizer "in the act of making loyal speeches and collecting a dollar a head off the negroes." Undaunted, African Americans continued to vote and run for office. "The radicals in Clark [sic] County have nominated an ignorant freedman to represent them," a Democratic paper complained in 1870.[16]

Faced with the reality of black political power, armed mobs fought to regain control. An 1871 race riot in nearby Meridian, in which white vigilantes killed dozens of blacks and ran out the white Republican mayor, foreshadowed a wave of anti-Reconstruction violence across the state. By mid-decade, white Democrats had overthrown Mississippi's biracial Republican government through fraud and force. The bloody counterrevolution prompted a congressional investigation, but white supremacists made no attempt to hide their intent. "Call it what you please," the *Shubuta Times* warned in 1876, "some call it the color line. It looks to us like the white line. It will be seen who in this emergency can choose to stand with the negroes against the whites. Mark them."[17]

Those who lived through Reconstruction recognized that violence undergirded white supremacy, and they handed down this lesson to future generations. Fifty years after the Confederate surrender at Appomattox, and three years before the first of the Hanging Bridge lynchings, Shubuta's hometown paper recounted whites' struggle against "a dangerous, ignorant foe...the negro." The editor recounted "amusing incidents," told to him by elderly locals, of prominent whites driving blacks from the polls with bricks, clubs, and guns. In another instance, vigilantes assaulted a black man for attending a white church service. "Having tied the negro," the editor noted, "they gave him a whipping he never forgot for many days." White violence, the article concluded, taught African Americans their place in the new order. "Every blow the white man struck the negro," the editor concluded, "later rebounded as a blessing to him."[18]

White supremacists bestowed these blessings freely, but black Mississippians clung fiercely to freedom's promise. "The vote is an awfully important thing," an elderly George W. Donald noted decades later. "I know it because I used to vote." Born into slavery in Clarke County, Donald cast his first ballot for Republican presidential candidate James Garfield in 1884, nearly a decade after white supremacist Democrats took back the state legislature. Six years later, African Americans in Clarke County ushered in 1890 with a rollicking anniversary celebration. "Emancipation is all the talk down here," a local black clergyman reported in January. "Emancipation for breakfast, dinner and supper."[19]

Black Mississippians did more than remember. In Clarke County and across the state, their determination to preserve their hard-won citizenship compelled white supremacists to usher in a slew of disenfranchisement schemes. Just a few months after black Clarke Countians kicked off the year with tributes to the Emancipation Proclamation, Mississippi's white Democrats gathered at the 1890 constitutional convention to accomplish what fraud and force alone had failed to do—eliminate African Americans from state politics. Through literacy tests, a poll tax, and a "good moral character" clause, they erected a web of obstacles to thwart black voters. Six years after George W. Donald cast his first ballot, county voters sent George L. Donald, a white man whose father once owned dozens of black Donalds, to represent them at the convention.[20]

White supremacists did not stop with disenfranchisement. The year following the 1890 constitutional convention, a train conductor ordered a black Shubuta pastor and his wife "into a smoking car, wherein white men were smoking, drinking, and telling vulgar jokes." A. B. Logan, who had purchased first-class tickets for himself and his wife, discovered the reality of the Jim Crow car. The state's new segregation laws called for separate accommodations on trains, but white men entered the newly established "colored" compartments at their leisure. "The race smarts under the sting of this injustice," the black Methodist *Southwestern Christian Advocate* reported in 1891. The New Orleans–based paper called on its readers across the Deep South to raise funds for a Supreme Court challenge. Five years later, when New Orleanian Homer Plessy's lawsuit reached Washington, the Court upheld the "separate but equal" laws that had spread to schools and other public accommodations.[21]

Violence proved essential to establishing this order, and lynching quickly emerged as a favored tactic. In the years between Mississippi's "redemption" from Reconstruction and the rise of Jim Crow, white vigilantes lynched scores of victims. Mobs in the Red Clay Hills, which comprised the northern half of Clarke County, killed at a rate unrivaled by other regions of the state. In the prairie and pinelands around Shubuta, white supremacists lynched political rivals, economic competitors, and suspected criminals with impunity. In 1883, a posse of twenty men seized a black man suspected in the murder of an "Irish peddler" and hanged him from a bridge in northern Clarke County. In 1890, Democrats in neighboring Jasper County assassinated F. M. B. Cook, a white Republican who courted black voters. Five years later, in her pioneering pamphlet *The Red Record*, native Mississippian and antilynching crusader Ida B. Wells provided ample evidence that her native state remained at the vanguard of southern racial violence.[22]

As white Mississippians laid the foundations for Jim Crow, locals in Shubuta built a new bridge. A Pratt truss, named for the Boston engineers who developed the style in the mid-nineteenth century, the span crossed a bend in the Chickasawhay that eventually curved in a southward crescent around the eastern edge of town. A sturdy and economical design common in turn-of-the-century Mississippi, the bridge's shoe-box-shaped skeleton of latticed steel beams and braces sat atop two sturdy concrete piers. Two miles north of Shubuta, the upper river bridge linked Clarke County's rural districts to a trading and shipping center in its heyday.[23]

Even before the bridge earned its infamous reputation, Shubuta's prosperity had already peaked. Farmers and lumbermen floated their harvests downstream when high water permitted, but the muddy river that flowed beneath the bridge remained a fickle artery. Every few years the Chickasawhay would flood. Knee-deep water covered the town's streets, and from their porches, residents watched debris and water moc-casins float by. At lower stages, the Chickasawhay became a gauntlet of snags and shoals, impassable by even the smallest skiffs. Just south of town, erosion from an eighty-foot bluff had narrowed the river's width to just fifteen feet. After spending several years and thousands of dol-lars in an attempt to "improve" the Chickasawhay, the federal govern-ment abandoned the project in 1916. Spanning a barely navigable river that connected steep banks choked with brush, the upper river bridge was no thoroughfare. The parallel highway and railroad bridges to the west skirted the river and crossed the smaller Shubuta Creek on their approach into town. Like the town itself, its impending decline delayed only by a war boom, the river bridge had passed its prime by World War I. Except for the trickle of country traffic that rumbled over it, the crossing was little more than a tranquil break in a densely wooded river bend (fig. I.3).[24]

Racial fear, like the river itself, occasionally overflowed. Just as concrete piers and steel beams kept the Hanging Bridge's rotting deck from col-lapsing into the muddy Chickasawhay, terror propped up Mississippi's caste system. Whites liked to boast that segregation and disenfranchise-ment had settled their racial problems, but Jim Crow demanded con-stant vigilance. Perceived threats to white control—political, economic, or social—continued to provoke deadly violence. The rash of racial terrorism that ushered in the twentieth century represented more than the birth pangs of a new order. Violence hovered over life in the Jim Crow South, and every outbreak served to remind African Americans

FIGURE 1.3

This postcard from the early twentieth century depicts the Chickasawhay
River as a scenic and viable waterway. Yet by World War I, federal
engineers had abandoned plans to "improve" the narrow and obstacle-
choked river for commercial shipping. "Shubuta on the Banks of the
Chickasawhay," n.d., item 2411, Forrest L. Cooper Postcard Collection.
Courtesy of the Mississippi Department of Archives and History.

of the price of stepping out of their prescribed place. The frequent yet
arbitrary nature of the violence gave it greater power, because black
southerners recognized that no one was immune from the mob's
wrath.

White supremacists also understood that violence served a higher
purpose than punishing individuals. Authorities and vigilantes alike
abused and executed blacks for offenses, real *or* imagined, that ranged
from trivial transgressions to serious crimes. Southern officials and newspapers typically depicted outbreaks of racial violence as open-and-shut
cases, complete with guilty black offenders, unidentifiable white assailants, and regrettable but justifiable retribution. Of course, the reality was
neither tidy nor reassuring. Frequently, black victims' greatest offense
was disregard for, or defiance of, the dictates of Jim Crow. In Shubuta,

where white vigilantes lynched six black victims in the span of twenty-four years, official accounts played up charges of murder and attempted rape. However, local African Americans—and anyone who dared to ask them—recognized that deeper fears fueled the killing.

Racial violence occurred with brutal regularity, but outbreaks increased at moments of crisis. During three eras of global war, racial turmoil erupted in Shubuta, Mississippi. International conflicts repeatedly opened a seemingly isolated community to the currents of world history and upset the status quo in the process. In each era—World War I, World War II, and Vietnam—whites in Shubuta and across the South worried that social and economic changes would disrupt their "way of life." In December 1918, reports that four black laborers had murdered their white employer seemed to confirm fears of a black uprising and the necessity of brutal violence. Twenty-four years later, economic anxieties and racial fears collided again when vigilantes lynched two adolescents accused of attempted rape. As black field hands and mill workers traded overalls for military uniforms, or migrated to cities in search of higher-paying defense jobs, local whites read of racial clashes in nearby cities and civil rights debates on Capitol Hill. In 1966, as the United States sank deeper into the Vietnam quagmire, racial violence erupted again in Shubuta—just a stone's throw from the Hanging Bridge.[25]

In each moment, African Americans recognized wartime threats to the racial status quo and seized opportunities to push for change. From Mississippi to Manhattan, African Americans exposed the contradictions between war rhetoric and grassroots realities. In 1918, and again in 1942, the United States embarked on global crusades to secure freedom and democracy while denying those privileges to millions back home. The World War I–era killings sparked a daring undercover investigation by an NAACP official just weeks before the fledgling organization's historic National Conference on Lynching. Twenty-four years after state and federal officials had ignored NAACP demands for an investigation, the Federal Bureau of Investigation (FBI) dispatched agents to probe the lynching at the Hanging Bridge. While the investigation yielded no convictions, concerns about America's global image and wartime unity forced the federal government to unprecedented action.

By the 1960s, the rumblings of Jim Crow–era civil rights campaigns had given way to a full-blown revolution. Seizing on the Civil Rights Acts of 1957 and 1960, African Americans in Clarke County and nearby Forrest County sparked the first federal voter discrimination lawsuits in civil rights–era Mississippi. After the passage of the Voting Rights Act of 1965, the number of black registered voters climbed from a tiny fraction to nearly half of the county's three thousand eligible African Americans in the span of a few weeks. Meanwhile, Clarke County became a testing ground for federal antipoverty programs staffed and administered by local black women. By 1966, a corner of Mississippi known previously for its lynch record had become a barometer for measuring the civil rights movement's political and economic impact. Much had changed, but racial violence persisted. As local blacks registered to vote, demanded access and service at local businesses, and collected paychecks for federal antipoverty work, their rising expectations sparked yet another round of attacks. And again, as the United States ramped up its Cold War crusade for freedom and democracy, wartime politics collided with civil rights protest. While that turmoil did not lead once again to the Hanging Bridge, the memory of past lynchings and the ongoing threat of violence hovered over the politics of race, citizenship, and economic opportunity in Shubuta and across the Deep South.

The grassroots activists of the 1960s shared with their forebears a vision of freedom shaped by racial violence, from legacies of white terrorism to the insidious brutalities of Jim Crow. The seeming disappearance of lynching suggested that Mississippi's ruling class had refined its strategies for maintaining power and fending off change. Yet in 1966, when African Americans in Shubuta launched a boycott of white-owned businesses and called for "black power" in the black-majority town, whites terrorized activists by night and beat demonstrators in broad daylight. The rise of a nonviolent mass movement, the passage of historic civil rights legislation, and the intervention of federal authorities inspired a backlash. After authorities locked up John Otis Sumrall, the fearless twenty-year-old who had introduced white volunteers to the nearby Hanging Bridge in 1966, an angry white crowd formed outside the county jail. Sitting in the same cell bloc where Ernest Green and Charlie Lang had waited in terror twenty-four years earlier, he listened through a barred window as angry whites milled about outside.

Across three generations, at three pivotal moments, a lonely river bridge became a symbol of a town's racial struggles and a nation's civil rights century. Racial violence connected an obscure corner of Mississippi to some of the most important activists, campaigns, and questions of the modern black freedom struggle. In Clarke County, local people did more than survive and endure. Through two world wars, they demonstrated Jim Crow's contradictions, vulnerabilities, and brutality. A generation later, as the nation's fleeting interest shifted to urban unrest, campus turmoil, and Vietnam, black Mississippians reminded America that Jim Crow's demise was incomplete. The ravages of that system—particularly poverty and its attendant ills—inflicted their own forms of violence long after the lynchings and beatings ended. The obstacles to freedom, as many rural black Mississippians defined it, were many. The country's commitment to overcoming these challenges had its limits.

The generations that followed Mississippi's civil rights era inherited an incomplete revolution and the echoes of a bloody past. Though abandoned and avoided, the Hanging Bridge still looms as a memorial to a story longer and more complex than many realize. The last lynchings there took place more than seventy years ago, and it is tempting to fill in the decades between then and now with an arc of inevitable progress. Yet the violence, in its various forms, did not end, whether we choose to remember it or not. When we put that forgotten violence at the heart of the story, we find a narrative more complicated than a steady march toward freedom. That story allows us to see more clearly black protest across generations, the connection between racial terrorism and subtler forms of repression, and a more truthful, if less triumphant, narrative.

PART I

1918

CHAPTER ONE

THE MOST ATROCIOUS
AFFAIR OF ITS KIND

On December 10, 1918, a sheriff's posse dragged Major Clark into the Meridian city jail. The men had driven nearly forty miles, and they would return home with a confession. Back in Clarke County, just outside of Shubuta, the twenty-two-year-old black farmhand's white boss lay dying from a shotgun blast. Local authorities hastily concluded that Clark had pulled the trigger, though so far their prisoner had steadfastly refused to confess. So the men stripped Clark naked, sat him atop a vise, and crammed his testicles between the metal jaws. As the vise tightened, Major Clark finally gave the men what they wanted. Ten days later, he swayed alongside three others, all suspected accomplices and all between the ages of sixteen and twenty-four, beneath a bridge over the Chickasawhay River.[1]

News of the quadruple lynching spread quickly. "Four Negroes Lynched by Mob at Shubuta," the *Jackson Daily News* reported. "Two of Shubuta Mob Victims Girls," announced a New Orleans paper. These dispatches, fed by local white officials to news offices in Mobile and Meridian, concluded that a confessed triggerman and his three accomplices had met their death "at the hands of unknown parties." None mentioned how authorities obtained Major Clark's confession, nor did they elaborate on the charges levied against the other three victims. Shaped and sanctioned by local authorities, the narrative that hit the newswires gave white Mississippians every reason to believe the story would quickly fade away. "The parties responsible for the execution of the negroes," the *Meridian Star* reported, "exercised extreme caution in carrying out their plans." Local white accounts dismissed both the possibility and the necessity of apprehending the vigilantes. "Shubuta was reported quiet today," the *Jackson Daily News* concluded, "No further trouble is anticipated."[2]

Walter White never believed the reports from Mississippi. In his New York office, the twenty-six-year-old NAACP staffer sat amid files stuffed with news clippings that told similar tales. Indeed, anyone who read the near-weekly lynching reports in 1918 could have recited the plot—the guilty black prisoners, the spontaneous and shadowy mob, the "overpowered" and blindfolded jailor, and the placid aftermath. The reports that White read in the New York papers, wired from Deep South news offices, simply summarized that all-to-familiar story. Yet these cursory descriptions raised White's ire and his eyebrows. The Shubuta mob had lynched *four* victims—Major Clark and his younger brother, Andrew, Maggie Howze and her younger sister, Alma—for the murder of Dr. E. L. Johnston, a wealthy landowner and retired dentist. As for motive, local authorities reported that Clark assassinated the Howze sisters' boss "at the instigation of one of the women who had had trouble with the dentist."[3]

That one word—*trouble*—caught the eye of a black newspaperman in Baltimore. W. T. Andrews, a Howard University–trained lawyer, had migrated from South Carolina in 1917 and established one of the nation's only black dailies. One of the first black editors to comment on the Shubuta lynchings, Andrews blasted the "Mississippi savages" two days before Christmas. He also questioned publicly the nature of the "trouble" that led Major Clark to murder a white man. Yet a black man in a Baltimore newspaper office relied on the same newswire reports as everyone else. Andrews needed facts to back up his suspicions, and southern white papers fell short. So he turned to the NAACP for help. "The reason for the killing of Dr. Johnson [sic]," he predicted, "would reveal that there was some facts that the lynchers desired to cover up."[4]

By the time Andrews's letter arrived in New York, Walter White had already boarded a southbound train. Nearly a year into his job at NAACP headquarters, the Atlanta native had spent much of those first months on the road. A former insurance agent and local NAACP branch leader, White had already proven himself a tireless recruiter and fearless investigator. Since February 1918, the light-skinned White had been infiltrating southern communities to probe lynchings and other abusive practices. Posing as a white man, the NAACP's secret weapon exposed the details that southern newspapers refused to print. In the process, he fueled the most visible national civil rights campaign in the association's brief history. On recruiting drives, he stirred black audiences with his "sleuthing" stories. Armed with his reports, the NAACP successfully lobbied congressmen to introduce a federal antilynching bill. Yet just weeks after Armistice Day ended fighting in Europe, the quadruple lynching in Mississippi obliterated any hope that southern mobs would stand down in the war's wake. The Shubuta lynchings lured White deep into the southern interior, a region hostile to, and largely untouched by, black activists' wartime organizing efforts. In rural Mississippi, the NAACP's future leader encountered southern blacks who defied the lynching routine. In telling their stories, he articulated themes that bound together black activists and local people in an ongoing battle against white supremacy.[5]

AN AGED AND RESPECTABLE WHITE CITIZEN

The press reports out of Shubuta told a tidy murder tale. This version of the story served not to indict a lynch mob, but rather to redeem the reputation of a dead white man and an entire community. According to the official account—authorized by local officials and wired nationwide by local reporters—some overzealous vigilantes had lynched four blacks for killing their white boss. Neither the murder victim nor the town bore any responsibility or guilt for the incident. "Those who participate in such affairs," a local editor concluded, "are not usually representative of the community in which they reside." The damage control began with the "wealthy retired dentist" whose death had sparked the lynching.[6]

Indeed, Dr. Everett Levega Johnston had once been a dentist. The "aged and respectable white citizen" came from one of the town's leading families. Although local papers failed to mention his lineage, Johnston's pedigree reached back to Clarke County's earliest days.

His great-grandfather, a federal Indian agent, had drafted a removal treaty that ceded eleven million acres of Choctaw land—a third of Mississippi's total area—to the United States government. Arista Johnston, E. L.'s father, took over the family farm after the Civil War and, by his own humble estimation, "made a success at it." By 1918, he farmed over two hundred acres, with an additional eight hundred acres of pasture and timberland. A Mississippi Delta cotton planter might scoff at these relatively modest holdings, but in a region of small farms and lumber mills Arista Johnston stood tall. Although the Civil War had cut short his formal education, Johnston earned the respect of Shubuta's small clique of professionals, merchants, and landowners. In 1899, Clarke County whites elected him to the first of three terms in the state legislature. By World War I, he had taken a turn as Shubuta's mayor and settled into a lengthy stint as a county supervisor.[7]

Arista Johnston's rise paralleled Shubuta's climb from a rough-and-tumble railroad stop to a bustling trade center. The largest town on the rail line connecting Mobile and Meridian, Shubuta served as a shipping point for cotton, lumber, and naval stores. By the turn of the century, the town's leading families had pooled their money to establish a thriving bank. Local lumber barons financed a twelve-mile railroad that hauled logs from forests east of town to Shubuta's sawmills. The town's largest lumber company, whose holdings included a foundry and machine shop, advertised its custom steam-fed engine in national trade journals. Despite its technological innovations, the Brownlee Lumber Company depended above all on cheap black labor. Along with its patented "Universal Twins" saw engines, the company boasted in a national machinery magazine, the mill required "three white men, 52 'niggers,' and 25 yoke of oxen" to churn out a steady stream of yellow pine boards. From the mills to the forests and the fields around town, Shubuta's white elite floated on a pool of cheap black labor. All week long, the area's black majority toiled as millworkers, farmhands, and maids. On Saturdays, black shoppers poured into Shubuta's bustling downtown to hand their meager wages right back.[8]

Despite its aristocratic veneer, Shubuta shared with neighboring towns a hard-edged racism shaped equally by the need for white control and the reality of economic rivalry. Poor and working-class whites, who competed for the crumbs that fell from the upper crust, guarded their racial privilege. Robert C. Weems, son of a wealthy Shubuta family and a boy during the World War I era, recalled that it "would infuriate the white carpenters" if a homeowner hired a black man for a repair job. "Every now and then," he recalled, "you'd hear about a black trades-man's tools getting stolen."[9]

For those fortunate enough to be born into Shubuta's leading fami-lies, black tradesmen posed no threat to their aspirations. Like his peers, Arista Johnston expected his sons to become college-educated professionals. And they did. E. L, followed by two younger brothers, graduated from Atlanta Dental College. By 1910, Johnston had set up his practice in downtown Mobile, married, and moved to the city's up-scale Spring Hill district. However, his life on the upper crust started to unravel. Rumors of Johnston's heavy drinking and "general inattention to business" spread back to Shubuta. By 1918, E. L.'s brother Ernest had relocated from Meridian to prop up his brother's floundering prac-tice. And E. L., his life and career in shambles, moved back home.[10]

Such was the nature of Dr. Johnston's retirement. Even if he could shake his drinking habit, his hometown offered few options to sal-vage his career. His younger half-brother Percy had already established a practice in town. E. L. briefly "peddled dentistry," neighbors noted with a mix of pity and derision, from a horse-drawn buggy. His rides through the rural districts netted him few patients. While local papers described the murdered dentist as an "aged" retiree, Johnston was just forty-five—still draft eligible—in 1918. By then, apparently, he had abandoned any hopes of reviving his career. When he registered for the draft just three months before his death, he scribbled down "farming" as his occupation.[11]

As Johnston managed his aging father's crops and cattle, his reputa-tion continued to plummet. Rumors of his "looseness with women"— talk that had started during his stint as an itinerant dentist—gave jealous men of both races reason to seek revenge. Back on the farm, Johnston's womanizing allegedly sparked a confrontation with one of his black workers. Major Clark, along with his younger brother

Andrew, had moved onto the Johnston farm to pay off the debt on a mule. Their father, a farmer from the county's northern end, had hired out his sons to work off the cost of his purchase. There the boys met Maggie and Alma Howze, two sisters who also lived and worked on the farm. After word reached Johnston that Major and Maggie—both in their early twenties—planned to marry, he confronted Clark and told him to leave her alone. Maggie, like her teenage sister Alma, was pregnant with Johnston's child.[12]

Rumors of the quarrel on the Johnston farm gave Major Clark a motive for murder, and no white investigator felt the need to delve deeper. Despite the fact that ten days passed between Johnston's death and the mob killings, most white newspapers did not report the murder, arrests, or confessions until *after* the lynching. Local authorities characterized the murder plot as on open-and-shut case. After Johnston fired the Howze sisters for an undisclosed reason, the women plotted the assassination with the Clark brothers. On the morning of December 10, while Johnston milked a cow, Major Clark shot his boss through a crack in the barn wall. The load of No. 4 shot tore through the back of Johnston's neck, instantly paralyzing him. When a doctor attempted to remove shot from his spinal column later that evening, Johnston died almost instantly.[13]

Despite local officials' attempt to sanitize their story, conflicting accounts had already leaked out. After shooting Johnston, the more detailed newspaper accounts noted, Major Clark did not flee. He alerted the Johnston family and, "pretending he had no idea who had fired on Dr. Johnston," helped to carry his mortally wounded boss into the house. Clark's ruse quickly fell apart, white officials later claimed. "He told so many conflicting stories," a town leader explained, "that he was arrested and confessed, giving the entire plot." That Major Clark would linger after killing his white boss, just days after a heated confrontation, seemed downright suicidal. And despite later claims of his prompt arrest and confession, a wire report from Meridian suggested that the killer's identity remained a mystery for at least several hours. The morning after the shooting, papers as far as away as Washington, D.C., carried reports that "a posse...with bloodhounds" was scouring the countryside for Johnston's "unknown assassin."[14]

When the authorities settled on Major Clark as their shooter, the other details quickly fell into place. After Clark's jailhouse confession in Meridian, the sheriff rounded up his brother Andrew and the Howze sisters. After they spent nine days in the county jail in Quitman, the sheriff transported the four suspects to a preliminary hearing in Shubuta. Most local papers later printed verbatim Major Clark's public guilty plea—none mentioned that lawmen had already tortured one out of him. "Yes sir, that's right," Clark allegedly announced at the hearing. "We agreed to kill Dr. Johnston and I done the shooting." The other three, local reports noted, never said a word.[15]

After the hearing, county authorities made a curious decision. Instead of returning the prisoners to Quitman, county authorities locked them in Shubuta's tiny jailhouse. The recently constructed county jail was no fortress, though it was certainly more secure than the square brick hut just off Shubuta's main street. With four "confessed" murderers locked in its two tiny cells, a single sheriff's deputy stood guard outside. Mayor J. P. Spence, who presided over the preliminary hearing, later denied any "undue excitement" before or after. "The trial was one of the most orderly he had ever witnessed," the *Meridian Star* reported, "not the slightest thing occurring to indicate that any attempt would be made to wreak summary vengeance on the prisoners." Despite the mayor's denials, the ten days between the arrests and the preliminary trial provided ample notice for would-be vigilantes. On Friday, December 20, the town's limited supply of spare rooms filled up quickly, and automobiles from surrounding counties rolled in throughout the day.[16]

The mob barely waited for nightfall. At dusk, a few men headed to the town's tiny power plant to cut the electrical supply. Sometime between six and eight o'clock—"official" accounts differed on such details—"something went wrong at the powerhouse and the town was plunged into darkness." On cue, more than a dozen automobiles converged on the jailhouse. The deputy sheriff walked out into the street and surrendered to the mob. A handful of men seized the prisoners from the jail and loaded them into a waiting car. Then the convoy rumbled down a dirt road toward the steel-framed toll bridge on the outskirts of town.[17]

Well into Saturday morning, the corpses of the Clark brothers and the Howze sisters swayed above the muddy Chickasawhay, two from one side of the bridge and two from the other. In town, local officials waited for the bodies to be "discovered" by a passerby before sending for the coroner. When county officials and curious onlookers finally gathered at the bridge, they sent for black townspeople to retrieve the bodies for burial. No one came. Eventually a gang of white men pulled up the bodies and loaded them onto a mule wagon. Back in Shubuta, the usual Saturday crowds of country folk milled about as a wagon loaded with corpses rumbled toward Will Patton's funeral parlor.[18]

Like the dead dentist, the town undertaker descended from a prominent local family. Will Patton's father, like Arista Johnston, overcame a meager education and established himself as a prosperous businessman. The elder Patton also enjoyed a national reputation among temperance crusaders, thanks to his successful campaign to rid Shubuta of saloons in the 1880s. In rhetoric that echoed the previous decade's plot to overthrow Reconstruction, W. H. Patton denounced the "saloonist" menace as an alliance of immoral whites and "illiterate negroes." By liberating Shubuta from "the great demon drink," Patton claimed another victory for the racial status quo. The merchant certainly appreciated the tenuous—and volatile—nature of white control. His antisaloon campaign received fawning coverage in local newspapers and temperance journals, but a lone newspaper article in 1897 announced, with no elaboration, that Patton had survived a stabbing by "a demented negro." Shubuta's violent edge persisted, but with holdings that included a large store, sawmill, cotton gin, and a funeral parlor, Patton had as much invested in the town's good name as anyone.[19]

When a quadruple lynching undercut that aura of order and progress, the town patriarch sprang to Shubuta's defense. Two days after local newspapers carried white officials' account of the murder and subsequent lynching, the *Laurel Leader* published Patton's version of events. The murder plot stemmed from a wage dispute, the "Prominent Citizen" reported. Maggie Howze had enlisted the help of her sister Alma and the Clark brothers—"his two most trusted servants"—over fifty cents a week in back pay. Like the Clark brothers, who worked to pay off the debt on their father's mule, Maggie Howze "owed for a Singer sewing machine." Johnston withheld a portion of her three-dollar weekly wage until she "cooked out the debt," as Patton put it. When Maggie quit, for reasons Patton did not disclose, she demanded the difference.[20]

After establishing the alleged motive, Patton rehashed authorities' account of the murder conspiracy. Maggie's sister Alma—nearly eight months pregnant—walked several miles into town to purchase the shell that killed Johnston. Andrew stood watch outside the barn, and Major fired the fatal shot from his hiding place inside. The subsequent lynching was "unfortunate," Patton noted, because death sentences surely awaited the four suspects. "This was the most diabolical plotted crime ever committed around this section," Patton declared, "and most of the community deplore the fact that the laws of the land were not permitted to execute these criminals legally."[21]

While the elder Patton preferred to wait for the courts to dispose of black convicts, his son reportedly exhibited less patience. Rumors spread that Will Patton was among the men who abducted and lynched the prisoners. Some later claimed that the undertaker had led the mob. Those rumors likely reached the relatives of the victims, who refused to retrieve the bodies that county officials had delivered to his funeral parlor. At the northern end of the county, neighbors warned Major and Andrew Clark's father that the mob had set a trap for him. If he headed down to Shubuta, he would be the next to swing from the Hanging Bridge.[22]

Whether out of fear, distrust, or defiance, the victims' relatives refused to claim the bodies for burial. Left with no alternative, Will Patton packed the corpses into crude pine coffins. Just outside the fence of the town's white cemetery, gravediggers prepared two large holes—one for the brothers and another for the sisters. On Sunday afternoon, less than twenty-four hours after the lynching, a work crew buried the dead without a funeral. Black townspeople avoided the sordid scene. Word spread through town that the gravediggers had seen movements in Alma Howze's abdomen. If medically impossible, that rumor embodied a tragic truth. In a few weeks, Howze would have given birth to her first child.[23]

A COMMITTEE OF NEW YORK NEGROES

When word of the Shubuta lynchings reached its New York headquarters, the NAACP fired off a telegram to Mississippi governor Theodore Bilbo. "Speaking in the name of its 155 branches and 42,000 members in 38 states of the Union," the association requested "information regarding any steps taken or contemplated by Mississippi authorities to uphold her laws against members of [a] mob who have so outrageously flouted them." Not quite ten years old in late 1918, the NAACP had increased its numbers exponentially during World War I, and made the antilynching crusade an immediate postwar priority and put the full weight of its growing clout behind it. None of this mattered to Mississippi's governor. He ignored the inquiry, until a local reporter asked him if he planned to respond to the well-publicized telegram. "No, not tonight," Bilbo declared, "I will tell them, in effect, to go to hell."[24]

Bilbo's reply typified the official state response to the Shubuta lynchings—such incidents were Mississippi's business and no one else's. The governor had pushed through a slew of progressive reforms, including the prohibition of public hangings, yet he proudly defended Mississippi's Jim Crow regime. "We have all the room in the world for what we know as N-i-g-g-e-r-s," the governor warned, "but none whatsoever for 'colored ladies and gentlemen.'" More pragmatic elites, like the editor of the New Orleans *Times-Picayune*, deemed Bilbo's language "coarse and unwise," but saved their harshest criticism for "a committee of New York Negroes" who aimed only to stir up racial trouble.[25]

Well before that "committee" became a household name across the South, the NAACP's surging membership and broadening reach shook the region's racial status quo. By 1918, the NAACP had established branches in every southern state. Walter White's arrival in 1918 marked a turn toward a more aggressive style of recruiting and publicity, and his undercover investigative work acquainted a national audience with the brutal realities of white supremacy. As he crisscrossed the South, White linked seemingly isolated rural communities like Shubuta to a wider network of activists and journalists. As he gathered intelligence for campaigns against discrimination and violence, he also uncovered black resistance in the darkest days of Jim Crow.[26]

White dedicated his life to an organization catalyzed and shaped by the struggle against mob violence. The NAACP organized in 1909 in the midst of rising antiblack violence across the country. A 1908 race riot in Springfield, Illinois, punctuated a rash of outbreaks aimed at black neighborhoods in northern states. As with previous incidents in Indiana and New York, the Illinois mob formed to lynch a black prisoner accused of assaulting a white person. After local police transferred the inmate, the Springfield vigilantes burned, looted, and lynched their way through the city's black neighborhoods. On Spring Street, a mob strung up an eighty-year-old man and poked at him with knives before torching his house and leaving him to choke to death on his own blood.[27]

Such gruesome scenes galvanized a loose coalition of white reformers and black activists. The NAACP's inner circle, a clique of predominantly white lawyers, journalists, and social workers, applied the Progressive formula of research, publicity, and reform to the race problem. With facts and figures culled from careful investigation, the NAACP would expose racial abuse and promote legal remedies. The founders charged the organization's lone black executive, W. E. B. Du Bois, with publicizing the association's work. As editor of *The Crisis*, Du Bois created a clearinghouse for lynching data and an outlet for the NAACP's investigative journalism. But before Walter White's arrival, *The Crisis* relied on a mishmash of black investigators, white allies, and private detective agencies to supply reports on mob violence. Each source had its limits. White contacts, whether liberal sympathizers or hired detectives, struggled to find willing black informants. Black investigators encountered greater obstacles. With Walter White (fig. 1.1), who, as the poet Langston Hughes once joked, looked like a "little Irishman," the NAACP added a secret weapon to its arsenal.[28]

A few years before the formation of the NAACP, mob violence on the streets of Atlanta lit a fire in White. When he was twelve, he and

FIGURE 1.1

Portrait of Walter F. White as a young man. His light complexion and
fair features allowed him to pose as a white man to investigate lynchings
and other racial abuses in the South. Visual Materials from the NAACP
Records. LC-USZ62-107019. Courtesy of the Library of Congress
Prints and Photographs Division and the National Association for the
Advancement of Colored People.

his neighbors huddled in their homes, rifles at the ready, as white mobs rampaged through the city's black neighborhoods. The Atlanta Race Riot of 1906, sparked by months of race-baiting political campaigns and white press reports of black attacks on white women, left an indelible impression on White. "I knew then who I was," he remembered later, "I was a Negro, a human being with an invisible pigmentation which marked me a person to be hunted, hanged, abused, discriminated against, kept in poverty and ignorance, in order that those whose skin was white would have readily at hand a proof of their superiority."[29]

If the Atlanta Race Riot exposed White to white supremacy's brutal excesses, his experiences as a fair-skinned African American convinced him of its absurdities. During his childhood, whites had erected a baffling array of laws and codes on the foundation of firm and definite racial distinctions. Yet White, with his "invisible" blackness, discovered at an early age the cracks in the color line and the logic that sustained it. The son of a mail carrier, Walter enjoyed a comfortable upbringing among the city's black upper class. Because of their fair complexion— so light that a census taker in 1900 mistakenly listed the family as white—Walter's family enjoyed privileges and courtesies that darker-skinned Atlantans did not. His mother shopped in white-owned department stores, where clerks called her "Mrs." and allowed her to try on clothes. Yet the ride downtown presented perils for Mrs. White and her daughters, Walter's sisters, who had to choose carefully whether to sit in the black or white section of the segregated streetcar. They encountered "embarrassing stares and remarks" from whites, White recalled, if they sat in the black section. If they sat in the front of the streetcar, however, they risked far worse if someone discovered their identity. Ultimately, the dilemma compelled Walter's father to buy his wife a buggy.[30]

As his mother's chauffeur, Walter witnessed the indignities and inconsistencies of Jim Crow firsthand. He learned that "passing"— whether to drink from a white water fountain on a childish dare or, later, to investigate a lynching for the NAACP—could be shockingly easy and deadly serious at the same time. The rewards—both for an ambitious young activist and the cause he served—seemed well worth the risk. By flaunting the color line, and subverting the South's supposedly inviolate social order, White mocked white supremacy's twisted logic and exposed the evils that propped it up. So, barely two weeks into his new job as the NAACP's assistant field secretary, White asked his boss and mentor James Weldon Johnson for permission to investigate a Tennessee lynching in person.[31]

A fellow black southerner, Johnson recognized the perils and potential of White's mission. In Florida once, some white men had almost lynched Johnson for talking with a light-skinned woman they believed to be white. The NAACP's first black field secretary, Johnson came on board in late 1916, just weeks after the association formally established an antilynching committee. The following summer, he personally investigated a lynching during a recruiting swing through the South. If White earned the confidence of local eyewitnesses, Johnson realized, the resulting exposé could be a bombshell. Yet if White was found out, he might well be the next lynching victim. Johnson had only known his young protégé a few months. Impressed by White's efforts on behalf of Atlanta's NAACP branch, one of the most active in the country, Johnson had lured the young man, who was then starting a promising career as an insurance agent, to work full time for the cause. He also did not want to lose his new recruit in his first month on the job, but he reluctantly authorized the first of what turned out to be many undercover trips.[32]

The gamble paid off. In Tennessee, and then in Georgia that summer, White honed the tactics that he would put to use in Shubuta at the end of the year. His insurance-agent training served him well, and he devised subtle tricks for coaxing secrets out of wary strangers. When White visited a southern town, he would hang around the general store or a local hotel, introducing himself as a traveling salesman or land speculator. Rather than pepper locals with lynching questions, he struck up conversations about politics or the weather. If a local happened to mention the recent lynchings, White feigned indifference and tried to change the subject. By doing so, as he knew, he encouraged boasting. Sometimes he would pretend to be bored or unimpressed. Once he claimed that he had heard of "much more exciting lynchings" elsewhere. "When local pride had thus been sufficiently disparaged," White explained, "the facts came tumbling forth."[33]

Those facts often tested White's composure. In Tennessee, an eyewitness described how a mob had castrated black sharecropper Jim McIlherron, chained him to a tree, doused him with coal oil, and roasted him alive in front of one thousand onlookers. White also learned the roots of local resentment toward the lynch victim—his relative prosperity, his years spent living up north, and his willingness to defend himself. The final trait, the sharecropper's determination to match a white attacker blow for blow, sealed his fate. "Any time a nigger hits a white man," a local explained to White, "he's gotta be handled or else all the niggers will get out of hand."[34]

A few months later, in southern Georgia, similar signs of black self-assertion sparked a lynching spree that left at least eleven dead. After a local black farmhand killed his white landlord in retaliation for a brutal beating, whites feared a rebellion. On the first day of the rampage, a mob seized two black men in Troupeville and shredded their bodies with over seven hundred bullets. The following day, the mob killed three more men, including the alleged mastermind of the conspiracy, Hayes Turner. When Turner's pregnant wife, Mary, threatened to swear out warrants for their arrests, the vigilantes hung her upside down from a tree, doused her with gasoline, and set her on fire. As the flames scorched her body, white men disemboweled Mary Turner and stomped on the writhing fetus that had tumbled to the ground.[35]

Having extracted the gruesome details from unsuspecting informants, White produced a series of exposés that raised the NAACP's profile and pressured reluctant authorities to respond. After local townspeople escorted him to Mary Turner's crude grave, which was marked by an empty whiskey bottle corked with a cigar butt, White phoned the governor's mansion in Atlanta and asked for a meeting. Posing as a reporter for the *New York Evening Post*, he strode into Georgia governor Hugh Dorsey's office and handed over his findings. The report disturbed Dorsey—an increasingly vocal lynching critic—but not so much as the realization that he had unknowingly hosted a black NAACP official.[36]

The gory details of southern mob violence, and the daring manner in which White collected them, made for compelling reading. The *Crisis*

35

and black newspapers nationwide reported his findings, as did some white publications. These stories also made White the NAACP's most popular speaker, and he increasingly juggled his ongoing investigative work with recruiting stops across the South. The organization's war-time growth owed much to its southern-born black staffers, who had spent much of 1917 and 1918 on extended organizing swings through the region. In two short years, membership in the region had swelled from a few hundred to several thousand. By heading south to investigate abuses and rally support, Johnson and White transformed the NAACP's image and broadened its support base. With a war in Europe winding down and racial violence in the United States on the rise, the association redoubled its efforts to maintain its momentum.[37]

The Shubuta lynchings highlighted both the extent and the limits of the NAACP's growth in Dixie. Most of the region's local branches sprouted in Upper South and Eastern Seaboard states, far from the black-majority counties of the southern interior. The handful of Deep South branches, like most of their counterparts to the north and east, thrived in larger towns and cities. By any measure, Mississippi—the "deepest" and most rural of southern states—posed the greatest challenge to the NAACP's movement-building efforts. The Magnolia State's lone branch, founded in Vicksburg in early 1918, endured constant harassment and lapsed into inactivity after whites ran several founding members out of town. These factors made White's journey into eastern Mississippi—nearly 150 miles from the NAACP's tenuous outpost in Vicksburg—more daunting, and potentially more significant, than previous lynching investigations. He could establish contacts within and fix outside attention on an area largely untouched by a growing national movement. But he could also get himself, and anyone who helped him, killed. "There will be some difficulty," he predicted, "in handling this matter." With that flourish of nonchalant bravado, White lit out for Mississippi.[38]

Such a Thing Can and Does Happen in America

White relied on a network of contacts and supporters cultivated during his previous swings through the region. By the end of World War I, the

NAACP listed among its southern membership some of the region's most prominent black professionals. This network provided White with local contacts, investigative leads, and shelter during his southern trips. Even before leaving New York, White had contacted a black Mobile dentist and NAACP supporter to look into Dr. Johnston's troubled background. The NAACP also reached out to Robert Church, Jr., a Memphis businessman and civic leader. Church's father, born into slavery in Mississippi, became the South's first black millionaire in the late nineteenth century. Robert Church, Jr., succeeded his father in business and established himself as the city's black powerbroker. In 1916, Church founded and funded the Lincoln League, a local Republican organization that quickly registered ten thousand black voters. The following year, Church spearheaded the formation of the Memphis NAACP branch and served as James Weldon Johnson's host and guide during a ten-day investigation of a nearby lynching.[39]

When news of the Shubuta lynchings reached New York, the NAACP authorized Church to hire a private detective agency to investigate. Given the mention of "trouble" between the murdered dentist and his female employees, the NAACP wanted to confirm its suspicions regarding "the real cause" for the murder. "We want to know," Johnson instructed Church, "if the impending motherhood of the younger woman had any bearing upon this quarrel...and also if there were any suspicions of illicit relations between the murdered dentist and the younger woman." Confirming such suspicions, and corroborating White's own findings through a white southern private eye, served the NAACP's desire for vivid and credible antilynching propaganda. As with previous investigations, the NAACP wanted findings it could deliver not just to sympathetic journalists but to southern officials and congressional allies as well. "Above all else," Johnson concluded, "a thorough and authentic investigation is desired—one upon which the strongest kind of fight can be waged."[40]

Local allies like Church provided intelligence for White's antilynching investigations and helped to stitch together the NAACP's southern support network. Every excursion into Dixie presented an opportunity to organize new branches and encourage existing ones. En route to Shubuta, White spoke to "two splendid Branches" in Chattanooga and Nashville. Dozens of black Tennesseans signed up at each meeting. At both stops, White requested appointments with white public officials. In Chattanooga, he had a "cordial" discussion with the state's newly elected attorney general about a pending antilynching bill in the Tennessee legislature. More daring still, White attended the gubernatorial inauguration in Nashville and unsuccessfully requested an audience with new governor A. H. Roberts.[41]

White's next public appearance proved the most successful. "I had an excellent meeting in New Orleans," he reported to an NAACP colleague, "and made the best speech I have ever made." Reeling from a bout with food poisoning, White nonetheless wowed the crowd gathered at the Pythian Temple Theater, packed beyond its twelve-hundred-seat capacity. On the platform behind him sat prominent businessmen, ministers, and the president of Straight University. To Johnson, his mentor, he wrote, "I reached your class once or twice, when I had to hold up my hand to stop the crowd cheering." After his speech, over a hundred new members paid their dues on the spot. "Their slogan now is '5,000 Members,'" White concluded, "and I think they will get them."[42]

If the New Orleans stop lifted White's spirits, the following day's train ride into Mississippi reminded him how much of the South remained beyond the NAACP's reach. White had called on some of Meridian's leading black citizens before venturing south into Clarke County. The city boasted a small but thriving black professional class. As in the Deep South's existing urban branches, White's recruiting targets enjoyed the financial independence and political connections that most southern blacks did not. The NAACP cultivated these contacts to gain a foothold in the South's most inhospitable corners. In Meridian, White sought out D. W. Sherrod, a physician and leader of the state's Black-and-Tan Republicans. While a nonfactor in state politics, the faction—whose name distinguished them from the rival Lily-Whites—provided black elites with access to patronage posts and national party politics. White deemed Sherrod, a delegate to the 1916 Republican National Convention, "a fighter" and potential leader. He met with several other potential recruits and talked them through the process of starting their own branch. Most important, the men provided a car and driver to take White on the final leg of his journey.[43]

White's mission into Clarke County took him off the beaten path of the NAACP's southern network of urban elites, and he anticipated he would have a more difficult time than on his previous trips. The lack of reliable accommodations and his Meridian hosts' warnings persuaded him to limit his investigation to a single day. Perhaps the minimal passenger train service—one northbound and one southbound departure per day—convinced White that he needed an automobile for a quick getaway. Whatever his misgivings, White rumbled southward, armed only with his wits and experience.

During his earlier lynching investigations, White relied on a repertoire of techniques to win over strangers. Before his first trip to Tennessee, he had requested press credentials from white NAACP stalwart and journalist Oswald Garrison Villard. He never returned them. Although he carried the credentials to use in a pinch, White preferred the guise of a traveling salesman to that of a white New York reporter. A press badge from the *New York Evening Post* occasionally helped to get him meetings with public officials, and might save his neck if he got into a jam, but a Yankee reporter poking around town certainly would raise hackles. In the wake of the Shubuta lynchings, a Mississippi paper argued that mob violence only encouraged "Northern newspapers" to persist with their "habit of saying nasty things about the South." Few local whites would willingly supply them with more material.[44]

The salesman ruse provided White with some advantages. The part came naturally to a former life insurance agent whose income once rested on his ability to earn the trust of strangers. On a practical level, it allayed white fears that their local secrets would end up in print. More important, it gave White believable and benign reasons for venturing over to the black side of town. A Yankee reporter who sought out black informants endangered not only himself but any black person he approached. But by posing as "a salesman for the Exelento Medicine Company of Atlanta," with its first-rate line of hair-straightening products, White could head into the "bottoms" of Shubuta without raising suspicions and risking lives.[45]

Shubuta proved more challenging to White than previous investigations. Although local papers had claimed that Shubuta quickly returned to normal after the lynchings, White encountered a town still on edge. White townspeople seemed impervious to his usual tricks, and he found no one willing to boast about the mob's exploits. Across the tracks, White made contact with T. H. Doby, a local black preacher, and Hattie Howze, the lynched sisters' cousin. The young woman's courage impressed White, who knew that she risked "join[ing] her cousins" by talking to a fair-skinned stranger about their fate.[46]

In contrast to press accounts that emphasized the lynchers' stealth and efficiency, White's black informants stressed the mob's brutality. Hattie Howze had heard that her cousin Maggie fought back even as the lynchers slipped a noose around her neck. Despite being five months pregnant, Maggie struggled to free herself from a dozen grasping hands and loudly protested her innocence. To shut her up, a member of the mob smashed her teeth in with a monkey wrench. A second blow cut a wide gash in the side of her head, White reported, "in which the side of a person's hand could be placed." One by one, Maggie watched as the lynchers tossed her younger sister, her fiancé, and her intended brother-in-law over the bridge railing. When her turn came, she did not go as easily. The first time her captors flung her over the railing, she caught herself on the side of the bridge. As she pulled her battered body back over the railings, the men tried again. Only on the third attempt did Maggie plunge fifteen feet to her death. The following day, Hattie Howze told White, mob members joked about how hard "that big black Jersey woman" fought back.[47]

Black informants provided vivid images of white brutality, but they also exposed white ambivalence and disunity. White press accounts stressed the guilt of the lynching victims and made no mention of alternate murder theories. Doby told White that Johnston's father did not believe that Major Clark had killed his son. Instead, the black preacher claimed, Arista Johnston assumed that a white man had killed his son in an argument over a woman. The killer knew of the spat between E. L. Johnston and his employees, White explained, and "felt that he could kill the dentist safely, and the blame would be put on the Negroes." The senior Johnston, black informants claimed, even attempted to intervene to stop the lynching. Rather than rejoice in vigilante justice, White reported, "the father was sick after the lynchings occurred."[48]

The gory details sickened White as well. That evening, on a train to Memphis, he scribbled the outline of his report. The next morning, at Robert Church's Memphis home, White typed out his narrative and mailed it to NAACP headquarters in New York. "I am sending you enclosed herein my complete report on the Shubuta lynching," White began, "which as you will see by reading it, is undoubtedly the most atrocious affair of its kind ever know[n]." Having infiltrated Shubuta, and lived to tell about it, White turned his attention to getting that story before a larger audience than ever before. "I believe that this can be done," his report concluded, "and that it will do great good to let [the] world know that such a thing can and does happen in America."[49]

A Martyr to the Cause of Negro Womanhood

The black press did not wait for White's investigation to denounce the Shubuta lynchings. "Most Inhuman Lynching of Year," announced the *New York News*. "Leading Citizens of Shubuta Take Two Sisters, One of Whom Was Affronted by Employer, and Two Brothers, Their Protectors, and Hang Them to [River] Bridge" The headline echoed the suspicions that drove White's undercover investigation and the alternative narrative that emerged even before he returned from Mississippi. Black journalists questioned the victims' guilt, raised the taboo topic of interracial sexuality, and celebrated signs of self-defense. Whereas white press accounts glossed over the mob's cruelty and absolved the better class of responsibility, civil rights advocates emphasized a more savage reality. White's investigation confirmed black suspicions and raised questions crucial to the antilynching campaign and the broader movement for civil rights.[50]

Although the black press relied on the same wire reports as their white counterparts, their interpretations diverged sharply. The white press took at face value the guilt of the victims. Even southern white journalists who denounced the lynching did not question the chain of events that landed the four victims in jail. In fact, several white editors deemed the lynching unnecessary precisely because the courts would have sentenced all four to death. "Conviction was reasonably certain," a southern Mississippi newspaperman argued, "and a legal execution would have been more impressive as a lesson to the criminally inclined." A like-minded Memphis editor reminded readers that the Jim Crow legal system rendered mob violence a brutal and embarrassing excess. "When will Southern people stop destroying themselves by lynching Negroes," he pleaded, "when it is so easy legally to punish a negro malefactor?"[51]

African Americans shared neither the presumption of guilt nor the confidence in southern courts. "An offense against the laws of the state is not even required to provoke an outrage," a black editor declared. "Mere suspicion is sufficient, so that the life of those unfortunate people is no more safe than a dog's running wild in the streets." White's investigation revealed that many townspeople believed that a white man had killed Johnston knowing that the black workers would be blamed. As with other aspects of the Shubuta story, the notion of a cover-up drew from a deep well of exploitation and mistreatment at the hands of white authorities.[52]

When African Americans challenged openly the integrity of Jim Crow justice, white southerners took notice. "According to the negro papers," a white lynching critic complained, "few, if any, negroes who are lynched are guilty of the crimes charged against them." In an unintended nod to the Shubuta case, he added, "Negro papers often suggest that a certain negro was lynched to cover up a crime committed by a white man." Given that such claims raised the question of white complicity, Mississippi papers took great care to absolve local authorities and townspeople of any blame. Despite the fact that the mob abducted the prisoners just off the town's main street, and barely an hour past sunset, the *Laurel Leader* claimed, "the mob worked so quietly and swiftly that few citizens were aware of it."[53]

African American newspapers openly challenged these accounts, and White picked them apart in his report. From the arrest of the four black youths to their burial ten days later, he outlined a leisurely and deliberate ritual that implicated lawmen, leading citizens, and ordinary citizens. Although he noted that some whites opposed, and may have even attempted to stop, the lynching, White described the killings as a community-sanctioned action. The dentist's shoddy reputation and the victims' motives mattered less than the necessity of racial control. "The fact that *a white man* had been killed by a *Negro*, whatever the cause of the killing, was enough to warrant lynchings," White argued, "for they felt that if the offenders were not made examples of, no white man who had wronged a Negro would be safe." While most local whites did not participate, White concluded, they all benefited. Shubuta whites closed ranks in the wake of the violence.[54]

If the "cause" of Dr. Johnston's death mattered little to the lynch mob, the dispute between the former dentist and his farmhands mattered immensely to others. Johnston's reported "trouble" with the Howze sisters cut to the very core of the South's lynching culture. Since Reconstruction, whites had played on fears of interracial sex and deployed images of beastly black rapists, bent on ravaging white women, to rally resentment and regain control of local government. In Reconstruction's wake, as white lawmakers unleashed a barrage of Jim Crow laws, fears of black-on-white rape justified continued violence. Even in the wake of the Shubuta killings, which had nothing to do with rape (at least black-on-white), the myth cast its long shadow. "Lynching is seldom, if ever, justified," a south Mississippi editor declared. But, he continued, "in the case of *one certain crime*, which is not necessary to mention here, there is a measure of justification for the white citizens who take the law into their own hands."[55]

Antilynching activists recognized the rape myth's volatility. Newspaper stories of black-on-white rape sparked the Atlanta Race Riot of 1906—White's earliest exposure to mob violence. Years before White joined the NAACP, courageous activists challenged the "rape-lynch" complex at great personal risk. In 1892, whites forced Mississippi-born journalist and antilynching crusader Ida B. Wells to flee Memphis after she publicly challenged "the old threadbare lie that Negro men rape white women." Six years later, during a race riot in Wilmington, North Carolina, a mob destroyed black editor Alexander Manly's printing press

43

after he denounced unfounded reports of black-on-white rape and, like Wells, pondered the possibility of *consensual* sex between black men and white women. By the time White went to work for the NAACP, the dismantling of the rape myth infused the organization's antilynching work. Like Wells and Manly before them, NAACP investigators chipped away at the white South's favorite justification for mob violence and Jim Crow itself.[56]

White's report had done much to expose and undermine the rape-lynch complex. None of his first three undercover investigations—in Tennessee, Georgia, and Mississippi—involved rape charges. But the Shubuta case did more than undercut the myth of the sex-crazed black marauder; it turned the language of rape and racial purity on its head. In Shubuta, White discovered, a white aggressor had forced himself on multiple black women. "The constantly repeated assertion of those who attempt to defend lynching," White declared, "is that this crime must be perpetuated in order to prevent violation of white womanhood in the South by Negroes and to keep the two races separate and distinct." Yet the case revealed "how well this rule is observed by those of the 'superior race' ... when it comes to illicit relations between *white men* and *colored women*."[57]

The Shubuta investigation fueled suspicions that Dr. Johnston sexually exploited his female workers. In the alternate narrative that emerged, the image of the predatory and possessive white womanizer replaced that of the lust-crazed black marauder. Black Baltimore editor W. T. Andrews flipped the rhetoric of rape and revenge. "Negro women," he announced, "have absolutely no protection from white monsters in the South." Andrews, who first publicly questioned "the nature of the trouble" between Johnston and his workers, did not wait for an NAACP investigation to question the sanctioned story. Like White, he had read enough evasive lynching accounts to doubt the "official" account of the Shubuta lynchings.[58]

White's findings echoed Andrews's presumptions. "In this section of the country," White lamented in the wake of his Shubuta investigation, "no colored girl or woman has any chance to remain pure; if she by her comeliness attracts the lustful desire of a white man." While most

awaken public sentiment and compel an official government response. His previous investigations had nudged America in the right direction, yet had failed to force legal or legislative action. This time had to be different.[63]

Others shared White's belief that Shubuta represented something darker and more foreboding than anything that had happened before. The New Orleans–based *Southwestern Christian Advocate*, a paper for black Methodists in Louisiana and Mississippi, noted "two things distinct about the lynching"—the killing of young women and the crude indifference of state officials. The victims' age and gender invited widespread condemnation. White referred to the dead as "children, for they were no more than children when they were lynched." While Major Clark and Maggie Howze were in their early twenties, their younger siblings were teenagers. Sixteen-year-old Alma Howze, the youngest of the victims, provided the most searing image of the whole affair—an unborn fetus writhing inside a corpse. That image, coupled with the sadistic beating of Alma's pregnant older sister, surpassed Mary Turner's notoriously grisly fate. If a Mississippi mob would slay not one but two pregnant women, then what horrors lay ahead?[64]

Mississippi's callous response undercut hopes that southern officialdom would unite in opposition to lynching. "What concerns the twelve million Negroes in this country," a black editor declared, "is that a group of four Negroes can be lynched, one of them a girl of 16 years, and that absolutely nothing will be done about it." Bilbo's "go to hell" reply dramatized this fear, and linked the mob to the governor's mansion. "Can there be any wonder," White fumed, "that lynching mobs kill Negroes as they would wild beasts[?]" Bilbo's defiant posture seemed all the more galling compared to developments in neighboring Alabama. The week after investigating the Shubuta lynching, White posed as a white *New York Evening Post* reporter to attend the trial of two white men indicted for hanging two black men in November 1918. While the all-white jury refused to convict, the mere fact that Alabama's governor had authorized the state attorney general to prosecute a lynching case stood in stark contrast to Mississippi's official indifference.[65]

Deep South blacks held out little hope that local juries would send lynchers to jail, but they drew a sharp distinction between Mississippi's defiance and the "law and order" stance of neighboring states. The taunting of racial reformers, a New Orleans editor warned, "encourages lynching" and "will make possible more." Bilbo's response, which drew sharp criticism from several white southern editors outside the state but virtually no public comment from Mississippians, marked the governor as "sympathetic with the law breaking, if...not the crime of lynching itself." The combination of depraved sadism and a heartless official response, a black critic warned, suggested that whites could slaughter "any number of Negroes, almost at any place without the least bit of fear" that they would face prosecution.[66]

The specifics of the Shubuta lynchings and fear of mounting violence fueled condemnations of the "worst" mob outrage in near memory. A black New York weekly declared that Mississippi "outrivaled the barbarism of Texas and Georgia by lynching two brothers and two sisters." Even when juxtaposed against the decade's two most historically significant lynchings, Shubuta stood alone. The 1916 public burning of Jesse Washington—in front of ten thousand onlookers in Waco, Texas—led directly to the formation of the NAACP's antilynching committee. After local whites distributed a postcard souvenir of the grisly event, W. E. B. Du Bois published the image of Washington's charred corpse in *The Crisis*. The 1918 Georgia killing spree that led to Mary Turner's death, documented in painstaking detail by White, generated unprecedented publicity for the NAACP and compelled declarations from southern editors, officials, and even President Woodrow Wilson. In San Antonio, a newspaper offered a $1,000 reward for the capture of Mary Turner's killers. If the Shubuta lynchings "outrivaled" these atrocities, as White and his journalist allies contended, their impact could be all the more significant.[67]

For White, Shubuta represented an opportunity to take the NAACP's publicity efforts to the next level. He had published accounts of his previous research in Tennessee and Georgia in *The Crisis*, and from there his findings had trickled out to black and white newspapers nationwide. After the Georgia lynchings, White had embarked on an eight-week investigation into "work or fight" laws across the South. These stat-utes, aimed at alleviating wartime labor shortages, permitted local au-thorities to round up African Americans on vagrancy charges and hand them over to white employers. In Shubuta, a local ordinance required all blacks between the ages of sixteen and sixty to carry an employment card. Anyone who could not prove that they worked at least five and a half days per week could be declared a "vagrant," fined up to fifty dol-lars, and sentenced to one to three months hard labor for the town.[68]

White's report on this abusive practice, unlike his previous lynching articles, ended up in a prominent white publication—the *New Republic*. With this publication under his belt, White hoped his Shubuta report would find a home in the mainstream press and score an unprecedented publicity coup for the antilynching campaign. To that end, he made every effort to verify the story. In Birmingham, White and John Shillady, the NAACP's white executive secretary, met with the private detec-tive hired by Robert Church. In the parlor of the fashionable Tutwiler Hotel, George Bodecker—former Birmingham police chief and son of a Confederate intelligence officer—dutifully reported his findings to his presumably white clients. Bodecker had tracked down a former Shubuta resident living in Birmingham who deemed Dr. Johnston "a worthless character" but hastened to add that "the best element in the county [was] opposed to the lynching."[69]

White returned to New York in search of a white paper willing to publish a graphic lynching account. He had his eye on the *Nation*, the liberal-left flagship once owned by Oswald Garrison Villard's father. Villard, the NAACP stalwart who had first lent White press creden-tials, wrote regularly for the magazine. White assured the managing editor that he had verified the facts with a white detective agency and minimized "the possibility of any action for libel," but the *Nation* po-litely passed along the piece to another magazine. While the editor agreed that the story "ought to be given wide publicity," he remained "doubtful whether this is the best place to handle it." Across town, the *Dial* and the *Independent* both declined the piece as well. The editor of the latter, a frustrated White reported back to the *Nation*, requested a revised essay "leaving out all horrible details."[70]

To White's dismay, New York's progressive white journalists balked at publishing the gory particulars. Perhaps, as his mention of libel suggested, White's decision to implicate by name local officials and prominent townspeople made editors uneasy. Or, possibly, they balked at his sarcastic invocations of American war rhetoric. He did, after all, title his report, "An Example of *Democracy* in Mississippi"—a nod to President Woodrow Wilson's wartime call "to make the world safe for democracy." Clearly, as White discovered, even the most sympathetic editors believed their readers to be too squeamish for his reportage. The young crusader was aiming for the public's heart; white editors worried that his lynching stories would hit them in the gut.

White's struggle to publish his Shubuta story provided a reminder that, despite its growth and innovations, the NAACP faced obstacles. As civil rights activists attempted to broaden their appeal and increase their influence, they ran up against the limits of public tolerance for racial reality and meaningful reform. Antilynching activists walked a fine line between exposing atrocities and alienating potential allies. Even the NAACP, which eventually published a condensed version of White's findings in *The Crisis*, eliminated all named references to white townspeople and local officials. The abbreviated report lacked the bite of White's original draft. Instead, the article—unattributed to White and retitled simply "The Shubuta Lynchings"—challenged "the meager facts as given in the press dispatches" with a clinical presentation of "the real facts of the case." While the NAACP carefully deleted White's more pointed commentary, they included a telling anecdote. After describing the abduction, hanging, and burial of the four victims, the article quoted local officials' leading "theory" as to the mob's motive. Noting that the next term of court would not start for three months, the authorities concluded in a widely quoted telegram, "the idea of the county being forced to care for and feed four self-confessed assassins of a leading citizen might have aroused the passion of the mob."[71]

"No more puerile and absurd an excuse has ever been given for a lynching" fumed White. "America has just passed through and is yet observing a period of food conservation. One cannot help but admire the originality of the lynchers and particularly their great patriotism in thus conserving food needed to save the lives of the Turks, Armenians and Germans by putting to death four helpless and defenseless members of a race that helped America with all of its resources to 'make the world safe for democracy.'" Even some southern white editors deemed the food excuse, in the words of a Louisiana newspaperman, "as flimsy a pretext as one could invent." Yet White saw something more sinister afoot. Since the United States entered World War I, mob violence had risen steadily. Faced with white southerners who perceived no fundamental conflict between patriotic fervor and racial terrorism, black activists attempted to link their cause with the nation's lofty war aims. As America made the transition from war to peace in the closing weeks of 1918, the Shubuta lynchings dramatized the stakes of this struggle.[72]

CHAPTER TWO

NOT MADE SAFE

In the weeks and months after the Shubuta lynchings, the threat of mob violence weighed heavily on James Yates. Like the Clark brothers, Yates grew up in the rolling pastureland north of Shubuta. To the west of his family's cabin, the Chickasawhay River rolled south toward the bridge where the brothers had been hanged. Just days before Christmas 1918, news of lynchings reports flowed upstream, and Yates pieced together the story from the rumors coursing through the countryside. By the time word reached his family's homestead—fifteen miles north of Shubuta—the body count had risen to nine. "Five men and four women were hung," he recalled, "their feet dangling just inches above the muddy water."[1]

Reports of the lynchings had spread far and wide, Yates heard, the gruesome particulars "written up in the northern newspapers." He never read one of those stories; the details mattered less than the message the mob sent. He could be lynched, he concluded, for anything— for "using the front door instead of the back door," for not moving off the sidewalk for "Miss Ann or Mr. Charlie," or for drinking out of the wrong water fountain. "If you were Black in Mississippi," Yates reasoned, "lightning would surely strike home sooner or later." Twelve years old in 1918, James Yates resolved then to leave Mississippi before a bolt struck him.[2]

Yates's ground-level view echoed in Walter White's reports on southern mob violence. Both portrayed Mississippi as a place of perpetual racial tensions and volatile racial passions. Rather than some tragic aberration, the Shubuta lynchings dramatized the constant threat of violence that served to shore up white supremacy. Following in the wake of a war "to make the world safe for democracy," civil rights advocates argued that the South offered its black citizens neither security nor opportunity. Having spent the war years investigating rampant discrimination and abuse, White gloomily concluded "that the white man of the South is absolutely incapable of practicing democracy so far as any case where the Negro is concerned." Until the United States could extend some protection to southern blacks like James Yates, White and his allies questioned President Wilson's lofty international agenda. "Ten thousand Leagues of Nations may be formed," White warned, "and the leaders of thought throughout the world may talk of democracy until the end of time, but as long as mobs can willfully murder in cold blood...as the Shubuta mob has done, the world is not a place made 'safe for democracy.'"[3]

From the hills of eastern Mississippi to the halls of Congress, African Americans attested to the perils they faced as the nation transitioned from war to peace. Yet in Clarke County, whites seemed oblivious to the disconnection between the Virginia-born president's soaring rhetoric and his native region's disregard for black rights. In the months leading up to the lynching, Shubuta's newspaper pondered "the inward meaning of President Wilson's immortal phrase"—*safe for democracy*. "Safety means security...from the forceful encroachment of others," editor J. E. Stovall explained. "Likewise democracy means freedom— of the individual, the group, the community, the state, the nation, the world—freedom in the enjoyment of life, liberty, and the pursuit of happiness." Without "a world wide recognition" of democratic principles, Stovall continued, neither Shubuta nor any other place would be made safe. "When all individuals and groups shall recognize the rights of all other individuals and groups, and concede them," the editor concluded, "then will the world be 'safe for democracy.'"[4]

This sermon on human rights and global security—straight from Shubuta's hometown paper—revealed the malleable rhetoric that civil rights advocates, militant white supremacists, and business-minded conservatives all invoked in their attempts to shape the postwar world. White and his allies recognized white southerners' ability to reconcile patriotism and prejudice, but hoped to sow seeds of doubt by showing how racial abuses undermined American credibility on the world stage. Until mob violence abated, a black New York editor declared three days after the Shubuta lynchings, "the presence of this country at the Peace Conference is a grotesque and hideous mockery." If whites in Shubuta fought to ensure security and self-determination worldwide, as they claimed, then civil rights advocates demanded they start at home.[5]

The competing visions of Wilson's humanitarian agenda—defined in sweeping terms of freedom and security—continued to clash in the war's wake. Racial violence played a crucial role in a process that played out locally and nationally. Wartime change encouraged many southerners to reinforce the racial status quo. However, the wave of violence that accompanied America's entry into World War I and intensified in its wake forced them to reevaluate how they managed white supremacy. In Mississippi, the war effort undercut a political faction that melded progressive reforms and racial demagoguery. Even as urban rioters and rural vigilantes nationwide attempted to force African Americans into their prewar place, business elites in Mississippi and elsewhere took steps to stabilize race relations. "Every lynching," a Memphis civic leader argued, "makes even the good negro feel less safe in his person and property." Warning that "the negro is not the only sufferer from the lynching habit!" the "law and order" advocate warned white Mississippians that mob rule would undermine their power and prosperity.[6]

As some white officials readily admitted, a combination of grassroots turmoil and negative publicity had forced their hand. The NAACP's antilynching efforts, coupled with a massive exodus of black southerners from the Deep South, pressured some farsighted Mississippians to seek to soften their state's image. "Is This an Invitation to Negroes to Move?" a black New Orleans editor asked in the wake of the Shubuta lynchings. His query captured vividly the reaction of those, including young James Yates, who accepted that invitation by the thousands in the World War I era. While civil rights activists and business-minded whites debated the state's obligations to its black citizens, African Americans across the state defied the notion that Mississippi was a place made safe. These migrants repeatedly cited discrimination and abuse as reasons for fleeing the South, and civil rights activists connected mass migration to mob violence at every turn. Faced with a national antilynching drive that portrayed Jim Crow as a vicious regime, pragmatic leaders took steps to rehabilitate the South's image and stem black outmigration. Ultimately, their campaign for law and order, like their wartime appeals to freedom and democracy, rang hollow. Even as the nation clamored for a "return to normalcy," unabated racial violence transformed rural Mississippi and the struggle to come.[7]

The Persecuted Subjects
of an Experimental Democracy

From the moment civil rights supporters learned of the quadruple lynching in Shubuta, they linked it to the politics of war, peace, and democracy. This strategy predated the United States' entry into World War I and accelerated with the president's stirring war address in April 1917. By entering the war on the side of democracy, Wilson declared, the United States could lead a crusade "to make the world itself at last free." Three months later, in the wake of a race riot in East St. Louis that left as many as 250 African Americans dead, nearly 10,000 black-clad marchers strode silently down New York's Fifth Avenue. Organized by the NAACP, the Silent Protest Parade highlighted the wartime spike in mob violence. The marchers' signs and banners juxtaposed idealistic war aims with the grim reality of white supremacy. "Make America safe for Democracy," read one. "We have fought for the liberty of white Americans in six wars," read another. "Our reward is East St. Louis." By aligning the antilynching campaign with Wilson's patriotic crusade, James Weldon Johnson informed the NAACP's branch leaders, public protest played a crucial role "in awakening and moulding public opinion in our favor."[8]

Despite hopes that wartime protests would turn the tide in the struggle against mob violence, racial attacks increased. By July 1918, the one-year anniversary of the Silent Protest Parade, southern vigilantes had already eclipsed the total number of lynching victims for the previous year. Indeed, the Shubuta lynchings marked a grisly milestone in this reign of terror. "In 20 months since the United States entered into the great war for democracy, and when the American people were dedicated to so high a purpose," the NAACP announced, "103 negroes have been lynched." Across the country, the black press emphasized the bloody landmark as well. "Century Number Reached December 20," a St. Louis paper announced. "When Four, Two of Which Were Women, Were Hanged to the Girders of a Bridge in Mississippi."[9]

For civil rights advocates and supporters nationwide, Shubuta provided a sobering measure of progress. Black journalists wove together wartime hopes and postwar heartbreak in their condemnation of the quadruple lynchings. "Is this the kind of democracy we have fought and suffered for," asked a New York editor, "and is this our reward for all that we have done?" In a published letter to the *St. Louis Post-Dispatch*, a prominent black Baptist minister cautioned that mob violence undercut American influence at the peace talks. "If, while America is wishing her form of government upon the Russians, Jugo-Slavs, Lithuanians, Germans, Austrians, and others, that system breaks down at home and such damnable outrages occur," the pastor warned, "they might fittingly say to us that they would rather be the subjects of an enlightened autocracy than the persecuted subjects of an experimental democracy."[10]

Walter White peppered his report on Shubuta with similar allusions to the war effort. Originally titled "An Example of Democracy in Mississippi," the narrative of the lynching doled out sarcasm and disgust in equal measure. Could "America dare even discuss any principles which remotely relate to democracy," White asked, as long as mobs murdered fellow citizens with impunity? Lest the United States boast of its superiority to the recently vanquished Germans, White argued that what happened in Shubuta "surpasse[d] in brutality and barbarism any committed by the Teutonic powers in Belgium and France."[11]

The conflation of bloodthirsty Germans and southern mobs proved more compelling, or at least less risky, than questioning the president's lofty rhetoric. For months, the United States government had bombarded Americans with images of German brutes bent on death and destruction. Now African Americans painted southern mobs with the same broad strokes. A Baltimore editor branded the Shubuta lynchers "our American Huns" and raised the specter of authoritarian aggression that the Allies so recently had beaten back. "With the passing of autocracy we had hoped that the spirit of Might Makes Right would go," a St. Louis editor lamented. "But the recent lynchings tell a different story." White's biting references to Wilsonian war rhetoric never made it into print, but his allusions to German brutality survived, though in diluted form. *Crisis* editor W. E. B. Du Bois had adopted a more practical and patriotic approach in the wake of his controversial "Close Ranks" editorial in July 1918. Hoping to increase black clout with federal officials, before the war Du Bois had called on African Americans "to forget our special grievances," stand "shoulder to shoulder with our white fellow citizens," and focus on "that which the German power represents today…death to the aspirations of Negroes and all the darker races for equality, freedom and democracy." As if to underscore this very point, *The Crisis* ran an abbreviated version of White's Shubuta report and inserted an excerpt from an American ambassador's "account of German lynchings" in France.[12]

Even as the "Huns"—German soldiers and American lynchers alike—trampled freedom, civil rights advocates declared, black soldiers fought and died for democracy. In the postwar months, black veterans became a powerful symbol of rising expectations and a tragic reminder of southern whites' determination to force blacks back into their prewar place. Even more than mangled field hands and ravaged maids, the image of the brutalized black soldier dominated World War I–era discussions of southern racial violence. The returning black veterans would incur white wrath, one black editor predicted, because "they will be imbued with the spirit of the thing they have been fighting for—Democracy." Inspired by this "new vision," he warned, "they will not feel like being kicked around like dum-driven cattle." The Shubuta lynchings, the editor concluded mournfully, offered a preview "of the reward that awaits the thousands of brave black boys on their return." If southern whites slaughtered defenseless youth at the slightest hint of defiance, how would they respond to proud black men in uniform? "What will be their reward for their true devotion to the Stars and Stripes?" the editor warned. "Will it be the lynchers' rope for them and their sisters?"[13]

In the weeks following Armistice Day, the black press mourned both soldiers and civilians who died at the hands of white mobs. No one seemed safe from a broadening postwar backlash. The week before the mob struck in Shubuta, Kentucky vigilantes seized a recently discharged army private and hung him from a tree. The ex-soldier had scuffled with a deputy sheriff who accused him of theft. Just a few days later, a uniformed black sergeant in Anniston, Alabama, narrowly avoided lynching after shooting two white streetcar operators who attacked him for sitting in the white section. After the mob struck in Shubuta five days later, talk of attacks on black troops mingled with reports of Mississippi's latest lynching. When Walter White arrived several weeks later, informants claimed that a brother of the lynched Howze sisters, another recently discharged soldier, disappeared as he walked home from the train station. Some said a white mob had lynched him. Others claimed that policemen forced the ex-soldier onto a chain gang.[14]

White could not substantiate these claims, and he eliminated them from his final report, but the rumors underscored how pervasive attacks on black soldiers had become. Reports of racial violence mingled and morphed in the postwar months. In editorials and investigations, antilynching advocates portrayed these seemingly isolated incidents as a coordinated effort to subdue soldiers and sharecroppers alike. Maintaining white supremacy had always been hard work, and racial violence had long served to reinforce the racial status quo. The sight of uniformed black men undoubtedly increased whites' sense of urgency. When black veterans returned to Clarke County, local officials demanded that they discard their uniforms within three days or face jail time. Through harassment, intimidation, and violence, a black Mississippi veteran lamented, white supremacists seemed determined "to blot out all memory of the war."[15]

The Shubuta lynchings, occurring in the midst of mounting violence against black soldiers, showed how quickly white Mississippians wanted to forget. Yet many had gone through eighteen months of war sensing no conflict between Wilson's war for democracy and white supremacy. Through relentless investigation, protest, and publicity, the NAACP and its allies hoped to convince government officials and the public at large that the war's end only made antilynching efforts more urgent. While the opening months of 1919 furnished dozens more incidents for the NAACP to investigate, the killings in Shubuta galvanized an antilynching campaign in the midst of a postwar transition. As the NAACP looked ahead to the challenge of securing the peace at home, it looked back across three decades of mob violence. In a final publicity push for its May 1919 National Conference on Lynching, the NAACP published *Thirty Years of Lynching in the United States*, a booklet finished just weeks after White's trip to Shubuta. In just over one hundred pages, it offered a sixty-page list of 3,224 documented victims between 1899 and 1918.[16]

The Shubuta lynchings dramatized the ongoing threat of unchecked and indiscriminate southern violence. Having capped off a year of mounting attacks—the highest recorded total of black victims since 1911—the quadruple lynching suggested that mob violence, whether measured in bodies or sheer brutality, showed no signs of abating. While the four in Shubuta represented more than half of Mississippi's seven recorded lynching victims in 1918, the NAACP pamphlet offered evidence of the state's unrivaled record of racial violence. In a thirty-year period, only Georgia claimed more lynching victims (386) than the Magnolia State (373). Per capita, however, Mississippi's lynching rate nearly doubled that of Georgia. More damning still, the state topped a chart of "Women and Girls Lynched." With the Howze sisters factored in, Mississippi claimed more than 20 percent of all recorded female mob victims.[17]

The lynching of pregnant women provided a gory climax to a section entitled "The Story of One Hundred Lynchings." Sandwiched between a statistical summary and that sixty-page list of lynching victims, the NAACP selected several dozen vignettes from its trove of files. Only four wartime incidents—including all three of those personally investigated by White—made the cut. The final lynching account summarized White's Shubuta findings—the "loose character" of Dr. Johnston, the pregnant Howze sisters, the quarrel with Major Clark, and the divergent theories surrounding the dentist's death. The passage closed with the fetus still wriggling in Alma Howze's corpse.[18]

The Shubuta example provided a concluding glimpse of mob victims, but a final vignette offered a glimmer of hope. Titled "Mob Leaders Go to Prison," the passage described a North Carolina judge's decision to sentence fifteen white men to prison terms for leading a lynch mob that killed four innocent bystanders. The vigilantes failed to lynch their target, a black prisoner locked up in Winston-Salem's city jail, because the mayor had called out guardsmen, police officers, and firemen to disperse the mob. The governor responded to the unrest by dispatching troops and artillery. The anecdote closed with the words of an unnamed "prominent business man": "We don't mean to be sentimental on this matter, but we aren't going to have our city's good name spoilt by a lynching."[19]

That juxtaposition of sadistic cruelty in Mississippi and successful antimob measures in North Carolina typified the NAACP's antilynching strategy. Where "sentimental" appeals failed to warm hearts, activists sought to cool heads. In every southern state—even Mississippi—powerful whites shared the North Carolina businessman's practical aversion to mob violence. They worried that lynching reports would scare away not only black laborers but northern investors as well. Even as mob violence repelled the money and manpower necessary to sustain their prosperity, it attracted the attention of black activists and their allies in Washington. By enlisting the support of those white southerners who feared lynching's political and economic consequences, the NAACP sought to broaden its postwar influence. In their search for white Mississippi allies, antilynching activists reached out to men who—like their fellow southerner in the White House—balanced their racial ideology with their commitment to ordered prosperity.

TO FOREVER ELIMINATE THE NEGRO FROM POLITICS

While white Mississippians debated the best way to handle the state's black majority, African Americans in Clarke County's "bush country" clung to traditions of independence and uplift. Local whites spoke longingly of the days before "reconstruction times," but James Yates's grandmother Lizzy Cherry described the end of slavery and the building of a free black community. When Union soldiers marched through Clarke County, Grandma Lizzy had watched a fellow slave lead the Yankees to her master, who was hiding in a nearby swamp with field hands, livestock, and the family silver.[20]

Like his mother, Yates's father had been born to formerly enslaved southerners, who migrated from Alabama to Kansas as part of the post-Reconstruction "Exoduster" movement. Gibson Washington Yates moved to Clarke County around the turn of the century. Yet like his parents, who fought Reconstruction-era racial violence with their feet, Gibson Yates yearned to slip free from Jim Crow's tightening grip. While his wife and young children stayed with Grandma Lizzy near Shubuta, Yates journeyed with three of his siblings to eastern Oklahoma and established a homestead just south of the all-black settlement of Boley. Although his father eventually returned to Mississippi, the family tradition of self-determination and black consciousness had a profound affect on James Yates. He recalled a letter from an uncle in Oklahoma "saying he had joined the Marcus Garvey movement. He was waiting, he said, for a ship to take him and others back to Africa." Black Mississippians did not have to venture to Oklahoma or Harlem to join Garvey's Universal Negro Improvement Association, which established hundreds of chapters across the South—including one in Clarke County.[21]

James Yates attended the same log cabin schoolhouse where his grandmother and mother had learned to read and write. James found his new teacher, an elderly ex-slave, intimidating and "outright nutty." Every election year, Professor Blakeney rode his mule twenty-five miles into Meridian and attempted to vote. He told his young pupils that a new day was coming in Mississippi, when "the Blacks and poor whites are going to get together" and vote in a new regime. "In less than one hundred years," the professor promised his students, "we will have a Black President of the United States of America!" Eventually, as Yates recalled, the white folks up in Meridian tired of chasing off the old man: "A few years before he died, some people worked him over good at the polling place...[and] he was never really well again."[22]

The intertwined threat of education, black self-determination, and interracial politics fueled a harsh political turn in the decades leading up the Shubuta lynchings. Fearing that the professor's pupils might take a similar journey from the schoolhouse to the ballot box, militant white supremacists argued that the 1890 disenfranchisement convention had not gone far enough. Led by convention delegate James K. Vardaman, a newspaper editor turned state legislator, they launched an all-out attack on black education. "There is no use to equivocate or lie about the matter," Vardaman boasted, "Mississippi's constitutional convention of 1890 was held for no other purpose than to eliminate the nigger from politics." Without decent schools, he argued, black Mississippians would never satisfy the voting requirements imposed by the new constitution.[23]

A potent combination of racial fear and regional rivalry fueled the assault on black education. Vardaman built a diehard following in Mississippi's eastern "hill" counties by playing on resentment of aristocratic Delta planters. In the process, he did more than anyone to cement east Mississippi's reputation for a particularly "mean" style of racial politics. Vardaman's school-funding scheme—which stipulated that white tax dollars would fund white schools, while black schools would rely only on tax revenue collected from blacks—played upon the strings of race, class, and region in unison. Because officials in the black-majority Delta counties spent most of their school allotments on superior schools for a smaller pool of white students, Vardaman's plan simultaneously undercut those counties' funding advantage and served his antiblack agenda. The segregation of school funding, much of which came from poll taxes paid almost exclusively by whites, ensured that black school allotments would decrease statewide. From his newspaper office and his seat in the state legislature—and through two failed gubernatorial bids—Vardaman put these proposals front and center.[24]

Vardaman's legislative allies—who elevated him to House speaker in 1894—embraced his hard-line white supremacy. Arista Johnston, one of Clarke County's most influential Vardaman supporters, championed the antiblack agenda in Jackson. The farmer-legislator eschewed

Vardaman's vulgar theatrics—in print, at least, he preferred *negro* to *nigger*. But even as he sent his five sons to college and backed unprecedented public school expenditures, Johnston blasted the state's "suicidal policy of black education." Johnston echoed Vardaman's proposals, though the prosperous farmer stressed economic stability and political control over crude racism. "Our efforts to educate the negro for the last thirty years [have] been successful only in ruining the labor and increasing the criminality of the state," he argued, "and if we continue this policy I wish to ask how long will be required to array a large negro majority at the polls and how long will it then take to re-establish the horrors of reconstruction times?" Alluding to Vardaman's campaign promises to overturn the Fourteenth and Fifteenth Amendments, Arista Johnston promised Clarke County voters that he would support any plan that would "forever eliminate the negro from the state and county politics."[25]

First among the "horrors of reconstruction times" that fueled Vardaman's rise to power was the specter of "social equality." The "White Chief" warned at every turn that black voting would lead to racial amalgamation and advocated racial terrorism to beat back this threat. "If it is necessary every Negro in the state will be lynched," Vardaman famously warned, "it will be done to maintain white supremacy." Such pronouncements unnerved the state's conservatives, who believed that Mississippi already had enough laws on the books to nullify any threat to whites' "social, industrial, or political supremacy." Vardaman's racial extremism, his critics argued, would undermine economic development and encourage blacks to flee the state. In his 1900 inaugural address, business-minded governor A. H. Longino not only rebuked Vardaman's attack on black education but proposed measures to curb rampant vigilante violence. Emphasizing "the unequaled advantages it offers capital by the way of profits in manufacturing," Longino argued, Mississippi would "never attain that magnificent degree of prosperity and grandeur of statehood, that of right should be hers, so long as public opinion permits the high-handed mob to treat the law with contempt, defy the courts and officers, and murder the people, without prosecution or punishment."[26]

The governor's call for law and order riled Vardaman supporters, who countered that public criticism of lynching only inflamed racial tensions. In the wake of Longino's call for "the suppression of mobs," Arista Johnston blasted the governor's antimob agenda in the region's largest newspaper. A bill that required the state to award damages to the families of lynch victims and to remove negligent law-enforcement officials, Johnston boasted, "was still-born dead in committee-room, and, I hope, buried so deep that it will never be resurrected." Not only had "the mere agitation of such a law...caused the number of lynchings to increase," Johnston argued, but black Mississippians bore responsibility as well. While Vardaman's critics attributed the spike in lynchings to inflammatory white supremacist rhetoric, his allies countered that mob violence was necessary to counter an imagined epidemic of black assaults on white women. This rape myth—which fed off Vardaman's argument that political and educational privileges only emboldened black men's "lustful" desires—pervaded the state's political culture. Like Vardaman, Arista Johnston rationalized mob violence as a justifiable punishment for black rapists. Two decades before his murdered son's alleged sexual transgressions flipped that rape myth on its head, the Clarke County farmer-legislator used the specter of the black rapist to discredit antilynching measures. "The only way to stop lynchings," he argued, "is to stop the crime for which parties are lynched, and God only knows how that can be done."[27]

This potent mix of racial fear and populist politics paid dividends in 1903, when Vardaman won the race for governor on his third attempt. A new direct primary law allowed him to take his message to the masses and bypass the small clique of state party leaders who had blocked his previous bids. Yet the rise of racial extremism exposed political divisions across the state—not only between the hills and the Delta but in communities across the state. The tension between pragmatic white supremacy and crude prejudice animated local politics as well as regional rivalries, as community leaders balanced the demands of racial control with the need for social and economic stability. In Clarke County, where Arista Johnston attempted to ride the White Chief's coattails into a third consecutive term in the legislature, prominent local whites criticized Vardaman's "extreme views" and made clear their preference for a governor who represented "the conservative business element." Questioning the wisdom of championing a "hostile attitude" toward blacks, local Vardaman opponents backed a lawyer from a prominent local family in his campaign to unseat Johnston. When the smoke cleared, Vardaman had failed to carry Clarke County and Johnston had lost his seat.[28]

Johnston never repudiated his support for Vardaman, who captured a seat in the US Senate four years after leaving the governor's mansion. Facing off against a powerful Delta planter, Vardaman capitalized on the twin-pronged strategy of regional class resentments and race-baiting theatrics. In Clarke County, Vardaman's base had swelled as the area's demographic and economic character shifted. Clarke entered the twentieth century a black-majority county, but lumber workers and mill employees swelled the local white population. Vardaman had that constituency in mind when he launched his Senate bid in nearby Meridian, where whites from Clarke and other neighboring counties cheered on the White Chief as forty yoke of oxen pulled his wagon through downtown. Supporters carried signs reading "Hillbillies" and "Rednecks." Some wore red bandannas around their necks to drive home the point. Vardaman, dressed in his trademark white suit and black Stetson hat, rattled off a list of racist pledges for the common man. He repeated his unrealized gubernatorial pledges to repeal the Fourteenth and Fifteenth Amendments, and told a story about a "big, black buck" who raped a white mother and her daughters in their rural farmhouse while the men worked in the fields.[29]

Vardaman carried seventy-four of Mississippi's seventy-five counties—including Clarke—and took his white supremacist crusade to Washington. The rookie senator threw himself into a southern-led campaign to segregate the nation's capital and purge the federal government of black employees. Whether in Mississippi or Washington, Vardaman declared, blacks "should not be permitted to share with white men in the government of white men." The senator arrived in Washington the same year as Woodrow Wilson, the first southern-born president since Reconstruction. Declaring the South "back in the saddle," Wilson's southern appointees segregated federal agencies and purged black government workers. To ensure that the Wilson administration did not hire any new black government officials, the US Civil Service Commission instituted a policy requiring photographs for all job applications. On Capitol Hill, southern lawmakers introduced bills to segregate Washington streetcars and prohibit interracial marriage. None supported these efforts more vigorously than Vardaman, who delighted supporters back home with his saber rattling.[30]

Like fellow southerners who considered themselves "progressive," Wilson balanced a commitment to Jim Crow with other political priorities. The Virginia-born son of a former Confederate chaplain, the president remained decidedly sympathetic to the southern status quo. First as a scholar, and later as a public official, he defended the racial order that white supremacists erected in the wake of Reconstruction as necessary and beneficial to both races. As he did the key components in his reform agenda, Wilson regarded segregation as a progressive innovation that promoted order and stability. On a practical level, the president had every reason to appease his southern Democratic supporters. Yet unlike Vardaman, the president balanced his racial convictions with an overriding commitment to wartime unity. Recognizing this tension, civil rights advocates emphasized the domestic and diplomatic liabilities of mob violence. Despite Wilson's prewar capitulations to white supremacists, civil rights advocates hoped that the war emergency would force the president to reconcile his zeal for global democracy with the need for racial justice back home.

Wilson remained decidedly aloof from black leaders. Nonetheless, he recognized the threat that mob violence posed to his global ambitions. For six years, the president had repeatedly declined black requests for a public condemnation of lynchings. But by 1918, with wartime race riots and lynchings on the rise, Wilson finally capitulated to concerns over diplomatic embarrassment and plummeting black morale. "We are at this very moment fighting lawless passion," Wilson declared in late July. "Germany has outlawed herself among the nations because she has disregarded the sacred obligations of law and has made lynchers of her armies." Speaking nearly a year to the day after the Silent

Protest Parade, Wilson took care not to offend his southern supporters by mentioning African Americans or singling out the region where the vast majority of wartime lynchings took place. Mob violence persisted "not in any single region, but in many and widely separated parts of the country," the president declared. Despite his unwillingness to take the white South to task, Wilson branded lynching a "disgraceful evil" that undermined his lofty war aims. "We proudly claim to be the champions of democracy," Wilson pleaded. "If we really are in deed and in truth let us see to it that we do not discredit our own."[31]

Wilson's words did little to curb mob violence. "So far is Shubuta from civilization," a black editor lamented in the wake of the lynchings, "that [it]...never hears of presidential proclamations, or pays any attention to them when it does hear." Wilson, keenly aware how carefully southern whites followed his words, refused to acknowledge lynching's overwhelmingly regional and racial character. Furthermore, government efforts to stoke patriotic fervor for the war fueled a national wave of vigilantism. Worried that domestic radicals could sabotage the war effort, Wilson acquiesced to a host of repressive wartime measures that mirrored the southern backlash against "subversive" blacks. Three months before Wilson's antilynching address, a mob near St. Louis killed German-born Robert Prager for making "disloyal" remarks at a socialist rally. The lynching, which one defense lawyer praised as a "patriotic murder," allowed Wilson to frame mob violence as a national problem. Meanwhile, mob violence from coast to coast provided a veneer of patriotism for white supremacists bent on policing African Americans. Back in Mississippi, vigilantes frequently harassed, intimidated, and attacked black Mississippians under pro-American pretenses. In Shubuta and elsewhere, as Walter White had documented, employers exploited wartime "work or fight" laws to force black men onto labor gangs and black women into white kitchens.[32]

Although racial abuses continued in the war's wake, Mississippi's most notorious white supremacist had overreached. As a self-appointed watchdog of the administration's segregationist policies, Vardaman had annoyed the Wilson administration by howling on the rare occasion when a black appointee surfaced. More galling to Wilson, and politically perilous to Vardaman, was the senator's opposition to American involvement in World War I. He opposed military preparedness and voted, with only five other senators, against the Declaration of War in 1917. As with his other controversial positions, Vardaman invoked white supremacy to defend his antiwar stance and shore up his base for the upcoming reelection campaign. He simultaneously attacked the draft for sending "arrogant strutting representatives of the black soldiery" to southern military bases and for leaving too many black men behind to ravish Mississippi's white women. As the war wound down and his reelection campaign ramped up, Vardaman called on white men to protect their wives and daughters from "French-women-ruined" black veterans.[33]

Race baiting could not save Vardaman from a patriotic backlash back home. In Shubuta, the local paper carried Wilson's public rebuke of the senator. "Wilson against Vardaman," announced a front-page headline. Three weeks after avoiding any mention of Wilson's antilynching message, the paper printed verbatim the president's carefully worded statement. He had no right to criticize Mississippi for reelecting the senator, Wilson warned, "but I should be obliged to accept their action as a condemnation of my administration, and it is only right that they should know this before they act." The heavy-handed reportage—the editor capitalized Wilson's more pointed phrases—worked in Shubuta and across the state. Vardaman carried less than a third of Mississippi counties and lost handily. However, Clarke County's majority of mill workers and small farmers bucked the statewide trend and voted for Vardaman.[34]

The virulent racism of the campaign did not abate with Vardaman's defeat. Through his Jackson-based weekly, the lame-duck senator fueled a postwar backlash with virulent propaganda. Convinced that the president and his in-state political rivals were "with the negro," Vardaman's tabloid churned out evidence of an imminent racial revolution. A few weeks before the Shubuta lynching, a full-page spread outlined "What the Negro Will Demand" after the war. "The thing to do is to prevent him from securing things that will destroy the white man's civilization," Vardaman warned. "It is time, has been time for years, for the white men to do something." A week later, decrying Japanese plans to protest the Allied powers' racial chauvinism at the upcoming peace conference at Versailles, the Vardaman camp maintained that force was the only language that would deter the "inferior races" from challenging white supremacy. "A gentleman would not visit a home where he suspected he was not welcome," Vardaman declared. "But a negro or other near-ape, will go any place where he is not barred by a club."[35]

The senator's recent defeat suggested that such crude appeals were losing their power, though election results did not save four black victims a few weeks later. Since Mississippi white supremacists codified segregation and disenfranchisement in the late nineteenth century, Clarke County's gentry had tried to walk the line between racial extremism and economic stability. While some locals clung dearly to the White Chief's virulent and volatile racism, Clarke County's white elite feared the economic and social consequences of becoming Mississippi's lynching leader. Radical white supremacy, and the spate of mob killings that it inspired, branded Clarke as a particularly vicious corner of the nation's lynching capital. Faced with accelerating black outmigration and racial disorder, white political and business leaders statewide scrambled to refurbish Mississippi's reputation. That strategy culminated in an unlikely scene—a white Mississippian presiding over the second day of the NAACP's National Conference on Lynching.

The Right Kind of Propaganda

Ultimately, the grassroots calculus of rural blacks impressed Mississippi's conservative establishment more than Wilsonian rhetoric. As he reeled from news of the Shubuta lynchings, James Yates did not mull over the hypocrisy of American war aims. Instead, he lamented the futility of life under Jim Crow. "At best," he concluded, "I would end up with a third-rate education, qualifying me for only the worst kind of jobs, that is, if I didn't cross the wrong white man and get myself killed." For Yates, the lynchings snuffed out any thoughts of a future in Mississippi. "After the incidents at Shubuta I had only one obsession," he recalled. "That was to get up North to magic places like Chicago and New York, where I'd heard there was some freedom, and where white folks didn't shoot you, lynch you, and insult you every day."[36]

Mississippi's business community called this "labor demoralization." The state had lost some impoverished and disillusioned residents during the previous decades, but through the first decade of the twentieth century Mississippi remained a magnet for southern black migrants. Recruited by planters to farm the fertile Mississippi River valley, African Americans still saw in Mississippi an opportunity for some level of prosperity and independence. Yet war mobilization and the subsequent spike in racial turmoil fueled a mass exodus. An estimated one hundred thousand blacks left Mississippi in the latter half of the 1910s. In 1920, for the first time in state history, the federal census reported *fewer* black residents than the previous one.[37]

African Americans in Clarke County left at higher rates than their counterparts in neighboring counties. Several months before the United States entered World War I, Shubuta's *Mississippi Messenger* lamented the promise of "soft work and good pay" that lured local blacks north. For a paper that almost never mentioned the town's black majority, the acknowledgment revealed how serious local elites deemed the problem. Falling cotton prices, boll weevils, floods, and the abuses of the farm-tenancy system forced many rural blacks to abandon the land, but discrimination and violence factored in as well. White constituents recognized the link between lynching and labor flight, and some urged their leaders to take action to stem the tide. "I am as fully a believer in the theory that this is a white man's country...as any citizen of it," a white Mississippian warned the governor in 1917. "But if we wish to see Mississippi prosper, the evils I have mentioned, and others that exist, must be corrected."[38]

Lynching loomed large among these evils. "The fear of the mob," black researcher and War Department adviser Emmett J. Scott warned in his study of wartime migration, "has greatly accelerated the exodus." James Yates's disillusionment echoed in black coverage of the Shubuta lynchings. Black newspapers—particularly those with heavy circulation in Mississippi—played on the anxieties of business leaders (fig. 2.1). The New Orleans–based *Southwestern*

Christian Advocate noted that Clarke County had already "lost a large number of its most faithful laborers." In the wake of the quadruple lynching, more would surely follow. "We sincerely hope," the editor declared, "that there will not be enough Negroes in Clarke County, Mississippi, to carry a pail of water two blocks, and that they will move out at the first opportunity." The *Chicago Defender*, wildly popular among the Windy City's transplanted Mississippians and those they left behind, crowed that the Shubuta lynchings had "dealt a vicious blow" to Clarke County's white employers. The paper, which Mississippi authorities regularly confiscated, aimed its economic forecast at business-minded elites and aspiring migrants alike. "Fields are void of workers," the *Defender* reported, "and crops are decaying for the want of attention."[39]

Such images haunted the handful of planters, businessmen, and clergy who gathered in Jackson barely a week after the Shubuta lynchings. Resurgent mob violence, combined with Vardaman's headline-grabbing rants, had some of the state's most powerful men worried. Mississippi had nearly made it through 1918 with three recorded lynchings, but the quadruple lynching in Clarke County more than doubled the year's death toll and shattered any illusion that the state had changed its ways. Fearing the consequences of more lynchings in the coming months, "Mississippi's strongest men" met to chart a new way forward.[40]

The Mississippians had help. Bolton Smith, a Memphis investment banker and civic leader, had traveled down with the editor of the city's leading newspaper. A few months earlier, after an upsurge in racial violence across his home state, Smith had spearheaded the founding of the Tennessee Law and Order League. Working through his extensive personal and commercial contacts in Mississippi, Smith argued that his neighbors to the south urgently needed just such an organization. "There is no question," Smith advised, "but that it is to the interest of the vast majority of planters in Mississippi to make the negro satisfied." With the aid of the "successful business man," the clergy, and the press, Smith argued, Mississippi's power brokers could stabilize a labor crisis quickly spiraling out of control. With high-sounding rhetoric and urgent economic concerns, these men founded the Mississippi Welfare League.[41]

THE REASON

FIGURE 2.1

Black activists and journalists regularly emphasized mob violence as a
prime motivation for black migration to northern cities. This argument
resonated with business-minded white southerners who feared a shortage
of cheap black labor. "The Reason," *The Crisis* 19:5 (1920): 264.

While financial concerns brought together an impressive roster of planters, businessmen, and corporate lawyers, the group invoked Wilsonian idealism and Christian charity in its founding statement. "A great change has come into the minds and hearts of the people of the world," the charter began. "The sacrifice and suffering caused by the world war have brought about a new era of altruism, and men of broad vision and adequate material wealth have awakened to a new conception of their duties to their fellow men." The triumphant war rhetoric contrasted their high-minded humanitarianism with the suspect patriotism and demagoguery of the Vardaman crowd. Indeed, the Welfare League's executive committee included men, particularly Delta planter-politician Leroy Percy and Jackson newspaperman Frederick Sullens, who had played key roles in the senator's downfall.[42]

The Mississippi Welfare League's founding statement offered a stirring yet purposefully vague set of proposals. They eschewed "radical remedies" for the state's current ills, and though the men stressed privately their commitment to "the spiritual, moral, intellectual and physical well-being" of Mississippians "regardless of race," they made no mention of lynchings or other abuses in their early press releases. In fact, they failed to mention any *racial* problems by name. Their manifesto, released to news outlets nationwide, urged "greater respect for the law" and pined for a day when "all our people may the more fully enjoy and appreciate the common blessings of life, liberty, and the pursuit of happiness." To that end, the league solicited contributions of $100 each from seventy leading citizens, just as Jesus, in the Gospel of Luke, sent out seventy men to tell the people that the kingdom of God had arrived.[43]

Seven thousand dollars seemed a paltry sum to usher in the kingdom, but the Welfare League's immediate goals were less lofty. With one salaried staffer, the organization announced itself a "clearinghouse" for Mississippians hoping to "promote public opinion toward the achievement of objects in common with its own." In other words, the Welfare League served as a public relations firm for employers hoping to stem the exodus of black laborers from the state. "From an industrial standpoint," the league's executive committee concluded, "we cannot progress unless we...educate our great laboring class to love their State, appreciate its advantages, and strive for its economical progress." To retain black labor and rehabilitate the state's image, executive secretary Jack Wilson argued, the league needed "to scatter the right kind of propaganda."[44]

The league's belated calls for a relatively enlightened approach to black labor retention revealed just how desperate Mississippi whites deemed the postwar crisis. Attempts to halt the exodus northward by fraud and force had failed, and the league's leaders proved receptive to risky new ventures. When the NAACP requested the fledgling organization's endorsement of its upcoming National Conference on Lynching, the league proved surprisingly receptive. Such an alliance might have seemed laughable just a few months before and would soon be unthinkable once again. However, for a brief moment in the wake of the war, the NAACP's eagerness to enlist southern white support for its antilynching efforts dovetailed with the Welfare League's desire to soften Mississippi's image. That the association's leadership remained largely white undoubtedly greased the wheels. Founding league member Fred Sullens made clear to NAACP officials that he opposed "any form of social or political equality." But the World War I veteran would at least acknowledge NAACP correspondence out of respect for Joel Spingarn, the organization's white executive board chairman. The two had served together in army intelligence during the war. Like most of the Welfare Leaguers contacted, Sullens believed the upcoming national conference would be counterproductive. "The proper place to discuss this question is in the South," Sullens warned, "and the proper persons to handle it are Southern men."[45]

Vardaman agreed. Back at the helm of his Jackson-based propaganda rag, the ex-senator denounced the upcoming conference as further proof that "Negroes are demanding social and political privileges which, prior to the war, they were apparently content to do without." While the White Chief conceded that "lawlessness causes trouble, interferes with business, and unsettles everything," he maintained that "there are some instances where nothing else will take its place. Lynching will continue as long as rapes and foul murder is [sic] committed by negro brutes."

Instead of demanding due process in the conviction and punishment of black suspects, Vardaman called on "the white men in every community in Mississippi [to] organize, select 25 or 30 of the bravest, and best men who will take these matters in hand." Rather than rely on "courts of law"—which forced "outraged" white women to recount their "guiltless infamy" in public—these upstanding vigilantes would apprehend the accused and "investigate" alleged crimes. "Before anybody is hung," Vardaman proposed, "they will know definitely that the person deserves hanging." In response to reformers' call to stamp out lynching, the White Chief proposed that Mississippians refine the practice.[46]

In spite of such shrill denunciations, NAACP ex-president and conference planner Moorfield Storey convinced a few white Mississippians to sign a preconference "call." The list of endorsements also included Georgia governor Hugh Dorsey, who had unknowingly welcomed Walter White into his office several months earlier, and former Alabama governor Emmett O'Neal. While the Mississippi signers—a Presbyterian lay leader, a railroad lawyer, and two Welfare League officers—lacked a political pedigree, NAACP officials recognized their symbolic importance. Conference planners had originally planned to have the Mississippi-born former attorney general Thomas Gregory read Walter White's investigative reports on lynchings in "So. Georgia [and] Shubuta." Instead, the NAACP invited the Mississippi Welfare League's only paid staffer to preside over the final day of the conference.[47]

Whatever convinced Jack Wilson to travel to New York, he clearly believed the move to be in the best interests of the league's publicity campaign. Carnegie Hall was no lion's den, even for a white Mississippian, as the NAACP had made every effort to build a national and nonpartisan gathering. Former New York governor and US Supreme Court justice Charles Evans Hughes, Wilson's Republican opponent in the 1916 presidential race, keynoted the opening session. Alabama's ex-governor Emmett O'Neal quoted former president Theodore Roosevelt, as he bemoaned the "mob spirit" sweeping the nation.[48]

The first day's only black speaker, NAACP field secretary James Weldon Johnson, tread where few white speakers dared. To challenge the myth that black rapists were to blame for lynching's persistence,

Johnson described the previous year's bloodiest incidents—all personally investigated by Walter White—in Tennessee, Georgia, and Mississippi. In none of these cases, he reminded the twenty-five-hundred attendees, "was a woman concerned at all as far as the crime of rape goes." The killings at Shubuta, where whites attempted to wash away the sins of one of their own with the blood of four black servants, capped the night's most pointed address. Amid a backdrop of pleas and platitudes, Johnson evoked the images of a castrated and charred Jim McIlherron, a disemboweled Mary Turner, and four battered corpses—Major and Andrew Clark, Maggie and Alma Howze—swaying from a Mississippi river bridge. "We need a little common honesty," he concluded. "This nation needs to humble itself before God. It needs to stop some of its loud boastings about humanity and democracy...until it is able to throw the arm of protection around the weakest within its own borders."[49]

Despite Johnson's castigation of Mississippi, Jack Wilson seemed pleased by "the splendid spirit" and lack of "radicalism" he encountered in New York. Echoing the president and other southern lynching critics, he stressed the national scope of mob violence and expressed relief that conference-goers "are broad and fair enough not to point the accusing finger at any particular section of the United States." As he presided over the second day's proceedings, Wilson readily deplored the sins of lynching "in whatever section they are found," and outlined the Welfare League's paternalistic approach to racial harmony. Likening the black race to "clay in the hands of the potter," Wilson explained how his organization planned to mold them. He had recruited "fifteen of Mississippi's outstanding colored men" to serve on an advisory committee. "It is pathetic," Wilson boasted, "to see how these men appreciate what I am trying to do for them." With their help, the league could convince the state's black residents they had "a better opportunity to be prosperous and happy in Mississippi than in any state in the Union."[50]

Lest anyone mistake his stand against lynching as an endorsement of "social equality," Wilson dispensed with that "bugaboo" immediately. "I do not want you to misunderstand me," he declared. "As a Mississippian, as a Southerner, there are certain traditions of my people that I must stand by." Wilson dismissed white fears of antilynching efforts as a "camouflage" for egalitarian reform, and he declared that black Mississippians desired no such thing. He cautioned northern reformers and black civil rights activists that white southerners alone could ensure racial peace. "We know best how to handle the situation," Wilson argued. "It must be done within."[51]

Wilson's Jim Crow apologia did not go unchallenged. NAACP stalwart William Pickens, the Yale-educated son of South Carolina slaves, challenged the southern white establishment's approach to antilynching reform. "The good man is in error who thinks he can endorse disfranchisement and segregation and 'Jim Crow-ism,' and still successfully oppose the mob," warned Pickens. "Mob members may be ignorant in some ways," he argued, "but they are too severely logical to overlook an inconsistency like that." In a defiant nod to the white South's demands for local control, Pickens castigated southern police brutality and called for federal antilynching laws. Then, he reminded Deep South whites of the source of their labor woes. "Southern people did not realize that so many laborers would be lost," the NAACP organizer declared, "by the mere killing of a few negroes each year."[52]

While these concerns over labor and profits had compelled white southerners to speak out against lynchings, Pickens contended that terrorism drove the South's racialized economy. "Lynching and mob violence are only methods of economic repression," he argued in a pamphlet published by the fledgling American Civil Liberties Union. "To attack lynching without attacking this system is like trying to be rid of the phenomena of smoke and heat without disturbing the basic fire." The slaughter of over two hundred Arkansas tenant farmers in February 1919, just weeks before the NAACP Conference on Lynching, heightened the urgency of Pickens's argument. The massacre in eastern Arkansas, which erupted in retaliation for the formation of the Progressive Farmers and Household Union, underscored the connection between economic control and mob violence.[53]

Pickens, who had grown up in Arkansas, contended that the same economic logic that fueled mass violence there drove seemingly isolated incidents across the country. "If we examine any, even the most complicated, of these 'race' troubles," he argued, "we will find some economic wrong at the bottom, some trouble about wages or work or property." While he did not mention the Shubuta lynchings specifically, the victims fit this profile. The Clark brothers worked for Johnston to pay off their father's debt on a mule. Maggie Howze's dispute with Johnston, a town leader alleged, stemmed from his decision to dock her pay by fifty cents a week to pay off her debt on a sewing machine. Presumably, when she quit, he had the prerogative to withhold the back pay, confiscate the sewing machine, or both. Regardless of what else transpired between employer and employee, white employers could wield credit as a cudgel. Lynching, Pickens argued, propped up "a cunningly contrived debt slavery."[54]

Pickens's antilynching arguments struck even some African American critics as "All-or-Nothing" radicalism. Still, Pickens did not deter southern whites' attempts to capitalize on the propaganda potential of the National Conference on Lynching. The unanimous passage of a resolution calling for federal antilynching legislation, in direct defiance of his pleas for local control, did not faze Jack Wilson. After the Welfare League leader announced his plans to plant "a publicity committee in every state in the South," the NAACP appointed him to head a task force charged with accomplishing that very goal. Wilson also sat on the committee that drafted the postconference "Address to the Nation," which decried lynching as "a menace to civilization." The influence of the NAACP's ambivalent southern allies permeated the brief declaration. While the drafters lamented that "local and state authorities offer only the feeblest objection to the actions of the mob," they avoided any mention of race, region, or federal legislation.[55]

In the wake of the antilynching conference, the NAACP and the Welfare League exploited the politics of security to divergent ends. The NAACP's annual conference theme for 1919, "To Make America Safe for Americans," invoked unrealized war aims and stressed the primacy of antilynching efforts. Back in Mississippi, the league's calls for a gentler Jim Crow regime took a backseat to its aggressive propaganda campaign aimed at black migrants. As "Red Summer" riots rocked Chicago and other northern cities, the Welfare League supplied the Associated Press and local Mississippi papers with reports aimed at "getting negro labor back from the north." In Clarke County, the *Mississippi Messenger* reassured readers that the Welfare League was "Formulating Plans for Return of Worthy Ones Who Have Been Misled." Those plans included offices in Chicago and St. Louis, the top destinations of Mississippi migrants, and a "publicity campaign" to counter "the evil and unfounded propaganda" of labor recruiters and black activists. In August, Jack Wilson visited Chicago personally in an attempt to convince transplanted Mississippians to come home. When his pleas fell on deaf ears, he returned with "two negroes of high citizenship" for a carefully orchestrated tour of Mississippi. A few weeks later, papers in Clarke County and statewide reported triumphantly that the men "declare themselves entirely converted from their previous stand and believe the south offers a fitting place of residence for negroes." With no hint of irony, Shubuta's hometown paper boasted that the unnamed Chicago blacks "discovered that negroes could walk on the sidewalks of Mississippi cities without being lynched."[56]

African Americans dismissed the report as propaganda. A black Mississippian reported that the Welfare League had escorted the "alleged Negro leaders" around the state "as if they had been convicts." Blasting their findings, the local informant reported "that racial conditions are worse in the South to-day than they have been in all the years of my life...and any one who reports to the contrary is false and a traitor to the cause of humanity." A black journalist in St. Louis cataloged the "hellish treatment" he witnessed during a recent southern tour and gave the Mississippi Welfare League a blunt ultimatum: "The South Must Repent!—Before Southern Afro-Americans in the North Will Return There to Live and Labor."[57]

Even in the wake of the summer's bloodiest race riot, black Chicagoans ignored the league's entreaties to return south. Meanwhile, their friends and relatives in Mississippi continued to head north. Welfare League press releases on white hostility and black poverty in Chicago, dutifully reported by Clarke County papers, failed to stem the tide. Indeed, the communities surrounding the bridge over the Chickasawhay River abandoned the state at record rates. The 1920 federal census, conducted just four months after the Welfare League's propaganda campaign peaked, revealed that Clarke County's black population had declined by nearly 30 percent since 1910. In a state that surpassed its southern neighbors in outmigration, Clarke County's black population dropped by four times the statewide rate. While black outmigration began in earnest in other parts of the state before 1910, migration from southeastern Mississippi paralleled the rise of racial tension in the war years. And while some blacks in other parts of the state fled rural poverty and repression for the relative safety of Mississippi's larger towns, Clarke County blacks saw little prospect for relief in nearby cities. Indeed, a wartime migration study reported heavy population losses in Meridian, Laurel, and Hattiesburg, and noted an even sharper decline in the surrounding rural areas. Rising wages in mills and on the farm, a telling sign of white employers' desperation, failed to stem the tide.[58]

The heavy population losses in the communities surrounding Shubuta, dramatized by black antilynching advocates, spurred belated pledges to curb racial abuse. However, James Yates and thousands of fellow black Mississippians had already concluded that the ravages of Vardaman-style politics—abysmal schools, bitter resentments, and brutal repression—choked out any hopes of advancement and security. This postwar backlash outlasted the Welfare League's brief moment in the spotlight and gave the lie to its refined rhetoric of racial goodwill. Indeed, Mississippi's white elite devoted more energy to repressing pro-civil-rights journalism than they did to developing effective counterpropaganda. As the antilynching campaign heated up in the postwar months, the state legislature banned the sale "of literature tending to disturb relations between the races." A black preacher fled the state after being beaten by a mob, fined, and sentenced to six months on a chain gang for selling *The Crisis*. Unable to wage even a propaganda battle without attendant violence, the Welfare League, and its promises of security, faded away.[59]

MY GOING-AWAY CLOTHES

Clarke County whites resented "the evil and unfounded propaganda" spread by civil rights advocates, but the looming threat of mob violence was neither rhetorical nor abstract. In the months following the

Shubuta killings, racial attacks occurred with frightening regularity and for any number of motives. Stories of mob violence in Shubuta terrified locals like young James Yates, but more direct scrapes with white vigilantes convinced him that he might be next. Around the time of the quadruple lynching, his uncle Willie escaped a similar fate.[60]

James's uncle worked in a Quitman sawmill. One day, he accidentally hit a white man with a piece of lumber. A gang of white workers tried to grab him, but Willie escaped. By the time he made it home, lynching rumors had spread through the countryside. Local merchants, anticipating trouble, stopped selling shotgun shells to black customers. The Yateses' neighbor, a European immigrant and social outcast, headed to town to buy them some ammunition. On his way out of Quitman, he spread the word that the Yateses would not go down without a fight. "Some of you will get killed by those niggers," he warned, "if you try to lynch that Willie."[61]

That night, James's father, uncle, and two black neighbors hid with loaded shotguns in a stand of trees. His aunt and grandmother spent the night in the chicken coop, while James hid with his mother and sisters under a rosebush in the back yard. "I pictured trucks filled with hostile Kluxers," James recalled. "That was one of the longest nights I ever endured" (see fig. 2.2). When morning broke, everyone emerged from their hiding places. The lynch mob never came. "It was like Freedom Day again for Grandmama," James recalled, "and she was dancing all over the house."[62]

The celebration was short-lived. Even as the Welfare Leaguers circulated reports of postwar racial harmony, ongoing mob violence undercut their sunny pronouncements. In 1920, on the Fourth of July, a gang of masked men riddled a railway mail clerk's body with bullets near Clarke County's northern border. The black postal worker, James Foster Spencer, had fought off an angry white supervisor with a knife as their train passed through Enterprise. Two white postal clerks beat Spencer unconscious and turned him over to local authorities when the train reached Meridian. Two days later, a gang of masked men seized Spencer as he rode to face charges in Clarke County. The *Meridian Star*, while stressing that the lynching took place in a neighboring county,

81

boasted that "the killing of the negro was the quietest and most orderly that ever took place in this section." The NAACP hoped that the killing of a postal worker might force federal intervention, but Postmaster General Alfred S. Burleson's inspector quickly dismissed the case as "completely within the jurisdiction of the state authorities."[63]

Two months later, a mob lynched another Meridian man just a stone's throw from James Yates's cabin. Local authorities had transferred Will Echols to Quitman for safekeeping after the state Supreme Court stayed his execution. That night, a mob raided the county jail, drove the prisoner down a lonely county road, and pumped his body full of bullets. The *Chicago Defender*, by now all too familiar with Clarke County, reported that the mob forced Echols to kiss a Confederate flag and yelled "To Hell with the Supreme Court" as they opened fire. Meridian officials again made every effort to distance their county's good name from Clarke's brutal record. Just as the Lauderdale County authorities "were not in the least to blame" for the Spencer slaying, the *Meridian Star* reported, "no blame can be attached to them in the lynching of Echols yesterday morning."[64]

The hairsplitting made no difference to Yates, who already deemed his home county a death trap. He quit school in his early teens, and squirreled away pennies for his journey north. Hard cash was hard to come by in his first job, at a Quitman brickyard, where the boss paid black workers in vouchers that could be redeemed for overpriced goods at the company store. When Yates asked for "real money" instead, a white man kicked him from behind and sent him flying into a pile of horse dung.[65]

The credit system and the violence that it perpetuated, as William Pickens had argued, trapped black laborers in a web of debt and abuse. However, whites employed other strategies to restrict black mobility. Despite the Welfare League's propaganda campaign, force quickly overtook persuasion as the preferred strategy for halting black migrants. In Meridian, the first stop on Yates's route north, white policemen routinely detained black train passengers on trumped-up charges. The city's lawmen joined in the propaganda war as well. In a testament to the role of black newspapers in promoting and facilitating migration,

COPYRICHT-1923.
THE HAMMOND STUDIOS,
MERIDIAN, AND JACKSON, MISS.

FIGURE 2.2

African Americans in Jim Crow–era Clarke County frequently
attributed racial violence to the Ku Klux Klan. Although the
post–World War I Klan's membership and influence peaked in northern
and western states, the Klan maintained a visible presence in southern
Mississippi during the 1920s. LC-USZ62-28024. Courtesy of the Library
of Congress Prints and Photographs Division.

Meridian's police chief ordered his deputies to confiscate the wildly
popular *Chicago Defender*.[66]

Undaunted, in 1922, sixteen-year-old James Yates put on his "going-
away clothes" under his dingy overalls and lit out for the Stonewall
train station. With two friends and two dollars in his pocket, James
trudged ten miles through the swamp rather than risk being spotted
along the roadside. In Meridian, as he waited nervously for the next
train, Yates fully expected a white policeman to haul him off to jail. In a
dingy Jim Crow car, just behind the train engine, Yates breathed easier
with every mile he put between himself and the bridge.[67]

Along with hundreds of fellow migrants from Clarke County, and thousands more from across the South, James Yates helped to reshape the politics of racial violence and civil rights by fleeing Dixie. Rather than a retreat, black migration represented the most immediate and historically significant response to World War I–era mob violence. As they moved to cities where they could and did vote, southern migrants shook up the politics of the urban North and boosted black clout in Washington. Even before World War I ended, the NAACP forged alliances with those congressmen who answered to northern black voters. St. Louis Republican Leonidas Dyer, sponsor of the first antilynching bill in American history, represented the city's largest black enclaves. As migrants from Mississippi and elsewhere poured into St. Louis in search of work and relative safety, these new voters forced politicians like Dyer to embrace unprecedented civil rights protections. Over the next twenty years, every congressional sponsor of federal antilynching legislation represented a northern or western state with a growing black constituency.[68]

Welfare League propaganda denounced outside "political forces" for slandering Mississippi, but unabated mob violence forced a growing number of white southerners to action as well. Unlike the antimigration boosters, these lynching critics advocated interracial dialogue and concrete reforms. In 1919, white moderates founded the Commission on Interracial Cooperation. Several years later, Jessie Daniel Ames, a leader of the interracial movement in Texas, founded the Association of Southern Women for the Prevention of Lynching. Arguing that southern mobs could no longer murder black men in the name of chivalry, association members lobbied church groups and political leaders to take public stands against racial violence. Throughout the 1920s, the number of southern lynchings declined steadily and the black pioneers of the antilynching movement claimed credit. W. E. B. Du Bois considered the southern interracial movement "one of the great results of the NAACP" and evidence that ten years of activism had "compelled the South to attempt its own internal reform." Meanwhile, Walter White—who ultimately investigated forty-one lynchings and eight race riots—churned out a series of books and articles based on his undercover investigations. In 1931, the NAACP's original secret weapon became its new leader. Antilynching legislation, despite unrelenting opposition from southern politicians, remained at the top of the organization's agenda.[69]

White's rise to the top of the NAACP coincided with a seismic shift in black politics. Northern urban voters, their ranks swelled by ongoing southern migration, abandoned the Republican Party for the economic appeal of Franklin Roosevelt's New Deal. James Yates, by then a registered voter in Chicago, recalled how "Black folks went wild" for the Democratic nominee. In 1934, a southern-born Chicagoan ran for Congress under the slogan "Forward with Roosevelt." The first black Democratic congressman in American history, Arthur Wirgs Mitchell personified this sea change in black politics. Six years earlier, three-quarters of black voters—including Mitchell himself—had cast ballots for Republican presidential candidate Herbert Hoover. In 1936, the same ratio lined up behind Roosevelt in his first reelection bid. Even before the votes were tallied, a Deep South editor gloomily predicted that white southerners would not share *their* party with northern blacks. "The shift of the Negro to Democratic ranks establishes him now as a possession to be retained or a prize to be sought in every election," Birmingham columnist John Temple Graves warned in the wake of the 1936 presidential election. "The future of the Democratic party here may depend upon what it is willing to pay for this prize."[70]

More black votes, prominent white southerners warned, meant more political clout for activists like Walter White. In 1938, two decades after his personal crusade against lynching began, White watched from the Senate balcony as New York Democrat Robert Wagner introduced a new antilynching bill. Southern senators, including former Mississippi governor Theodore Bilbo, responded with the longest filibuster since 1893. For six weeks, Vardaman's ghost returned to Washington, as southern senators stalled a vote on the antilynching bill with a barrage of white supremacist rhetoric. Bilbo, who had shied away from racial fireworks since World War I, urged the federal government to ship American blacks back to Africa. Twenty years after scoffing at the NAACP, Bilbo declared its latest antilynching bill "the entering wedge to…civil rights and social equality by the Negroes." Although Bilbo and company succeeded in killing the bill, those back home warned that greater battles lay ahead. "I believe you men will see," a southern Mississippi supporter warned, "that the fight *has just started.*"[71]

In Clarke County, that fight seemed just a bit less distant than it had twenty years before. Local blacks felt such seismic shifts only faintly, though racial turmoil and black migration had forged a link between urban North and Deep South that would shape future civil rights battles. Before it was over, black ballots would provide the balance of national political power. By demonstrating how sordid tales of southern violence infused national debates over racial violence, and by proving that no community was beyond the growing reach of black political influence, activists and everyday southerners in the World War I era defied Jim Crow at the height of its reign. In the late 1920s, a black pastor from Shubuta helped to relocate dozens of congregants to his adopted home of Albany, New York. Like James Yates, who also relocated to New York from Chicago, those transplanted migrants cast ballots and remembered their southern roots.[72]

For Yates, the journey led overseas. In a rehearsal for the global war against fascism that would pull in the United States and tens of thousands of black servicemen, Yates joined the Abraham Lincoln Brigade—a racially integrated volunteer unit—and drove supply trucks and ambulances in the Spanish Civil War. Ignoring the United States' official neutrality in the struggle between the Nazi-backed Nationalist rebels and the Soviet-supported Republican forces, Yates and several dozen African Americans joined an international coalition of leftist volunteers. He returned home a few years later and "joined up to fight Hitler," but military officials barred him from overseas service because of his time in Spain. Two decades later, as the branch president of New York's Greenwich Village–Chelsea NAACP, Yates organized food and clothing drives that sent several tons of donations to civil rights activists in Mississippi.[73]

One did not have to leave to resist. Back home, Yates's family kept alive traditions of self-reliance and self-defense. Like his son James, Gibson Yates had left the Deep South in search of a better life—first as the child of Exodusters, and later as a black settler in eastern Oklahoma—but ultimately carved out a homestead in Clarke County. Like the Yates family, the McRees kept a shotgun at the ready, but they also refused to relinquish all traces of political life. Nearly two decades after Walter White's fact-finding mission to Shubuta, Sylvester McRee wrote the NAACP head in May 1935 for "information as how to perfect a local branch of your organization here in Clarke County, Miss....Noticing the many things that this organization has done for the advancement of our race, we thought that we would get in the fight." As a second world war unleashed a new wave of racial turmoil, the bridge across the Chickasawhay River again focused attention on Mississippi's freedom struggle.[74]

PART II

1942

CHAPTER THREE

THE WAY YOU TREAT YOUR NIGGERS

On the evening of October 6, 1942, an unfamiliar sound interrupted the familiar echoes of shuffling feet and clanging metal in the Clarke County jail. From his upstairs cell, Isaiah Shine heard sobbing children. Then he saw them. Policemen hauled two boys up the stairs and tossed them into Shine's cell. That evening, a deputy sheriff's posse had rounded up Charlie Lang and Ernest Green, fourteen and fifteen, in Shubuta for "chasing" a white girl. By nightfall they sat trembling in a jail cell, charged with attempted rape.[1]

Isaiah Shine was no more a criminal than the jailed boys. A black sawmill worker, he had entered the army in January 1941 as part of the first peacetime draft in American history. When the Japanese attacked Pearl Harbor in December 1941, Shine was stationed at Fort Polk, Louisiana. One night, while on guard duty, he spotted someone staggering toward his post. When the man ignored orders to halt and identity himself, Shine shot him dead in his tracks. He soon discovered that he had killed a good friend, out on pass and stone drunk.[2]

After the shooting, Shine lost his mind. He would "go off," a relative remembered, ranting and raving for no apparent reason. Most of the time he was calm and lucid, but he could lapse suddenly into hallucinations and hysteria. The army discharged Shine and sent him to Mississippi's State Insane Hospital at Whitfield. The doctors, concluding that Shine was "harmless," sent him home to stay with relatives. After Shine started wandering off—he ended up in Hattiesburg on his last excursion— local authorities locked him in the county jail while they waited for Whitfield to readmit him. By the time the police brought in the two boys on the night of October 6, Shine had languished in his upstairs cell for several weeks.[3]

Six days later, just after midnight, the jailer entered the cellblock with several white men close on his heels. As the boys begged for their lives, Shine sprang to his feet. "Don't take them!" he shouted, "I'm the one that wants to go! I want to get out!" When Shine called the town marshal by name, the man pistol-whipped him. As the kidnappers dragged the boys down the stairs and out to a waiting caravan, the marshal entered an adjacent cell, locked the door, and tossed the keys out into the hallway.[4]

THE WHITES ARE GETTING WORRIED

War mobilization inadvertently sent Isaiah Shine on a downward spiral that started with a draft notice and ended in a psychiatric ward. Thousands more young men—from Clarke and other rural Deep South counties—poured into training camps, shipyards, and wartime boom towns across the region. With that rapid mobilization came a mania that, like Shine's descent into madness, made it increasingly difficult to separate reality from imagination. Across the South, white southerners began to see signs of black defiance at every turn. In rural counties like Clarke, they grounded these fears in reports of distant protests but also in the changes they observed around them. The racial anxieties unleashed by war preparations set off a chain of events that led again to Shubuta's bridge.[5]

After Pearl Harbor, the outmigration of draftees and defense workers from rural counties transformed the Deep South. Like Isaiah Shine, many local draftees reported for induction at nearby Camp Shelby, the largest military training center in the world. The half million soldiers that passed through the base transformed sleepy Hattiesburg into a boom town. Meanwhile, the Gulf Coast's shipbuilding industry exploded. Mobile, Alabama, a bustling port city and the terminus for the lone railroad to pass through Shubuta, saw its population shoot up 60 percent during the war. Clarke County natives, just a three-hour bus ride away, joined the rural migrants who poured into Mobile in search of lucrative defense work. As the city's shipbuilding jobs increased for-tyfold, Mobile reeled from extreme overcrowding, food shortages, and mounting racial friction. Although rampant discrimination excluded black migrants from all but the worst jobs and housing, many white migrants lashed out at perceived threats to their power and privilege. Indeed, government officials blamed the port city's racial tensions on "extremely anti-Negro" whites from rural inland counties. In August 1942, one of those white migrants—a twenty-nine-year-old bus driver from southern Mississippi—gunned down a uniformed black soldier. The killing—the worst of several clashes aboard Mobile's city buses—nearly led to a NAACP-led boycott. The local branch called off its plans only after the bus company conceded to some of its demands, including the disarming of its bus drivers.[6]

Stories of racial conflict spread across southern Mississippi. Sara Craigen Kennedy, a white Mississippi-born investigator who surveyed racial attitudes in the fall of 1942, cataloged rampant rumors of clashes on public transportation. "Everyone, when you mention the race ques-tion, begins reciting these incidents," Kennedy reported. "Fear of up-setting the status-quo is in their voice." In one rural community, whites claimed that blacks had hijacked and stolen a bus in Hattiesburg. On the road to Gulfport, another small-town resident claimed, "a nigger tried to get on the bus before a white man, but the driver fixed him up." These stories filtered back to Shubuta and other southern Mississippi towns with every war worker or soldier who returned home for a weekend visit. Yet one did not have to venture into larger towns and cities to encounter unsettling changes—real and imagined.[7]

At their core, wartime race rumors reflected a white fear of losing control of black workers. From the city to the countryside, the need to maintain a cheap and deep labor pool continued to drive racial politics. Wartime mobility and rising black expectations made this imperative much more difficult. Black men traded mill and farm work for mili-tary service and more lucrative wartime jobs. To compound whites' labor worries, the money that black soldiers and defense workers sent home allowed some sisters, wives, and mothers to quit low-paying work in white homes. Compounded by growing fears of racial agitators, this sparked some of the most outlandish wartime rumors. In rural Mississippi and across the South, southern whites blamed the sudden shortage of black help on "Eleanor Clubs." Named for—and blamed on—President Franklin Roosevelt's controversial wife, widely reviled in the South for her pro-civil-rights sympathies, this imaginary network of black domestics supposedly encouraged its members to demand higher wages and refuse to show up for work.[8]

With their alleged motto, "A white woman in every kitchen by 1943," the mythic Eleanor Clubs dramatized the connection between everyday interactions in small southern towns and seemingly distant racial controversies. Whites in Shubuta and surrounding communities attributed rising racial friction to "the servant problem" and described black domestics' clandestine activities in vivid, if always secondhand, detail. "Those Eleanor Clubs have upset my mode of living," complained a white housewife, who lamented her lack of "leisure time" and her mounting list of chores. "Finally the sheriff had to go down there and tell them they'd better get back to work or else!" Despite claims that local lawmen had raided clandestine meetings and threatened domestics—perhaps a wistful allusion to the "work-or-fight" laws of the World War I era—black women seemed surprisingly unfazed. "My old Louise, I'd had her ten years, has stopped now because her son's sending her money," a white woman in southern Mississippi complained. "It's just horrible now."[9]

Such complaints reflected tangible local tensions and a keen awareness that wartime changes threatened the racial status quo. "With Negro women spending more money, and refusing jobs in the kitchens of whites," a wartime visitor to Shubuta observed, "the impression quickly got about that Negroes were getting 'uppity' and 'out of their place.'" Other rumors linked the racial unrest to the turmoil engulfing the globe. In one tale, a black washerwoman refused to fetch her weekly load of laundry. "I'm waiting on Mr. Hitler," she told her boss, "When he gets here I won't have to wash for you but you will have to wash for me." As in previous moments of crisis—Reconstruction, World War I—fear of a social order turned on its head fueled white anxiety. "The greatest horror of any of the people, from the top of the social and economic scale to the very bottom, is social equality, and the fear of having to associate with Negroes on any plane other than the servant-master plane," Sara Craigen Kennedy reported after visits to Clarke and other southern Mississippi counties. "The idea of a Negro holding a position of authority over any white person is the most unthinkable and the most terrifying [*sic*] that they can imagine."[10]

Social equality, of course, meant race mixing, and sexual anxieties made wartime rumors all the more volatile. After the Mobile bus shooting, which stemmed from an argument between two men, rumors spread that the white driver had murdered the black soldier for sitting beside a white girl and getting "fresh" with her. Across the Gulf South, whites swapped stories of black men accosting white women on buses and trolleys. In one version of the story, the black soldier sat down beside a white woman, threw his arm around her, and told her what he would do to her "after all the white men are gone." These rumors fed off a widespread belief that the military was inducting whites at far higher rates than blacks. That myth rested on yet another—that nearly all black men carried venereal diseases. Draft boards were turning away black men in droves, read a typical complaint wired to Washington from New Orleans, "because they are all diseased." Wartime rumors of sidewalk propositions collided with the age-old specter of the marauding black rapist. "You know, there are more niggers than white people around here anyway," a white Shubuta woman explained to a houseguest. "But now that all the white men are being drafted and they're not drafting so many negroes, it's just getting to be a very dangerous situation."[11]

All these rumors sharpened the town's violent edge. "The whites are getting worried," a black undercover journalist warned, "with their young menfolk going off to war and leaving the white women unprotected." But townspeople did more than trade stories. Convinced that wartime opportunities and civil rights agitation had undermined black deference, some locals took it upon themselves to reinforce white supremacy. In Shubuta, a local merchant took to whipping blacks in the back of his store. James McRee, a black preacher's son, typified the "uppity" attitude that local whites resented. "When I'd go to buy something, I didn't scratch my head and grin," McRee recalled, "I just told them what I wanted." Locals reckoned McRee had spent time "up north" to act the way he did. He had not. After the storekeeper bragged that he would teach McRee a lesson, the young man confronted him. "Now, they told me you said you was gonna whoop me," McRee warned, nodding toward the stockroom at the back of the store. "One of us won't come out if you try it." The storekeeper left McRee alone, but in the early fall of 1942 he went after Buddie Smith with an ax handle when the young black man questioned his math. Smith snatched the club away and held several angry whites at bay—at least until the deputy sheriff arrived and hauled him off to jail.[12]

Buddie Smith's scrape with the storeowner took on a new meaning a few weeks later, when word spread that two black boys had accosted a white girl. Racial clashes stoked a fear that wartime change could lead to racial disruption. In that atmosphere of danger and uncertainty, where threats to the status quo seemed more imminent and widespread than ever before, a rape rumor set off a furious chain reaction. In Clarke County, a gathering white backlash claimed its youngest victims yet.

He Was the Nigger We Wanted

Like many rural black southerners, Ernest Green and Charlie Lang embraced the opportunities that war mobilization offered. For adolescents in a small southern town, that meant scavenging for scrap metal and old tires. As Fats Waller announced in his hit song—recorded just ten days after Pearl Harbor—you could "Get Some Cash for Your Trash." Government-sponsored drives for rubber and metal scrap inspired the boys to scour scrap heaps and roadsides around Shubuta. During one such scavenging adventure, the town marshal arrested the boys for "stealing" a tire from a junk pile. Since both boys were minors—Ernest was fourteen and Charlie had just turned fifteen—the lawman turned them over to their white employers. Floyd Hudson, who owned the local drug store, kept Ernest busy with errands and odd jobs. The local barber who employed Charlie as a shoeshine boy fired him after the run-in with the police.[13]

Beyond odd jobs and scrap gathering, Ernest and Charlie had scant options. Shubuta's black children, kindergarten through tenth grade, attended a six-room schoolhouse. The county paid five teachers a pittance to serve the 160 students who crowded into the crumbling building. Only three teachers in the county's black schools possessed a college degree, and two of them worked in Shubuta. The school stayed in session six months a year, whereas the rural county schools routinely shut down so that children could work in the fields. Yet like its counterparts across the county, Shubuta's school lacked accreditation. For students who made it past the sixth grade, the average for Shubuta's black students, their only hope for a legitimate high school diploma was to leave the county altogether.[14]

Neither Ernest nor Charlie had that chance. Although the boys were fourteen and fifteen respectively, they had only reached the second grade. Charlie could barely write his name. Both boys lived in rundown houses in the "bottoms," just a stone's throw from the Southern Lumber Company yards. Green lived with his mother and sister—his father had recently moved up to Meridian. Charlie's father worked on a railroad section gang, which kept him away for long stretches, and his mother had moved to Hattiesburg. So Charlie spent most of his time roaming the streets of Shubuta, and he rarely went anywhere without Ernest. On October 6, 1942, they wandered down to a concrete highway bridge just south of town.[15]

As Charlie and Ernest scavenged around the bridge, Dorothy Martin made her way home from school. Dorothy, who had just turned fifteen a week before, lived on a hill just south of the bridge. As she approached, she saw a boy emerge from underneath. Charlie may have startled her, but she would have recognized him. In addition to shining shoes and roaming the road around Shubuta, Charlie would do odd jobs for any white man—including Dorothy's father—who would pay him a few pennies. As she admitted later, she never saw Ernest.[16]

Whatever happened as she passed over the bridge, no one—except, perhaps, Dorothy—thought much of it. A white couple in a passing sedan noticed the girl crossing the bridge and the boys rummaging around it. They saw no reason to stop. Charlie headed back into town and hitched a ride into the woods with Ed Manning, a black pulpwood hauler who occasionally needed his help. Ernest went home for dinner and then headed to the picture show with a friend. Up the hill, Dorothy Martin arrived home around four o'clock in the afternoon.[17]

Jim Odom was working on a pickup truck in front of his convenience store when Dorothy's mother dragged her across the road a few minutes later. In addition to his store on the Wayne County line—just across the road from the Martin's home—Odom operated the Shubuta sawmill where Dorothy's father worked. Odum had other sources of income as well. A bootlegger, Odom had spent the summer of 1941 locked up in the Wayne County jail on a liquor charge. The previous year, county authorities had jailed him for contempt after he "lost his head during the trial."[18]

Given Dorothy's allegations, cooler heads likely would not have prevailed. But when she told the hot-tempered Odom that "a little nigger, bareheaded, white shirt and dark pants," had made a lewd threat and then chased her across the highway bridge, he went looking for the town marshal. Odom found Ed McLendon in the mayor's office around five o'clock. A Shubuta native, the fifty-six-year-old McLendon had worked in lumber yards until he ran for town marshal. Worn down from a life of sawmill work, McLendon suffered from a variety of ailments. Friends like Murray Paul Stewart, a twenty-three-year-old merchant's clerk who had just enlisted in the army, often drove him on his rounds. After hearing the girl's story, McLendon and Stewart went looking for Charlie Lang.[19]

By the time that Dan Martin returned home, word of his daughter's allegations had spread through town. Martin had moved his family to Shubuta just months before, after he landed a job at Odum's sawmill. If old-money families like the Pattons and Weemses represented Shubuta's establishment, the Martins represented the county's new white majority. Even as black migrants poured out of the county in the decades after World War I, white migrants arrived looking for lumber and textile jobs. Clarke County sawmills employed more workers per capita than all but two other Mississippi counties. Thanks in large part to Stonewall's denim plant—a rarity in the Deep South—Clarke had a higher percentage of textile workers than any county in the state. These jobs lured poor- and working-class whites off the farm and into the mills, where they rubbed elbows with black workers. Every day, Dan Martin and a handful of millhands—white and black—rode to work and back in the bed of Odum's truck. When he stepped off the truck that October afternoon, his boss was waiting.[20]

According to local gossip, Dan Martin and his mill-worker brothers had "led somewhat rough lives" and were regarded as "booze heads." Dan's brother Fred, who lived up in Stonewall, was widely regarded as the meanest drunk. Dorothy's story sent Dan into a sober fury. Odum quickly filled him in and drove him to a lumber yard where McLendon was waiting on Ed Manning—a black pulpwood cutter—to deliver a load. Along with Stewart, his driver and frequent on-duty companion, the impromptu posse set out to find the truck. On a dirt road outside of town, they came upon Manning's broken-down truck. Charlie Lang sat in the back. With no explanation, the men loaded Lang into their car and drove him back to Odum's store.[21]

Back at the store, the men called Dorothy over to identify the boy. Like other crucial elements of the story, the details mattered less than the allegations. All those present reported that Dorothy identified Charlie as the one who threatened to rape her and then chased her across the bridge. From there the stories started to diverge, but the inconsistencies did not dissuade the posse. "I took [the] nigger back to the bridge," McLendon reported, "and tried his foot in the track." At some point— those present later differed on *when* and *where* he confessed—Lang described a premeditated plan to rape Dorothy Martin at the bridge. He had not only waited for her, McLendon later claimed, but had followed her from town. When he jumped out at her, McLendon reported, "the little nigger said: 'Oh, you needn't run, because I'm going to (obscene).'" At no point, then or after the fact, did anyone claim that Charlie came within six feet of the girl.[22]

Dorothy never mentioned an accomplice, but at some point Charlie allegedly did. "Lang told me about Ernest Green," Stewart claimed, "that he was the nigger we wanted." When McLendon's posse pulled up to the Greens' house, with Charlie in tow, Ernest had already gone to bed. His mother answered the door, and McLendon asked to speak to Ernest. He had some questions about Charlie Lang, he told her, and he would have Ernest back directly. Mintora Green never saw her son again.[23]

Back at the store, Dorothy denied that she had seen Ernest at the bridge. By one account, the boys turned on each other. "One would try and deny it," Stewart claimed, "and the other would deny it and blame it on each other." A highway patrolman, who had arrived in the middle of the interrogation, reported that the boys "had also intended to include Jim Odom's young daughter in this attempt to rape." While Charlie outlined the plot in breathless detail, the lawman reported, "Ernest Green denied any participation whatsoever."[24]

With a confession in hand, Martin demanded that McLendon turn the boys over to him. The town marshal, worried that he could be implicated in such a plot, decided instead to carry them to the county jail in Quitman. McLendon loaded the boys into the back seat of Stewart's car, with Dorothy Martin's father seated between then. Odom followed behind with the highway patrolman. With the boys locked up in Quitman, the men returned to Shubuta. The next morning, McLendon returned to the county jail. "Green said he had something to tell me," the town marshal claimed, "that he was under the bridge and that Charlie was going to drag her under the bridge and one hold her for the other."[25]

Back in Shubuta, alternate accounts of the incident spread around town. On the black side of town, locals believed the boys had played a childish prank, like frightening Dorothy with a captured frog. Others claimed that Dorothy, not the boys, had initiated a conversation. While nearly all accounts of the incident noted that at least one passing motorist had spotted the trio at the bridge, African Americans heard that a traveling salesman from Mobile had stopped in Shubuta after seeing Dorothy Martin chatting with a black boy by the side of the highway. "That's the way you people up here treat your niggers," he supposedly teased. The suggestion that Shubuta whites did not know how to keep blacks in their place—or lacked the guts to do so—provided both motivation and justification for action. The measure of manhood was revenge, and any other course threatened to embarrass or discredit white male authority in a time of crisis. Rumors spread that Dorothy Martin later denied the allegations against the boys. Her father, perhaps fearing greater humiliation, allegedly whipped her and told her to keep quiet.[26]

As the week wore on, the jailed boys' families could do little to intervene. County authorities refused to let relatives see the boys, unless they could post the $1,000 bond. Two days after the arrest, Mintora Green went to Hudson's drug store to ask if Ernest had been working when the alleged rape attempt took place. The druggist had never had any trouble with Ernest, but he knew better than to challenge local authorities. "Don't talk to me about it," Hudson snapped. "Go home or you'll liable to get hurt yourself talking about it."[27]

The following Monday, five days after the arrest, Hilliard Lang headed downtown to beg someone to post bond for his son. As he neared the old well, a lumber truck pulled up with two uncovered corpses sprawled across the bed. Charlie lay beside Ernest (fig. 3.1). Nooses still gripped their necks.[28]

A MATTER OF INTERNATIONAL IMPORTANCE

The next morning, the phone rang in FBI director J. Edgar Hoover's Washington office. Noting "several news items appearing in the New York papers," the Justice Department's fledgling Civil Rights Section served notice of the latest wartime lynching. Later that afternoon, Assistant Attorney General Wendell Berge elaborated in a pointed memo to Hoover. "As you know," Berge wrote, "there has been received from the President an instruction that lynching cases should be investigated as soon as possible; that the results of the investigation be made public in all instances, and that the persons responsible for such unlawful acts be vigorously prosecuted." Furthermore, the Justice Department's second-in-command added, the "extreme youth" of the latest mob victims demanded "special attention." The next day, less than forty-eight hours after two lynched corpses rolled into Shubuta on the back of a pulpwood truck, Hoover ordered FBI agents to Clarke County. He demanded an investigation report in two weeks' time, "without fail."[29]

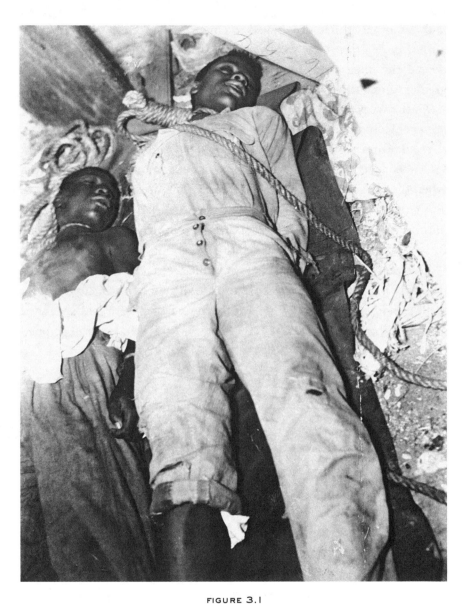

FIGURE 3.1

The bodies of Charlie Lang (left) and Ernest Green (right) after delivery
to Patton's Undertaking Establishment in Shubuta. A white tire shop
owner from Meridian snapped the photograph and sold it to a newswire
service. Courtesy of Bettman/CORBIS.

The official response to the Shubuta lynchings reflected a sea change in the federal government's handling of mob violence. For decades, no presidential administration had dared to interfere publicly in the South's racial affairs. Despite mounting pressure for legislative action and federal policing, Franklin D. Roosevelt remained decidedly aloof from antilynching activists throughout his first two terms. Yet the rising clout of civil rights advocates and the looming threat of war had forced subtle yet significant shifts in the administration's approach to mob violence. In 1939, the year after southern senators killed an antilynching bill that had sailed through the House of Representatives by a three-to-one vote, Roosevelt yielded to pressure from black activists and their white allies—including his wife—by replacing his attorney general with the racially progressive Frank Murphy. The former Michigan governor and Detroit mayor promptly established a Civil Liberties Unit within the Justice Department's Criminal Division. This office, soon renamed the Civil Rights Section, monitored racial violence and other abuses. Lacking a legislative mandate to prosecute lynchers, the new unit worked to build cases against local officials who aided and abetted mob action.[30]

With the tacit approval of a president who still feared alienating his southern base, the fledgling division prodded an equally ambivalent FBI to action. In the summer of 1940, the Justice Department dispatched an FBI agent to western Tennessee after local whites murdered a local NAACP official. The unprecedented move, urged on by the association's national leadership, seemed less momentous once Walter White discovered that a known leader of the lynch mob had escorted the federal investigator on his search for black witnesses. Predictably, the investigation went nowhere. Despite the failure of the Tennessee case, the specter of war strengthened the hand of civil rights activists and sympathetic officials who argued that mob violence gave aid and comfort to America's enemies. At a 1940 hearing on a new antilynching bill, an NAACP official quoted a Nazi newspaper that characterized American treatment of blacks as less humane than German treatment of Jews. The following summer, in anticipation of Roosevelt's meeting with Winston Churchill to draft the Atlantic Charter, Walter White repeatedly telegrammed the British prime minister to remind him that racial discrimination undermined the Allied war effort.[31]

Fears of another wartime surge in racial violence crystallized just a few weeks after Pearl Harbor, when a mob seized a black murder suspect from a jail in Sikeston, Missouri. First, the vigilantes riddled Cleo Wright's body with bullets. Then, in broad daylight, the lynchers dragged his corpse behind a car, doused him with gasoline, and set him on fire. Pictures of Wright's charred corpse, surrounded by scores of onlookers, appeared in newspapers across the country. For the Civil Rights Section, the Missouri incident dramatized its diplomatic rationale for lynching prosecutions. With the country now engulfed in a global war against totalitarianism, arguments against lynching seemed less abstract and more urgent than the NAACP's prewar appeals. The Civil Rights Section's head deemed the Sikeston lynching "a matter of international importance and a subject of Axis propaganda." In the Pacific Theater, he warned, the Japanese were bombarding the Allies' darker-skinned colonial subjects with American lynching stories.[32]

These arguments primed the Justice Department for a surprisingly swift response to the Shubuta lynchings. In their directives to the FBI, top Justice Department officials emphasized not just prosecution but also *publicity*. The demand that "the results of the investigation be made public in all instances" reflected the department's desire to counter charges of federal apathy. Noting the "numerous inquiries" about the lynched "negro boys," Justice Department officials urged immediate and conspicuous action. Antilynching activists had spent decades building a formidable publicity machine, and news of the latest atrocity had already hit the national newswires. With a quick and convincing response, the Justice Department could insert itself into that story. As for the investigation itself, Hoover bowed to Justice Department strategy that hinged not just on identifying the ring leaders but also on determining "any dereliction" on the part of local officials.[33]

On both points, federal officials found an unlikely ally. In Jackson, Governor Paul B. Johnson issued not only a routine hand-wringing statement of regret but also a public call for investigation and prosecution. Twenty-four years earlier, Mississippi governor Theodore Bilbo had told the NAACP to "go to hell" for requesting such a probe. Now, in 1942, Governor Johnson denounced the lynchings as "murder" and publicly castigated Clarke County's sheriff for lax security. "It was his duty," Johnson declared, "to notify the governor so the prisoners could be protected." Perhaps in anticipation of outside criticism, Johnson quickly dispatched an investigator to the scene and met personally with federal agents at the governor's mansion.[34]

That Johnson's words and actions contrasted sharply with those of Theodore Bilbo was no accident—the two had been political rivals since Johnson defeated the outgoing governor in a 1918 congressional race. While both men came from humble southern Mississippi backgrounds and built political careers on common-man appeal, the Hattiesburg lawyer shunned Bilbo's flashy style and racial theatrics. As governor of a state brimming with training camps, air bases, and shipyards, Johnson promoted his law-and-order approach as practical and patriotic.[35]

After meeting with the surprisingly cooperative governor, the federal agents—all from the FBI's Jackson field office—set out for Clarke County. By all accounts, Fortner Dabbs was the man they needed to see. After Ed McLendon had delivered the boys to the county jail, his counterpart in Quitman had assumed responsibility for them. Dabbs, the county seat's town marshal since 1936, had given a boilerplate account of the boys' abduction from the county jail. Dabbs, to quote a local press account, had been "overcome by a ruse." Someone claiming to be a constable had called him, Dabbs maintained, and said that he had a prisoner to deliver. The county employed no full-time jailer, and only four men—Dabbs, the sheriff, and two deputies—had keys. So Dabbs drove over to the jail, where shadowy figures threw a blanket over his head, pinned his arms down, and snatched his keys. After the gang of men dragged the boys from their cell, they locked Dabbs in an adjacent cell and sped off into the night.[36]

While Dabbs willingly played the hapless jailer for the press, the veteran town marshal wielded far more power than his humble title suggested. A farmer and cattleman with a spread just outside town, Dabbs had considerably more experience and clout than Clarke County's first-term sheriff—an alcoholic fuel franchise owner named Lloyd McNeal.

However, Dabbs had his own baggage, and his spotty reputation had spread beyond his local fiefdom. When FBI agents dropped in on the local circuit judge on their way to Quitman, the veteran jurist confided that Dabbs had "on numerous occasions, abused and mistreated negroes in the community." At one point, a grand jury had investigated Dabbs's treatment of black inmates in the county jail. More alarming still, Dabbs dodged conviction in a murder conspiracy trial in 1931 after one of his white tenants turned up dead.[37]

For Clarke County's black citizens, that mysterious murder offered another sordid tale of Jim Crow justice and confirmed Dabbs's ruthless reputation. In January 1931, local authorities had arrested George McKinnis, an illiterate black tenant farmer, for the murder of his white neighbor, Ozie Wilkerson. Both men farmed land owned by Dabbs. The ensuing trial uncovered that Dabbs had paid the premium for the murdered man's life insurance policy and, according to McKinnis, had arranged for his black tenant to kill him. Strangely, after having admitted to murdering a white man in cold blood, McKinnis received the lenient sentence of life in prison. Several months later, at Dabbs's trial, the black inmate recanted his claim that he had been his landlord's hit man. The newly elected circuit court judge, a member of Quitman's courthouse clique, promptly dismissed the jury. "Friends of Mr. Dabbs," the local paper reported, "staged an impromptu celebration at the abrupt ending of the trial, gathering around him and shaking his hand."[38]

That a penniless sharecropper could escape lynching—let alone a legal execution—for killing a white man raised suspicions in Quitman's black community. The accusations against Dabbs did not stick, but the rumors persisted. The leading theory posited that Dabbs had cut a deal with McKinnis, who implicated and then exonerated his former landlord. When the state penitentiary released McKinnis to independent supervision, barely a decade into his life sentence, rumor became local black legend. None of this derailed Dabbs's law enforcement ambitions. Four years after he stood trial for murder, Clarke County voters elected him to the first of several terms as town marshal. With friends in high places, Dabbs enjoyed the loyalty of the local establishment. "That he is making one of the best marshals Quitman has ever had," the *Clarke County Tribune* gushed in a 1938 reelection endorsement, "we feel sure everybody will readily admit."[39]

Local whites again closed ranks around Dabbs in the wake of the Shubuta lynchings. Although white officials in Meridian advised FBI agents that Dabbs "knew something of the proposed removal of Lang and Green from the jail and the lynching," the town marshal and his loyal constituents played dumb. For starters, Dabbs downplayed local racial tensions and his own checkered past. He had "worked negroes all of his life," Dabbs said, and he had "never had any difficulty" with them either on his farm or on duty. As for the story he gave the papers, Dabbs stuck to the script. A ringing phone woke him around one in the morning, Dabbs claimed, and the caller claimed to be the constable from the nearby village of Pachuta. Several minutes later, a shadowy figure claiming to be the constable showed up at his door. Still believing the man to be a constable, Dabbs headed to the courthouse in his pickup truck. There the kidnappers wrapped him in a blanket, took his keys, and locked him in a cell while they made off with the prisoners. Dabbs repeatedly denied that he had seen anyone's face. Darkness provided a convenient excuse while outside, but Dabbs also had a ready explanation for his inability to recognize any abductors once inside the jailhouse. The women's cell had a faulty light socket. The cell block was so dark, Dabbs explained, "I could not say if he was a negro or a white man."[40]

As soon as the captors sped off, Dabbs and Isaiah Shine, the "crazy negro" in the adjacent cell, shouted for the town's night watchman. The town's only on-duty official from sundown to sunup—and the extent of the security when the lynching party raided the jail—the watchman doubled as the nighttime clerk at Quitman's hotel. Rather than patrolling the courthouse grounds, the watchman was chatting with a hard-drinking oilman when he heard cries coming from the jail. Once freed from the cell, Dabbs called up the sheriff and the county attorney. Gathered at the sheriff's office, along with the night watchman and the half-drunk hotel guest, the men decided against an immediate search. "The sheriff," Dabbs said, "did not know what to do until daylight."[41]

When morning came, Dabbs and Sheriff McNeal drove down to Shubuta. They stopped first at Ed McLendon's house, but the town marshal and ex-officio deputy sheriff had slept in. "His wife did not want to wake him," Dabbs claimed, and apparently neither did they. On their way out of town, the lawmen stopped by the drug store where Ernest Green had worked, but Hudson told them that he "had no idea" where the men might have taken the boys. With that, the men called off their search. "Mr. Dabbs had to do some farm work," FBI agents noted, and McNeal "had not eaten breakfast."[42]

WHAT A NEAT LYNCHING

Ed McLendon woke up late on October 6. By his own admission, it had been a long night. As he walked into town, a friend slowed down to offer him a ride. The driver winked. "I heard there was a necktie party last night."[43]

No one who knew anything about the night's events had let on. In Shubuta, whites waited for a black pulpwood hauler to spot the bodies on his way out of town. Then the news spread quickly. Now that the bodies had been "discovered," McLendon hitched a ride out to the bridge. Two different men claimed to have driven him, including Murray Paul Stewart. "We got out of the car and saw the niggers hanging there," Stewart recalled later. "There was just a bunch of people looking at them so we went on back to town." As they drove back down the dirt road into Shubuta, McLendon noticed cars headed out to the bridge. By the time he rolled back into town, Sheriff McNeal had returned. Together, they drove out to the bridge. McLendon estimated the crowd at twenty—all white. McNeal believed it had swollen to forty "men, women, and girls" from as far away as Quitman. The sheriff recognized Mr. Showers, from the county agent's office, who wanted to take his wife down to see the gory spectacle. His secretary had tagged along as well.[44]

The boys hung from opposite sides of the bridge—directly across from each other and centered above the muddy river below. The sheriff estimated they had dropped fourteen feet before the taut ropes snapped their necks. He noticed no scars, marks, or bleeding. An onlooker re-marked aloud "what a neat lynching" it had been. The general feeling in the crowd, he concluded, was that the boys had "gotten what was coming to them." With the bodies still hanging, the local justice of the peace assembled a coroner's jury on the spot. With a pencil, he jotted down their verdict on a scrap of paper—death "by being hanged to Chickasawhay River Bridge east of Shubuta by parties unknown." Then, as McLendon put it, the sheriff and several onlookers "pulled the little niggers up" and loaded them into the open bed of a Chevy lumber truck. "I couldn't help," the deputy explained, "on account of my asthma." Someone spotted Dan Martin, the avenged girl's father, in the crowd. "Don't be so particular about getting those bodies down from the bridge," he allegedly shouted. "If I get there, I'll cut off their heads."[45]

As the truck rumbled toward town, McLendon and McNeal set off "in search for the niggers['] parents." The officers ran into Charlie Lang's father, Hilliard, on the main street of Shubuta. Hilliard Lang had heard news of a lynching just moments before the pulpwood truck rolled to a stop in front of Shubuta's old well. He caught a glimpse of his son, and then staggered back toward home. When McLendon stopped him, he refused to claim the the body. Mintora Green, Ernest's mother, declined as well. "She advised the officers that she did not want the body, nor did she wish to see…her dead son," her FBI interviewer noted. Instead, she "desired the County to stand the expenses of the burial." Left with no alternatives, the lawmen deposited the bodies in the shed behind Will Patton's funeral home. While a black work crew dug two graves just outside the white cemetery fence, Patton removed the ropes from the boys' necks and packed them in cheap pine boxes, their hands still tied behind their backs. "He received the bodies after 9am," agents noted after speaking with Patton, "and they were in the ground by noon."[46]

McLendon did not linger for the unceremonious burial. "I went home and went to bed," he said. Shubuta's top lawman had even less patience for federal agents. The investigation, McLendon warned them, "was going to result in more lynching of negroes." As for his whereabouts the night of the lynching, McLendon told agents that he was on duty that night. Around ten, Murray Paul Stewart drove him to Waynesboro. "Just to be drivin'," he said. "We did not stop there, just drove around and come back." Otherwise, McLendon claimed that he had sat around the mayor's office until four in the morning, chatting with Stewart and listening to the radio. Other than a couple locals hopping on or off the overnight bus to Mobile, he said he saw no one else that night.[47]

At a Missouri army base, an agent questioned Stewart, who had reported for duty just days after the lynching. Stewart's account of the night's events hewed so closely to McLendon's, the agent advised, "as to give color to the possibility that he may have collaborated with James Edward McLendon concerning an agreed set of facts." Still, six hundred miles of separation made the task more difficult. On their late night drive, Stewart recalled, they stopped at a "nigger juke joint" in Shubuta and an all-night diner in Waynesboro. The agent noted the "minor inconsistency."[48]

Back in Shubuta, white townspeople did their best to avoid similar slip-ups. The late-night bus passengers, on their way to and from defense jobs in Mobile, provided alibis for the likeliest lynching collaborators and casual indictments of the boys' character. Whites corroborated McLendon's characterization of the boys—especially Charlie Lang—as delinquents. James Pace, the town's white barber, deemed his former employee a "pretty sorry negro" and catalogued a list of offenses—stealing, swearing, and assorted mischief. Then again, Pace informed investigators, "the general condition concerning the negroes in the community was bad." Both Dan Martin and Jim Odom claimed that Lang had attempted to rape a nine-year-old black neighbor.[49]

While white townspeople closed ranks around the likeliest suspects, black townspeople undermined the cover-up in subtle yet significant ways. They rejected white attempts to paint Ernest Green as a troublemaker, remembering him instead as "a good, quiet boy" who "never gave anyone any trouble." Most agreed that Lang had been a "mischievous boy," but they chalked this up to boredom and desperation. Missie Hailes, the grandmother of the little girl whom Lang allegedly assaulted, claimed instead that the boy had slipped into her house to pilfer food. "He was hungry most of the time," she recalled.[50]

Black informants challenged white attempts to defame the dead boys, but they knew better than to implicate their killers. Federal agents pressed Charlie's father for names, but Hilliard Lang refused. "He was afraid," an interviewer noted, "that some men might come some night and take him out for a hanging." When asked to "guess" who in town might take part in a lynching, Lang replied simply, "Mr. Will." Why, the agent asked, did he suspect Will Patton, the local undertaker? "He had heard," the agent noted, "at different times over a period of years, that Patton was involved in the last lynching in that vicinity."[51]

Neither the agents nor anyone else seemed interested in revisiting the crimes of the previous generation. Yet a couple of white informants attempted to point the agents toward the latest lynchers. The town's postmaster confirmed the obvious—that Dan Martin had spearheaded the revenge killing. The hard-drinking lumber mill worker, he confided, "was the type of person who would become incensed over a matter of this type and take the law in his own hands with the assistance of relatives." In Quitman, an old man pulled aside an agent. He had gone to see the dead boys for himself, he claimed, and had heard several names mentioned in connection with the lynchings. A small gang, including Martin, his brother-in-law, two sons-in-law, and Ed McLendon, had abducted the boys. Hoping to nail down further details from the unusually talkative informant, the agent stopped by later. "His wife said that he had left home," the agent noted, "and she had not heard from him since." Around town, agents noted a "general consensus" among white townspeople that the old man "was mentally deficient due to his injuries suffered during the World War Number I."[52]

The mysterious informant's disappearance capped off a week of dead ends for the diligent, if tepid, FBI investigators. The agents, whom a local editor endorsed as an "impartial and efficient Edgar Hoover fact-finding squad," served the interests of public relations over prosecution. Locally, blacks deemed the investigation a "show" and held out little hope for justice. While hints of what happened at the bridge lay buried in a pile of confidential government files, African Americans again looked elsewhere to get the truth out.[53]

THESE PREJUDICES ARE BORN IN US

For black activists, Clarke County proved even tougher to crack in 1942 than in 1918. NAACP youth director Madison Jones, who passed through Meridian in the wake of the lynching of Charlie Lang and Ernest Green, reported that "negroes and whites are not talking, and feeling is tense on both sides." Rumors that the FBI had dispatched a "Negro federal man" had locals on the lookout for inquisitive and unfamiliar blacks. Given the danger and difficulty of an on-the-ground investigation, black activists turned to a trusted white ally. Victor Bernstein, they knew, did not spook easily. A native New Yorker, Bernstein had spent the late 1930s working as a foreign correspondent for the Jewish Telegraph Agency. As Berlin bureau chief, he had covered the Nazis' prewar persecution of German and Austrian Jews—and talked his way out of multiple SS interrogations. Back in New York, Bernstein went to work for the left-leaning *PM*—New York's daily picture magazine—which frequently shared Bernstein's stories with northern black newspapers. A few weeks before the Shubuta lynchings, Bernstein had toured the South to investigate rumors of a racial crisis and the likelihood that it would turn to bloodshed. Southerners were "doing more than their share to win the war," Bernstein reported. "But when you go South and hang around awhile asking questions and drinking beer and cokes with new-found friends, you get the uneasy feeling that the war the South is fighting isn't the same war that the rest of the country is fighting."[54]

Wherever he went, Bernstein ran up against the "artificially contrived bugaboo of almost every Southerner." Whether he asked about employment, housing, or education, he lamented, "somehow the argument winds up with threatened rape and the sanctity of southern womanhood." In Birmingham, Bernstein riled the secretary of the Chamber of Commerce. "There's one thing you can put in your pipe and smoke," the man told him. "There's no white man down here goin' to let his daughter sleep with a nigger, or sit at the same table with a nigger, or go walkin' with a nigger....The war can go to hell, the world can go to hell, we can all be dead—but he ain't goin' to do that." Across town,

Bernstein chatted with a supporter of the recently organized League to Maintain White Supremacy. "It occurred to me, at this point," Bernstein noted, "that the swastika is no prettier when entwined with magnolia blossoms."[55]

Just a month later, Bernstein headed to the Magnolia State. The *Pittsburgh Courier* had tapped the white reporter to cover Mississippi's lynching spree. Fresh on the heels of the FBI investigation, Bernstein rolled into Clarke County. If the sight of a Yankee reporter raised some hackles in Quitman, Sheriff Lloyd McNeal seemed eager to help Bernstein write the story he wanted New Yorkers to read. The sheriff's reputation had suffered in the wake of the lynching. The governor had chastised him publicly for failing to provide or request protection for the jailed boys. McNeal, the sheriff's counterpart in neighboring Lauderdale County divulged to the FBI, had little law enforcement experience and a drinking problem to boot. Rumors reached Meridian that Clarke County's sheriff, a fuel franchise owner just two years into his term as sheriff, "has often been intoxicated while on duty." By the time FBI agents and other curious visitors arrived, McNeal had sobered up.[56]

The sheriff met Bernstein in a parked patrol car. He was polite enough, but he wanted to set a few things straight. "First off," he began, "the papers got the ages wrong, sayin' they were 14." This had been a sticking point for the local authorities. McNeal and other county officials had made the same false claims to FBI agents, who dutifully confirmed the boys' ages—Ernest Green was fourteen and Charlie Lang was fifteen—at the Bureau of Vital Statistics. But McNeal had his mind on those New York readers. "You better put it down," McNeal insisted. "Them niggers wasn't 14, they were maybe 16 to 18."[57]

The sheriff recounted the boys' arrest and arraignment. Two days after McLendon and his posse drove their prisoners to Quitman, the sheriff scheduled a hearing in nearby Pachuta. He dragged the boys before the same justice of the peace who, four days later, assembled the coroner's jury at the bridge. "They got a fair-and-square hearin'," McNeal maintained. "They confessed to attempted rape."[58]

Bernstein asked if the boys even understood the charge. McNeal laid out the premeditated rape plot. Unlike the accounts of the arresting posse—all of whom pegged Lang as the aggressor and admitted that Dorothy Martin never saw Ernest—the sheriff's story reversed the boys' roles. "Green said he was planning to grab her," McNeal claimed to Bernstein, "and bring her down under the bridge to the other nigger." Like every other white account of the alleged ambush, McNeal confirmed that neither boy had actually touched Dorothy Martin.[59]

As for the abduction and lynching, McNeal stuck faithfully to the town marshal's well-rehearsed story. After the kidnapping, the sheriff claimed, they organized a search party and scoured the county for the boys. The discovered the bodies at the bridge, and immediately launched an investigation. "But you know how it is," McNeal added dryly, "people don't like to tell on their friends."[60]

Bernstein asked how the locals felt about the lynching. "We're all for law and order here," the sheriff declared. "Of course, we got some good folks who get kind of wild." As for what had sparked that wildness, the county sheriff invoked a familiar wartime lament: "Them niggers is gettin' uppity, you know."[61]

Bernstein walked across the street to the local newspaper office. The *Clarke County Tribune* had rehashed county officials' version of events in a terse front-page article on the lynchings. "Just a straight story," the editor told Bernstein—no editorials and no follow-ups on the promised investigations. "None of the better people around here believes in violence," he assured Bernstein. Still, the newspaperman saw no use in rocking the boat. "Seems to me my best policy is to forget it, now."[62]

Besides the sheriff, no one seemed eager to speak with the New York reporter. Someone in Jackson had recommended another local contact, an "educated fellow" who might shed some light on the lynching. If the leading citizens opposed lynching, Bernstein asked this man, why had they not made any public statements? "I haven't talked to anyone about it," he responded. "I've got other things on my mind." Bernstein made a note not to identify the man in his story. "Everybody in Quitman seemed to have things on his mind," he concluded. "I wondered whether one of those things was the fear of being called 'nigger lover.'" As for Shubuta, a Quitman man warned Bernstein to stay away. "It wouldn't do them niggers any good," he warned Bernstein, "to be seen talking to you."[63]

Bernstein kept moving. He had other things on his mind as well. Indeed, by the time he arrived in Clarke County, another mob had struck merely thirty miles from the bridge. Five days after the Shubuta lynching, vigilantes in Laurel seized Howard Wash from the Jones County jail and hung him to a nearby bridge. On Friday, October 16, a local jury had convicted the middle-aged black farmhand of killing his white boss. Wash's lawyer argued that his client had acted in self-defense, and the strategy swayed at least one jury member. Because the jurors disagreed over Wash's punishment, the judge could not legally sentence him to death. So that night, just hours before the inmate's formal sentencing to life in prison, a mob took matters into its own hands. An estimated one hundred vigilantes stormed the jail, "overpowered" the guards, and dragged Wash into the darkness. The next morning, local authorities found him dangling above Tallahoma Creek.[64]

With three dead in one week, Mississippi now had a lynching spree on its hands. The Laurel lynching not only kept the state in the national headlines but also lured investigators and journalists away from the bridge over the Chickasawhay. Indeed, no sooner had federal agents arrived in Clarke County than a new directive arrived at their Jackson office. From a prosecutor's standpoint, the Laurel lynching proved far more promising to Justice Department officials than Clarke County. Whereas only a handful of men—"not a mob within the legal means of the term"—had abducted the two boys from the Quitman jail, Howard Wash was lynched by a large crowd. In addition to the greater likelihood of identifying mob members, the Laurel case also proved more conducive to the department's strategy of prosecuting negligent local officials. "Delinquency by the state officers is glaring," a top official informed the attorney general. Given that "the jail was Federally approved, fireproof, mob-proof," he concluded, only "the jailor's failure, either through cowardice or connivance, to turn a key in a lock sent Howard Wash to his death." As Clarke County officials conspired to cover their tracks, distracted federal officials turned hopefully toward Laurel. "The Howard Wash case presents a real opportunity to establish Federal jurisdiction in lynching cases," the Civil Rights Section advised, "and we should vigorously prosecute it to that end."[65]

While federal officials held out more hope for justice in Laurel, Bernstein discovered the same mix of ambivalence and hostility there that he encountered in Clarke County. The *Laurel Leader-Call* had denounced the lynching of "the brutal murderer, Howard Wash," but local citizens seemed just as eager as their Clarke County neighbors to sweep the killing under the rug. A white minister lamented the lynching as "a blot on the community," but confided to Bernstein that he had decided against speaking out from the pulpit. A local businessman agreed that lynchings embarrassed Mississippi, but he quickly lapsed into the familiar litany of racial rumors and wartime anxieties. "We got to keep the niggers in their place," he insisted. Bernstein asked if "hanging from a bridge" was the place he had in mind. "No responsible person in Laurel favors lynching," he shot back; "we could settle our problems fine if you'd leave us alone."[66]

In Jackson, Governor Johnson acted quickly to prove that Mississippi could indeed "solve" its lynching problem. The week's events had tightened the screws on the governor, who had already chastised Clarke County officials for permitting a double lynching. After Wash turned up dead, the governor dispatched investigators, state troopers, and two companies of his State Guard to Laurel. "The courtyard is bristling with soldiers," the *Laurel Leader* warned. "Tear gas bombs, hand grenades and riot guns, glistening bayonets, are in readiness to cope with any trouble that may come up." The next day, state troops transferred five black inmates from Laurel to the Jackson city jail for safekeeping. Later that day, the governor sent several carloads of state police to Hazlehurst to head off a manhunt for a black murder suspect. If the townspeople had caught up with the fugitive before the state troopers, the week's body count likely would have risen.[67]

Johnson backed the show of force with more law-and-order rhetoric. In a move that surprised civil rights sympathizers and white supremacists alike, the governor publicly welcomed the FBI to Mississippi. The week after the Shubuta lynchings, US attorney general Nicholas Biddle announced the ongoing Mississippi investigations and pledged "relentless prosecution" of suspected vigilantes. "If the federal government...can be of assistance to the state," Johnson responded, "I shall welcome any investigation it wishes to make."[68]

The governor's stance intrigued Bernstein, who ended his swing through the state in Johnson's Jackson office. The gaunt figure across the desk from him, Bernstein observed, seemed "sincerely distressed." The lynching controversy piled yet another burden on the ailing governor. Legislative fights over his reform program, which included old-age pensions and free textbooks for schoolchildren, had worn Johnson down. He would die in office fourteen months later. But mob violence, which embarrassed the state and discredited his progressive agenda, raised his ire. The governor patted a stack of papers on his desk—letters, he informed Bernstein, "from all over the South praising my stand."[69]

Despite the good press, Johnson's antilynching stance invited criticism. In a state where allegiance to white supremacy and "states' rights" were articles of faith for public officials, Johnson's enemies claimed that he had betrayed Mississippi. Blasting the governor's "startling stupidity," *Jackson Daily News* editor Fred Sullens likened his FBI "invitation" to "asking Congress to go ahead and pass that obnoxious anti-lynching law." The veteran newspaperman, who had once traded punches with Johnson in a Jackson hotel lobby, never missed a chance to ridicule the governor. Sullens had a long-standing beef with antilynching advocates. He had witnessed a dozen mob killings, the editor boasted in 1942, and had never seen an innocent man lynched. Just as he had done after the 1918 bridge lynchings in Shubuta—and many times since—Sullens rejected attempts to curb mob violence through legislation. "Laws to prevent lynching do more harm than good," he maintained. "They get the people so wrought up they are liable to do most anything."[70]

That impulse, Sullens argued, was not savage but chivalrous. Decades after his father's generation mobilized rumors of lustful black brutes to rally support for white supremacy, the Jackson editor clung to the myths that drove mob violence. "There is something so honorable in the Southern men," he told a skeptical investigator, "that they cannot tolerate the thought of a white woman having to go into court and tell the gruesome details of an attack. Lynching gives the man what he deserves, capital punishment, and spares the poor woman the ordeal." The governor, Sullens argued, should remember the *real* victim in Shubuta: Dorothy Martin. "One's first thoughts should be about the hideous memory that poor little girl must carry in her mind until the end of her days," Sullens opined, "rather than spilling a lot of maudlinism over mob violence." The governor had betrayed this code of chivalry, and asked Mississippi "to surrender her sovereignty" in the process. "Because two depraved negro youths were lynched," the editor fumed, "Gov. Johnson is seemingly willing to tell the Negro-petting Yankees and racial agitators of the North to come on in and take charge of our government."[71]

Bernstein had read these editorials, and when he met the governor he complimented him for his "firmness and courage" in weathering criticism from white supremacists. Johnson paused, sizing up the Yankee reporter before elaborating further. "I don't know you, and I don't know how much you know about the South," the governor continued. "You know we have certain prejudices down here." Johnson had walked a fine line for a couple of weeks—balancing "law and order" with the dictates of white supremacy—and he had caught hell along the way. He wanted Bernstein's northern readers to understand a few things. "Now you know these prejudices are born in us," Johnson explained. "You know there's nobody down here would sit down with a Negro and eat with him at the same table. You know we'd rather die first, don't you?"[72]

Seamlessly, the governor transitioned from his horror at the prospect of an integrated dinner table to his affection for black Mississippians: "There's no one down here in Mississippi got a friendlier feeling for the Negro than I have." He gestured to a picture of Abraham Lincoln on the wall behind him. "I guess I'm the first Governor of this State would have that picture on his wall." Unlike the Great Emancipator, however, Johnson believed that the South should be left alone. Like other white Mississippians, Johnson lapsed into the familiar rundown of wartime racial anxieties: "Our feelings towards the Negro are our own business, and certain people in the North are trying to make it their business." Singling out "the President's wife," Johnson raised the specter of the subversive Eleanor Clubs. He repeated the claim that the military drafted whites at far higher rates than blacks. "There are counties," he warned, "where the Negroes outnumber the whites 10 to 1." With black majorities and racial tensions increasing "almost daily," Johnson argued that outside meddling only inflamed Mississippi whites. "We're a very proud people...and you just make us mad that way."[73]

"I'm bitter against lynchings," Johnson concluded, "but they are our problem, and we've got to handle them our own way." The governor paused. He could probably guess what the Yankee reporter might write. Nothing had been "handled" yet. The governor made some stirring public statements, the State Guard patrolled a couple towns, but these efforts netted no indictments or convictions. The governor insisted that he lacked the power to do more. He could not punish local officials or call special grand juries. Ultimately, he argued, the only solution was education. "We've got to teach our people to have respect for law and order," the governor concluded. As he parted ways with the governor, Bernstein's thoughts returned to the dead boys in Clarke County. "I wonder what their mothers are thinking now," he wrote, "about education as a cure for corpses swinging in the wind."[74]

A MERE FIGMENT OF HIS IMAGINATION

Back in Clarke County, the Justice Department investigation had ended with a whimper. Despite glaring holes in the testimonies of lawmen and likely suspects, local whites showed enough of a united front to discourage investigators. In Washington, the head of the Civil Rights Section doubted the possibility of indictments, but suggested that a grand jury hearing might mollify antilynching activists. "At least," section head Victor Rotnem advised the attorney general's office, "the record will then disclose we have done our utmost." Of the department's twin-pronged strategy of prosecution and publicity, only the latter seemed to offer any favorable outcomes.[75]

Privately, federal officials and investigators agreed that fewer than six men—"probably relatives of the girl"—abducted and lynched the two boys. A quick check of the local phone company's records confirmed that no one had called Town Marshal Dabbs, as he had claimed, just before the raid on the jail. That lie alone did not give the feds a case, but it validated their suspicions that Dabbs "might possibly have been in league with the parties who took the negroes from the jail." As for willing witnesses, the feds had none. Or, at least, none who posed a threat.[76]

During the FBI investigation, agents repeatedly asked Quitman residents if they had heard or seen anything suspicious on the night of the lynching. While most said no, several claimed they had heard "the cries of a crazy negro" but thought nothing of it. One woman, an agent noted, "paid no attention to these cries as he was always hollering." Locals knew that the "crazy negro"—Isaiah Shine—had been locked up days before and was waiting on a transfer back to the state mental hospital. Despite the fact that he had witnessed the abduction first-hand, no one seemed too worried about his testimony.[77]

The day following the lynching, Shine's uncle walked by the county jail to catch a glimpse of his nephew. From his second-story window, Shine kept up a constant chatter with passersby. "I told 'em to take me, don't take the boys!" he shouted. "I wanted to get out!" Someone had hit him, Shine claimed, "across the head with a pistol!" Local blacks believed a local lawman had struck the inmate to shut him up. If any of those men—Dabbs, McNeal, or McLendon—deemed Shine a real threat, they could have easily disposed of him. His claims could be dismissed as the ravings of a lunatic, but his presence proved unnerving all the same. Besides, his story was spreading fast on the black side of town. So local authorities made a few calls, and the State Hospital quickly made room. "I don't believe he stayed two days," a relative recalled, "before they rushed him right on to Whitfield."[78]

Several days later, agent John Falkner—author William Faulkner's cousin and the Jackson FBI office's lead investigator—drove out to Whitfield to see Isaiah Shine. A doctor welcomed him in and summoned an orderly to fetch the patient. The staff deemed Shine "harmless," but insisted "that no reliance whatever could be put in anything he said, since his mind and memory were in such a condition that he would be unable to draw any distinction between fact and imagination." Shine's behavior seemed to confirm the warning. When he entered the room, Falkner noted, he "snapped and saluted in a military fashion." He told the agent about his time "out on vacation"—how he had wandered off to Hattiesburg and then "gone to stay at the jail for Sheriff McNeal." He talked about the two boys that came to stay with him for a while. They said they had been arrested "for chasing a little white girl," Shine recalled, and he believed that they got what was coming to them. Agent Falkner asked how many men came for them. "There were twenty-five," Shine replied. Did he know any of them? "He then replied," Falkner reported, "that the only individual he knew was the man who hit him, but that the man who hit him was his best friend, and he was not mad at him and would never tell anybody who he was, even if he was hung for it."[79]

Shine then "wandered off" to other topics, but Falkner pulled him back. Now visibly "wrought up and nervous," he told of a huge mob of "both negroes and whites" that showed up in broad daylight and pelted the jail with stones. After busting out all the windows, they called for him to "hold up Lang and Green so they could shoot them," but Shine scolded them and the mob dispersed. That night the mob came back. The less sense he made, the more fantastic the story became. Yet Shine kept returning to a single salient point—that he knew the man who had hit him.[80]

Eventually, Falkner stopped the interview. Shine had become more distressed with every sentence. When the doctor told him he could go, the patient again snapped and saluted. Shine asked Falkner if he would like to buy some war bonds, and the orderlies led him out of the room. The doctor reminded Falkner that nothing Shine said could be relied upon, because "it was impossible to tell what was fact and what was a mere figment of his imagination."[81]

CHAPTER FOUR

A MONUMENT TO
"JUDGE LYNCH"

On an October night in 1942, Roy Wilkins sat with friends in a Harlem apartment. Around the living room, smartly dressed professionals chatted and cradled highball glasses. Some sipped soft drinks, while others "had a jigger or two of a stronger stuff," as Wilkins put it in his weekly column for Harlem's leading black newspaper. Like Wilkins, a forty-one-year-old veteran journalist who served both as the NAACP's assistant secretary and as editor of *The Crisis*, these were "typical middle class Harlemites." One of them devoted her after-work hours to the American Women's Voluntary Service, whose uniformed members sold war bonds, organized scrap drives, and built air-raid shelters for children. Another volunteered for the Red Cross, though the agency insisted on segregating African Americans' donated blood from that of whites. One man, a physician, was preparing to report for enlistment, and another had just received his draft notice. Besides Wilkins, no one at the gathering was in the "race relation[s] business." But the newspaper lying on the coffee table had fixed their attention on Mississippi's "lynch-famous town of Shubuta."[1]

"Mob Storms Jail," the *Amsterdam Star-News* announced, "Drags 2 Boys, 14, to Their Death." Below the subheading, a cartoon depicted two shirtless and barefoot black boys hanging from a bridge. From the far bank of the river below, a jackbooted German soldier saluted the spectacle with a hearty "Heil Hitler!" (fig. 4.1). On the bridge that loomed above the dangling corpses, at least one member of the white mob appeared to return the gesture. In 1918, the Shubuta lynchers were "American Huns." In 1942, they were Nazis.[2]

Answer to the Poll Tax

FIGURE 4.1

Black activists and journalists invoked the rhetoric and imagery of the "Double V" campaign in their response to the lynching of Ernest Green and Charlie Lang. More specifically, they pointed to domestic racial controversies—in particular the pending anti-poll-tax legislation in Congress—as a catalyst for a violent southern backlash. "Answer to the Poll Tax," New York *Amsterdam Star-News*, October 17, 1942, 1.

"It makes you wonder why the hell you should fight for a country that does that," the doctor fumed. A "pretty brown-skinned woman" spoke up next. "When I think of my husband breaking up his career, leaving me and our little girl, going off to fight in some jungle to save this country so those so-and-so in Mississippi can lynch children," she sighed, "I just HATE white people." Others vented their frustration, Wilkins noted, in language that "would not look well in print." With little recourse in Washington, and certainly none in Mississippi, Wilkins lamented, it seemed their only outlet was to "talk, cry, and curse."[3]

Wilkins knew better, and so did his friends. What he heard in that Harlem apartment, the NAACP staffer warned in his weekly column, "was being said by Negroes all over the United States—Negroes in overalls, in white coats, in cotton dresses, in evening gowns. By doctors of philosophy and by illiterate field hands." Cartoon depictions of "two kids, swinging from a bridge," and a photograph of two corpses tossed in a truck bed, sparked a fury that poured forth in editorials, speeches, petitions, and telegrams. The response fueled fears that plummeting black morale would sap America's fighting strength. Three thousand miles from Wilkins's Harlem apartment, a reader clipped a photograph of the two lynched boys from a black Los Angeles weekly and mailed it to the White House. "These happenings," he warned President Roosevelt, "are the reasons our boys resent fighting for our country." In Baltimore, prison guards clipped that photograph out of the *Afro-American* for a different reason—they feared that black inmates would riot. From coast to coast, evidence of black anger and disillusionment poured forth. "Today," an Illinois NAACP branch president declared, "the average Negro would rather give $5 to bomb a mob of Mississippi lynchers than to donate 5 cents to bomb a regiment of Japs or Germans."[4]

Mob brutality certainly undermined black morale, but denunciations of lynchers as Nazis fueled black determination. "Yes, the colored people will fight across the seas," Wilkins pledged, "and also this hateful thing here at home. Nobody should forget that or underestimate it." Invoking the rhetoric of the "Double V"—victory over fascism abroad and Jim Crow at home—Wilkins stood at the vanguard of a wartime pressure campaign that forced black civil rights into the political spotlight. Like the federal officials who dispatched investigators to Clarke County, African Americans emphasized the diplomatic liabilities of racial violence. As they attempted to wield that wartime leverage to their advantage, black activists understood that white supremacists would resist. The "Defiant South," New York's leading black newspaper lamented, would lose a world war—and fight another civil war—before it accepted black equality. "Millions of people in the South," the *Amsterdam Star-News* announced, "are now deprived of their civil and political rights, burned at the stake, and subjected to scores of other abuses and indignities from the hands of an un-American, un-Democratic bloc of citizens who would rather see Hitler win the war than to give Negroes the right to live like free men in the United States."[5]

Such claims might seem sensational, but the investigators who traveled south after Shubuta's latest bridge lynchings encountered white supremacists who defined the wartime race crisis in exactly those terms. Like Victor Bernstein, who warned that white southerners were fighting a different war than other Americans, the investigators who tried to make sense of the latest Shubuta lynchings encountered predictions of race war at every turn. White fears and resentments reflected more than wartime rumors and "natural" prejudice. Southern whites, like African Americans, read the papers. News of antidiscrimination directives from the White House and civil rights bills in Congress, not to mention an unprecedented federal lynching investigation, convinced many whites that they had a fight on their hands.

Responses to racial violence—black and white—mattered. They reflected the increasingly high stakes of World War II for civil rights advocates and white supremacists alike. As stories and images of wartime lynchings spread across the country, Americans projected their own hopes and fears onto two boys' dead bodies and a rusty river bridge. For black activists, Mississippi's "Kid-Lynchers" and their bridge demonstrated the un-American and inhumane logic of white supremacy. For many white southerners, the killings foreshadowed the bloodshed that they believed would spread across the region if racial agitators did not back down. For black mothers and fathers, the killing of Ernest

Green and Charlie Lang suggested that no one was safe from that gathering backlash. And for Roy Wilkins, the bridge took him back to the place where his family's freedom struggle had begun and where the future of that fight would be determined.

The Work of the Mob Goes On

The grandson of enslaved southerners, Roy Wilkins opened his autobiography with the sentence: "I was not born in Mississippi, but my story begins there all the same." Born in St. Louis and raised in Minnesota, Wilkins remembered vividly his visits to his grandfather's tenant farm on the outskirts of Holly Springs—hometown of the antilynching crusader Ida B. Wells. Sold and separated from his mother when he was nine, Asberry Wilkins spent much of his youth working in the cotton fields. Asberry was a teenager when the Yankees first marched through northern Mississippi and allowed him an opportunity to seize his freedom. He remembered casting a few Republican ballots before Mississippi's white Democrats launched their campaign to overthrow Reconstruction and—in their words—"suppress the Negro and keep him in the position where he belongs." Despite his political past, local whites considered Asberry Wilkins a "good nigger." As Roy Wilkins explained, "My grandfather had to keep his head down—or get his neck stretched."[6]

Wilkins's father, however, was a "bad nigger" in the eyes of whites. Willie Wilkins had no patience for farm life, and even less for Jim Crow. "The family's first hell-raiser," as his son later remembered, Willie worked his way through Rust College—a local black Methodist school—only to settle for work as a porter. After a run-in with a white farmer on a lonely dirt road, which started when the man called Willie a nigger and ended when Willie left him bloodied and groaning in his own wagon bed, Asberry Wilkins loaded his son and daughter-in-law on the first northbound train. His parents fled Mississippi, Roy Wilkins later learned, "one step ahead of a lynch rope."[7]

As a young man, Roy Wilkins discovered that leaving the South did not mean leaving the mob behind. Wilkins had just finished his freshman year at the University of Minnesota when a mob in Duluth lynched three black circus workers in 1920. After police arrested the men for allegedly assaulting a local white man, an estimated five thousand vigilantes stormed the city jail and hung the men from a light post. "This was Minnesota, not Mississippi," Wilkins remembered. A generation and a thousand miles separated him from his father's "escape from Judge Lynch," but the Duluth lynching drove home for Wilkins "what Du Bois had been writing about. I found myself thinking of black people as a very vulnerable *us*—and white people as an unpredictable, violent *them*."[8]

As with his NAACP predecessors James Weldon Johnson and Walter White, Wilkins's southern roots and his family's scrapes with mob violence shaped his outlook and his activism. If his northern upbringing distanced him from the daily threat of lynching, he never forgot what sent his parents fleeing north. The first black reporter for the University of Minnesota's student paper, Wilkins worked at newspapers in St. Paul and Kansas City before taking a job with the NAACP. Having lived across the urban North and Midwest, Wilkins understood the national reach of discrimination and violence. Try as he might, he could never fully leave Mississippi behind. From Minnesota to Missouri to Manhattan, Wilkins saw the state's bloody imprint—and his family's history of struggle—wherever he went. In 1942, the newspaper on his friend's coffee table brought him back, once again, to where his story began. His father had escaped a Mississippi mob. Two boys had not been so lucky.

By World War II, Wilkins had already been a professional activist for a decade. Hired as the organization's assistant secretary after Walter White succeeded James Weldon Johnson as executive secretary in 1931, Wilkins assumed editorship of *The Crisis* three years later after W. E. B. Du Bois's stormy departure. As the organization's chief lieutenant, propagandist, and backroom negotiator, Wilkins helped to engineer a wartime civil rights campaign. In June 1941, he joined White and Asa Phillip Randolph, head of the Brotherhood of Sleeping Car Porters and founder of the March on Washington Movement, in a tense Oval Office meeting with President Roosevelt. Faced with the prospect of one hundred thousand black protesters descending on the nation's

capital for a July rally, Roosevelt offered an unprecedented concession. In exchange for Randolph calling off the march, Roosevelt issued
Executive Order 8802, which barred racial discrimination in the defense industries and established a temporary Fair Employment Practices
Committee to review grievances. Randolph, a veteran activist and a
master of pressure politics, deemed it the most important presidential
action on black rights since the Emancipation Proclamation.[9]

While the fair employment committee raised some black hopes,
Wilkins remained pessimistic that another global crusade for democracy would pay any more dividends than the last. Noticeably absent
from the president's proclamation was any mention of discrimination
in the armed forces, and neither the march movement nor the NAACP
expected concessions from the military brass. However, the War Department, like the president, considered black morale and manpower an
urgent concern as war loomed. The same day that the Japanese attacked
Pearl Harbor, Wilkins arrived in Washington for a meeting of military
officials and black newspapermen. "The War Department," Wilkins recalled, "wanted us to buy the idea that a little cheerleading was all it
would take to keep black men in fighting trim." More interested in
public relations than reform, the top brass offered no concessions. The
army, Wilkins complained, "wanted as few black soldiers as possible."
They wanted black *recruits*, but preferred to outfit them with shovels
rather than rifles. As in World War I, many military officials and southern politicians believed that black servicemen should be used for labor
and support roles rather than in combat. The army's new air corps
wanted no black recruits, and the navy, Wilkins complained, "was only
in the market for mess attendants." Racial discrimination permeated
the national defense program—white supremacists insisted on segregated blood banks and even Jim Crow air raid bunkers. "So far as I
was concerned," Wilkins scoffed at the bunker proposal, "any white
folks who thought they were too good to jump into a shelter alongside
their black neighbors deserved to be blown to hell."[10]

Wilkins left the conference convinced that the federal government
would do little to protect black soldiers and civilians. Measured against
a catalog of ongoing injustices, Roosevelt's concession to the March on

Washington Movement seemed a momentary lapse rather than a turning point for civil rights. Yet black activists had their own list—an ambitious reform agenda that took aim at discrimination in the armed forces, on the shop floor, and at the ballot box. "Policies of racial discrimination divide us and aid the enemy," the NAACP announced in the wake of the Pearl Harbor attack. "The man who discriminates against Negroes is a Fifth Columnist." Invoking the "Double V"—a rallying cry coined and promoted by the black press—the NAACP warned that "the dictator armies may be defeated by a Jim Crow Navy, a Jim Crow Army, a Jim Crow Air Corps; but the dictator idea will never be defeated by Jim Crowism." While black activists a generation earlier had emphasized the Huns' naked aggression, World War II–era activists emphasized Nazi ideology. "If racial discrimination under Hitler is wrong," the NAACP argued, "racial discrimination in America is wrong." This time, white supremacists' *beliefs*—not just their brutality—were called into question. The image of a Nazi saluting the Shubuta bridge put this argument in sharp relief.[11]

Lynching remained a galvanizing issue for African Americans, but during World War II other campaigns competed for public sympathy and political traction. The campaign for federal antilynching legislation had elevated black civil rights to national prominence, and activists recognized that racial violence undergirded the South's Jim Crow regime. Nonetheless, after two fruitless decades of lobbying Congress and the White House to take action against lynching, and faced with the inevitability of an unrelenting southern filibuster, black activists looked for more promising avenues for racial reform. The fair employment victory, along with legislative and legal challenges to segregation and disfranchisement laws, siphoned attention and resources from the antilynching push.

At the same time, activists recognized lynching's power as a propaganda tool. When, just a few weeks after the bombing of Pearl Harbor, the mob in Sikeston, Missouri, shot Cleo Wright, dragged his corpse through the streets, and set it ablaze, the black press printed photographs of the victim's charred corpse on front pages from coast to coast. To federal officials' dismay, the Axis powers also seized the story.

Echoing black activists' warnings that mob violence undermined the war effort, the head of the Justice Department's Civil Rights Division reported that Missouri vigilantes had tarnished America's global image and strengthened the hand of Axis propagandists. That diplomatic reality compelled the president, who had long resisted calls for federal intervention in lynching cases, to dispatch federal agents to Sikeston.[12]

Despite the brutal slaying of Cleo Wright, black activists worried that public concern and political interest would decline along with the annual body count. The steady drop in recorded lynchings—from twenty-six in 1933 to four in 1941—led many to conclude that the antilynching movement was a victim of its own success. Years of negative publicity and political pressure had not forced federal action, they argued, but outside criticism had compelled southern states to take concrete steps to curb mob violence. Predictions of lynching's imminent extinction undercut efforts to mobilize public sympathy and push for legal protections. Some activists argued that lynching had not disappeared but had simply "gone underground." For every Cleo Wright, brutalized and butchered by a large mob in broad daylight, civil rights advocates argued that dozens of African Americans died at the hands of small posses who killed under cover of darkness. Often with assistance from local lawmen, a few men abducted, executed, and—frequently—disappeared blacks for minor offenses and perceived slights. Antilynching activists attributed this tactical shift to the threat of negative publicity and possible intervention by state or federal authorities, but they also argued that the "new technique" was more pervasive and harder to fight.[13]

For proof, civil rights supporters looked to Mississippi. As the nation prepared for war, the NAACP dispatched Howard Kester, a white southerner, to investigate a pair of suspicious killings in Canton. In one case, a reported robbery of a white lumber mill worker sparked a manhunt that led to the random assassination of a black passerby. After a bullet tore through twenty-two-year-old Claude Banks's skull as he drove home from a party, the posse jailed his companion, beat him, and swore him to secrecy before releasing him hours later. When a reporter drove over from nearby Jackson, local police prevented him from photographing Banks's corpse.[14]

Several months later, a black lumber mill employee turned up dead after a scuffle with his white foreman. Joe Rodgers had questioned rent deductions—for a house in which he did not live—from his weekly paycheck. When the white foreman responded by punching him and swinging at him with a shovel, Rodgers wrested the weapon away and struck him with it. The next morning, a white constable "discovered" Rodgers's corpse—naked, bound, and beaten to a pulp—washed up on a riverbank. The editor of the local paper, who also happened to be Canton's mayor, made no mention of the mysterious death. Both incidents, Kester reported, followed the logic employed by vigilantes in Shubuta in 1918: "A white man had been attacked by a Negro. A Negro must pay, the right Negro if possible, but a Negro at whatever costs." The old rules remained, even if the tactics had evolved. "Lynching is entering a new and altogether dangerous phase," he concluded. "The old mob is disappearing but the work of the mob goes on."[15]

Kester's Mississippi exposé foreshadowed the lynchings in Shubuta and the future of antiblack violence. In Shubuta, as in Canton, white mill workers—friends or relatives of the accuser—abducted the accused or attacked a suspect with help from local authorities. The posse did its work in the shadows and counted on collusion and cover from the white community. In Clarke County, as in Canton, whites attempted to contain the story and enforce black silence through intimidation. Dozens of similar incidents, the NAACP asserted, occurred every year with little press coverage and no response from state or federal authorities. These killings, they argued, proved that lynching would never die out without federal intervention. Despite black activists' multipronged wartime campaign, racial violence remained at the core of the struggle. In October 1942, a letter from a familiar place arrived at the national headquarters. "Writing the association," an anonymous informant from Clarke County wrote, "reporting the lynching of two 14 year old negros...hanged from the river bridge where 4 other persons was lynched several years ago."[16]

A COUNTER-CAMPAIGN TO HOLD
THE NEGRO IN THE DITCH

The investigation request landed on the desk of the nation's most famous lynching investigator. Walter White, however, had retired from undercover work. Twenty years after infiltrating Shubuta, the NAACP's executive secretary spent most of his time on speaking tours and lobbying blitzes. The head of the association for over a decade, White had become a fixture on Capitol Hill and something of a national celebrity. Across Dixie, white southerners now knew his name and—after he made the cover of *Time* magazine during the 1938 filibuster of the antilynching bill—his face. There was no chance of him ever "passing" again, certainly not in Shubuta. He considered calling up Howard Kester for another fact-finding mission. Then Roy Wilkins mentioned "an attractive young woman with a broad Alabama accent" who had dropped by the office just a few weeks before. She was looking for a job.[17]

Sara Craigen Kennedy did not fit the mold of an aspiring NAACP staffer, though her potential as an undercover lynching investigator proved irresistible. Born in southern Mississippi, Kennedy moved to Tuscaloosa, Alabama, after her father died unexpectedly. A fixture in the society section of the hometown paper, she seemed like a precocious but perfectly typical white southern teenager. In high school, she won a prize from the Daughters of the American Revolution for her essay "What the Statue of Liberty Means to Me." Two years later, she enrolled in the University of Alabama and joined a sorority. A summer spent working for a social service project in Manhattan piqued her interest in racial discrimination, and two subsequent summers spent working at a Harlem settlement house deepened her concern. The outbreak of war strengthened her conviction that "race prejudice" undermined national unity and endangered "the preservation of the principles of democracy."[18]

A month after she dropped by the NAACP office, and a week before the Shubuta lynchings, Kennedy wrote to Walter White. In response to wartime reforms, Kennedy argued, white supremacists had launched "a counter-campaign to hold the Negro in the ditch." The twenty-two-year-old

University of Alabama graduate submitted an "outline of a suggested trip to survey this counter-campaign, its methods and its effect on the Southern white populous [sic]." Through her study, she hoped to determine whether the wartime spike in violence and extremism was "part of an organized, carefully carried-out program of terror and intimidation...to make Negroes fearful of insisting on equal rights of any kind."[19]

Any other week, White might have tossed such a proposal aside. The association had plenty of contacts who were far more qualified for such a project. What it did not have was a white Alabama sorority member willing to investigate a lynching. With wealthy relatives and family friends scattered across Mississippi—including in Clarke County—Kennedy had remarkable connections, the kind that could help the investigation and provide unique insights into the recent wave of racial violence across the South. "Her family background," a staffer noted, "[makes] it possible for her to enter casual discussion with members of the southern ruling class." The NAACP secured an endorsement letter from the head of the Atlanta-based Southern Education Foundation, and prominent sociologists E. Franklin Frazier and Guy B. Johnson agreed to help Kennedy design a credible questionnaire. "In order to measure the subject's attitudes towards Negroes," Kennedy noted, she devised twenty statements and weighted responses on a five-point scale. Some statements gauged "traditional reactionary thought concerning Negroes"—"*White people as a race are just naturally smarter than the colored race*"; "*The Lord intended for Negroes to be the servant class*"—while others assessed white reactions to campaigns against lynching, employment discrimination, and segregation.[20]

A survey of southern racial attitudes had its merits, though White made clear the trip's immediate objective—"to start at Shubuta, Mississippi, and vicinity to get all of the facts she can." White hoped Kennedy might even get to Dorothy Martin, the boys' alleged accuser and intended victim. The study, he reminded his new hire, "is merely an instrument to get at the truth....[Y]ou need to guard against a too academic approach instead of a blood-and-flesh one." Kennedy was a novice, but she was no fool. She recognized the dangers that the trip posed—both to her and her controversial employer. Rather than correspond directly with White—"because of the nation-wide recognition of his name"—Kennedy sent her field reports to Odette Harper, a black Bronx native who went to work for the NAACP the same month. Kennedy advised Harper to write her in longhand and use a pseudonym. "Don't mention anything in your letters about NAACP," she suggested. "You can make suggestions about my trip, merely as an interested friend for instance.... *You get it.*" Kennedy's field reports, scribbled on notebook paper or typed up on hotel stationery and addressed to her friend "Milly," trickled back to NAACP headquarters as Kennedy made her way to Mississippi.[21]

When she reached Shubuta, Kennedy headed straight to "the biggest, richest house in town." Mary Weems, a distant cousin, was the middle-aged matriarch of Shubuta's wealthiest family. The unmarried daughter of the town banker, "Miss Mary" had strolled the city streets of Europe and cruised through the Panama Canal, and her stately home stood in sharp relief to the hardscrabble cabins and sawmills of Shubuta. "I'm sure that her comfort and the inheritance from her father were built on the poor white and colored," Kennedy noted. Even so, Mary Weems used her family's small fortune to smooth over the roughest edges of Shubuta's racial order. She put up the money for the town's black schoolhouse and doled out scholarships for local youth to attend the state's black Methodist college. Every Wednesday, she conducted Bible classes and a course in home nursing at a local black church. "She is said to be honestly concerned about the Negro in Shubuta," a black wartime visitor conceded, "and tries, as much as she is able, to compensate for the defalcations of other members of her race."[22]

Kennedy received a warm welcome at the Weems House. The small banquet in her honor went smoothly, Kennedy noted, "until...Mary asked me what my public opinion survey was about." Kennedy's mother had phoned ahead, and she must have mentioned the job—at least the details that her daughter had shared with her. The rookie investigator kept her cool. She was "a little worried," Kennedy admitted to her host, because her survey "was on the subject of Negroes."[23]

With that, Kennedy reported, "Mary hit the ceiling." She wanted to know everything—who had sent her, who she worked for, and if she had come because of the lynching. Kennedy kept up the ruse she would repeat whenever she ran across suspicious or hostile whites: "I said I hoped the people would realize that I had nothing to do with the survey, I was merely hired to walk around and check people's responses to the statements." She had "no interest in the problem whatsoever," Kennedy said, "and didn't give a hoot what they thought." If anything, she added, her questionnaire would "show Mrs. Roosevelt and other such northerners what the Mississippians feel about their Northern ideas." As for her stop in Shubuta, Kennedy added, "I just thought it would be nice to visit you all while I'm in Mississippi, but I'm on company time so I thought I'd better work tomorrow." Although the survey was about "ideas on the race problem in general," she conceded, "I thought it would be interesting here because of the lynching."[24]

"Child," Weems sighed, "no one will talk to you. They'll freeze up the moment you say *nigger*....And it might even be dangerous for you." Besides, she added, a "crowd from Quitman" lynched the boys anyway. With that, Kennedy's host quickly changed the subject. Later, after the other guests had left, Weems "opened up a little more." The boys were fourteen, she said, not "the hiked up ages" that local officials later claimed. She did not think the boys were guilty of attempted rape. "There's no telling," she muttered, "what sort of pressure was put on them at the magistrate's hearing to get them to 'confess' to such a thing." Still, the town matriarch pivoted, the blacks *were* "getting out of hand lately." Weems lapsed into a familiar refrain of wartime anxieties—the draft taking away "all the white men," the blacks outnumbering the whites, and rumors of imminent revolt. "The week before the lynching, while those boys were in jail," she claimed, "some niggers went in the hardware store and bought up every knife in town." Kennedy asked her host to complete the questionnaire, but Miss Mary had already said too much. "All she knew was that they all hated lynching and hated Mrs. Roosevelt," Kennedy reported. "And she went to bed."[25]

The following morning, Kennedy lingered—"just being sociable to regain some of her confidence." Nonetheless, she decided "not to press the issue" around town. Just outside of Shubuta, on the road to Quitman, she pulled over at a farmhouse. A white man and his sister agreed to take the survey. "They both answered the questionnaire 100% anti-Negro," she reported. Eight black families worked the farm and lived in cabins nearby. "They told me they both believed in treating niggers right," Kennedy noted, "paying them what you promised to pay, not over-working them." When she read the question about "the need for some organization to protect white supremacy," however, the farmer cracked a smile. "We've got us one around here like that," he said. Then, Kennedy reported, "the man began telling me how they have to 'mob' Negroes occasionally to keep them in their place."[26]

The rookie investigator seized her chance. The NAACP had sent her a dispatch from a black staffer who had inquired about the lynchings during a recent recruiting swing through Meridian. A couple of the victims' cousins, boarders at the city's black high school, claimed that the boys had been mutilated with pliers and screwdrivers. The white farmer had seen the bodies, and he was in a boastful mood. So she plied him for gruesome details. She had never seen a lynching, she said, although they had one back in Tuscaloosa when she was younger. "I was out of town and missed it," she sighed. "I think it would be real interesting, but I hate to see blood."[27]

"Oh this one wasn't bloody," the farmer replied. "They just plain hanged them...broke their necks." Seemingly perplexed, Kennedy responded, "I thought they usually cut them up some." There was no need, the farmer explained, because "these boys didn't resist at all." If they had, he added, "they would have fixed them up good, I guess." Kennedy asked him why he thought the victims did not put up a fight. "Oh, they were just kids," the farmer replied.[28]

The white farmer seemed quite familiar with the details; the conspirators had made no attempt to hide their handiwork. To the contrary, the farmer claimed, the party that retrieved the bodies had taken a few detours on their way to the undertaker. "Some men put 'em on a truck," he noted, "and rode all around the school building and over town." At that point, the farmer's sister spoke up. Another sister was Dorothy Martin's teacher. She was at school the morning after the lynching, when the truck rolled by on its way into town. "It was pretty exciting at school that Monday," the woman noted. "Sis could hardly keep the children in their seats: they were always jumping up and running to the windows to see the truck hauling those boys around." Martin stayed home the next day, she added. "I guess she didn't know till Monday morning when she got to school that they had been mobbed."[29]

Kennedy's contacts in Quitman offered no eyewitness accounts. However, they provided ample evidence of an increasingly tense mood. The town's "refreshingly liberal" Methodist minister, Kennedy reported, had criticized a local sawmill owner for mistreating black workers and worked with his congregation "to stimulate clear thinking on the race issue." The minister mentioned that "he had several of the women of the missionary society reading books on the subject," but since the lynching "all of the women have lost interest." Kennedy asked why Clarke County whites "seemed to feel more intensely against the Negro" than other places, and the reverend blamed the tension on the FBI investigation. "Then he started a monologue on his pet peeve," she noted. "Northerners who know little or nothing of our problems in the South and hav[e] their own solutions of how we should handle our affairs." The preacher rattled off the usual suspects—the president's fair employment order, his wife's "Eleanor Clubs," and the "Northern Negro soldiers" who provoked clashes on southern buses and trains. The president and Mrs. Roosevelt, he added, were "going out of their way…to encourage Negroes to rebel." The "thinking people of the South," were trying to deal with the problem, he complained. "If they'd only realize that and leave us alone."[30]

Kennedy heard this refrain constantly during her fact-finding trip. In her search for signs of racial progress, she sought out relatively "liberal" whites—newspapermen, educators, and clergy. Almost all were tight-lipped and resentful. "Any publication of the problem only stirs it up," Meridian's school superintendent, a man named Dr. Ivy, argued. Like the Quitman preacher, he argued that only those "who live right here in the situation" could "solve" an explosive issue that had accumulated a list of intentionally vague and euphemistic names—*the race problem, the racial situation, the negro question*. Like most of those she spoke with, the Meridian school administrator was long on problems and short on solutions. "Dr. Ivy lives in the situation," Kennedy reported. "He made no suggestions of how to solve it."[31]

Despite the praise heaped on Mississippi's governor for his response to the lynchings—and, increasingly, *because* of it—Paul Johnson had soured on "the race question." When Kennedy called on the governor, he lost his temper. "A Northern reporter came down here not long ago and interviewed me," he snapped, and "misinterpreted every thing I said, so I'm not going to say anything at all to you." The governor "was going to have me shown out of his office," Kennedy noted, "But then he started talking." He was not in a "liberal" mood. He had paid a price for welcoming the FBI's lynching investigations, and the kudos from Yankee reporters and civil rights activists had only embarrassed him further. "If you want to quote me on anything, let it be this," he fumed. "Those agitators are trying to make more white people black...get Negro men to have white women and white men to have Negro women. The *whole* thing is social equality."[32]

Back in Pearl River County—her childhood home—Kennedy saw signs of a looming backlash. Hosted by two of her father's old Klan buddies, she heard talk of reviving the Invisible Empire. Its services would be needed when the war ended, one townsperson predicted, "like it was after the last one, after them niggers came back from France thinking they were as good as white people." Others believed that they could not wait that long. Race rumors and Washington politics had convinced them that they were on the brink of war at home. No one fanned those flames more than Pearl River County's infamous native son—US senator Theodore Bilbo. In the wake of the bridge lynchings, he had a new cause to champion—the poll tax.[33]

KID LYNCHERS AND POLL-TAX MOBSTERS

By the time Kennedy reached her hometown—and Bilbo's—Washington's most notorious white supremacist had launched a filibuster against the most controversial legislation to reach the Senate since the 1938 anti-lynching bill. Like the earlier measure, the bill to abolish the poll tax had sailed through the House of Representatives by an overwhelming margin. The House vote took place on October 13—the day after the lynchings. Eight southern states, including Mississippi, still levied the tax, which discouraged poor whites and nearly all blacks from registering to vote. Advocates for repeal argued that, by keeping an estimated eleven million southerners off the voter rolls, the poll tax gave the region's congressmen disproportionate power on Capitol Hill. To highlight the imbalance, the *Poll Tax Repealer* pointed out that the thirty-two congressmen from four Deep South states received fewer combined votes than the two congressmen from Rhode Island. With only a few thousand supporters, southern lawmakers could rise through the ranks to chair committees and kill legislation that affected millions of Americans.[34]

Such arguments were lost on southern conservatives, who denounced the new bill as an attack on white supremacy. As Congress drew close to a vote—and Clarke County vigilantes prepared for a lynching—southern Mississippi congressman William Colmer claimed that the anti-poll-tax bill's "direct object" was "to enfranchise the Negro in the South." John Rankin, a veteran east Mississippi congressman and the House's crudest race baiter, deemed the legislation part of "a long range communistic program to change our form of Government and…to take the control of our elections out of the hands of white Americans." When his tirade failed to sway his colleagues, who voted three to one to outlaw the poll tax, Rankin laid down the gauntlet. "You are now creating a second front," Rankin cautioned his colleagues. "You are waging war against the white people of the Southern States."[35]

The same morning that Rankin predicted a southern backlash, papers nationwide reported that Mississippi whites had already struck back. "On the eve of the congressional action on the Anti-Poll Tax bill to 'enfranchise' some 4,000,000 Negroes in eight Southern States," announced Harlem's leading black newspaper, "the South opened the first gun of its reprisal by lynching two 14-year-old colored boys." The cartoon below, the image of a jackbooted Nazi saluting the lynchers, carried the caption "Answer to the Poll Tax." Across town, a rival daily blamed Rankin and his congressional allies for "inciting" racial violence with their "hysterical" speeches against the anti-poll-tax bill. Ernest Green and Charlie Lang, New York's pro-civil-rights press concluded, had died at the hands of "poll tax mobsters."[36]

Mississippi white supremacists and civil rights supporters agreed on little, but both sides claimed that controversy on Capitol Hill had sparked racial violence. "This Clarke county lynching reflects in measure cheap and dirty national politics," argued a Meridian editor. "Vote-hungry national leadership has purposely stirred up the issue of race prejudice." While he considered lynching "indefensible," the newspaperman heaped blame on northern politicians—and their black constituents—for the atrocity in neighboring Clarke County. Yankee congressmen, he argued, had struck down the poll tax to secure "Southside Chicago [and] Harlem colored votes." Such charges played on the pervasive belief that a cabal of black agitators had hijacked the Democratic Party, and that northern cities bursting with southern black migrants had swung the balance of power away from the South. This political shift, Mississippi's white elite contended, threatened to "scuttle many decades of mutually happy inter-racial unity and cooperation in the South." Unless northern agitators relented, they predicted, the violence would continue. "Washington is sowing tragic seed," warned the *Meridian Star*. "We must harvest bitter fruit."[37]

Despite their claims of persecution, white Mississippians and their allies across the South enjoyed enormous power in Washington. As soon as the anti-poll-tax bill cleared the House, Mississippi's senior senator threatened to filibuster for thirty days straight to kill it. Just four years removed from a southern filibuster that lasted nearly seven weeks, few doubted that Bilbo's poll-tax comrades would rally to the call. And while the former governor was a polarizing figure back in Mississippi, Bilbo's stand for white supremacy paid political dividends. Traveling across southern Mississippi, Kennedy encountered nearly universal support for the filibuster. Other than the statement about the abolishment of segregation, no items on her questionnaire provoked stronger reactions than those about the poll tax. An "over-whelming majority" of respondents opposed any attempt to get rid of the tax, she reported, because they believed "they would lose white supremacy in the state if Negroes were allowed the vote." This "great fear" united whites who otherwise agreed on very little. In the senator's hometown, Kennedy chatted with "one of the most liberal people here" about the anti-poll-tax bill. "This is the first time in my life I agree with Bilbo on anything," he admitted.[38]

In Clarke County and across southern Mississippi, whites echoed the ominous predictions of their representatives in Washington. A Quitman man reported "almost as much bitterness now as in Civil War days," and blamed the racial tension on "the federal government trying to take our poll tax away." The predictions compelled a white minister in nearby Hattiesburg to telegram Bilbo. "The day they pass a law to let negroes vote in the south, I fear it will cause the worse war we have ever had in the USA," he warned. "I am not alone, it is [the] talk everywhere."[39]

While his constituents predicted civil war, Bilbo linked his filibuster to the global crusade against fascism. "In making this fight against the unconstitutional anti-poll tax bill," the senator declared, "I feel that I am as much a soldier in the preservation of the American way and American scheme of Government as the boys who are fighting and dying on Guadalcanal." The senator's supporters echoed this argument— that white supremacy was not only constitutional but patriotic—in piles of letters and telegrams. Mississippi soldiers urged him to make sure they did not return home, as one army private pleaded, "to a state made corrupt and changed by legislation such as the anti-poll tax bill." Even some whites who could not afford to vote cheered Bilbo's filibuster. "As a poor Southern Farm boy," a southern Mississippi constituent wrote, "I would rather give up my privilege of voting than have ignorant negroes getting in politics and destroying our democracy." If forced to choose between enemies foreign and domestic, as Kennedy discovered on her trip to Mississippi, whites repeatedly claimed they would "rather be under Hitler's rule than under a Negro's."[40]

At the same time, Mississippi's white poll tax supporters drew parallels between Nazis and "Northern agitators." Like the NAACP and the black press, white Mississippians argued that a war for democracy was raging at home and abroad. And like the "agitators" they denounced, defenders of white supremacy argued that racial strife undermined the war effort. Hoping to deflect criticism in the wake of the lynchings of Charlie Lang and Ernest Green, Mississippi's governor blamed the racial unrest on "disturbing elements...which have in mind only one purpose, that of aiding the Axis powers." By talking up the "negro problem"—a dilemma that the governor claimed did not exist—these subversives hoped to sap Americans' resolve. "Let's get to the root of the evil," he urged, "and blast from our borders the disturbing influences and elements."[41]

Johnson's rhetoric, more tepid than Bilbo's racist harangues, had its limits. When Jim Crow's critics branded white supremacy as un-American, most white southerners resented the attack on their patriotism. But when civil rights advocates argued that racial violence sabotaged the war effort, many white southerners agreed. Mark Ethridge, a native Mississippian who had risen from a Meridian reporter to the editor of the *Louisville Courier-Journal*, warned that the "inexcusable" Clarke County killings "plays into the hands of Axis propagandists who mention lynchings prominently among their instances of white democratic hypocrisy." Mississippi had an obligation, Ethridge argued, to counter that charge with swift and decisive action. Moderate whites answered the editor's call with a full-page spread in Mississippi's largest newspaper. In the wake of the October lynching spree, seventy-one clergy, educators, and civic leaders—fifty-nine of them white—warned that unchecked violence would make Mississippi "a bridgehead of fascism in America." Lynchings not only had a "disastrous effect on the morale of our own people," the petitioners declared, but also on "the more than 600,000,000 allies of colored races."[42]

This diplomatic calculus compelled President Roosevelt, who had studiously avoided public comment, to admit that mounting racial strife portended a crisis. The same day that a chain gang buried Ernest Green and Charlie Lang—whose lynching Roosevelt would never publicly acknowledge—the president announced in a fireside chat that America's enemies were waging a "war of nerves" on the home front. "They have spread falsehood and terror," he warned. "They have fomented suspicion and hate between neighbors; they have aided and abetted those people in other nations—including our own—whose words and deeds are advertised from Berlin and from Tokyo as proof of our disunity." Having recently returned from a national tour of training camps and war factories, the president decried "prejudices and practices"—citing specifically the reluctance "to hire Negroes"—that undermined unity and exacerbated "the manpower problem." Only by overcoming these obstacles could America achieve "the kind of victory that will guarantee that our grandchildren...may live their lives, free from the constant threat of invasion, destruction, slavery, and violent death."[43] The address fell short of an explicit denunciation of lynching, but black activists played up the tragic irony of Roosevelt's "war of nerves" rhetoric. Two dead boys in Mississippi, Walter White telegrammed the White House, "are as much sabotage of our nation's war effort as a bomb in an airplane factory or shipyard." NAACP field secretary Daisy Lampkin, who was directing a membership drive in Chicago when the lynching news broke, marveled that Mississippi "would lynch two 14-year-old youth" seemingly in anticipation of the president's address (fig. 4.2).[44]

Like government officials, civil rights supporters emphasized the boys' age—a measure of southern depravity and plummeting black morale. "When a race-mad mob of morons lynches a couple of adolescents," fumed a northern white editor, "one begins to wonder if even a colored infant in its crib is immune from the perverted wrath of such sorry specimens." Talk of "kid lynchers" resonated with black parents, who responded to the atrocity with fear and fury. "Hurt over the way they murder those kids," read a hastily scribbled protest letter from soldiers in the all-black Ninety-third Division. In a letter that likely never reached the president's desk, they demanded protection for "the ones we left at home." Petitions from the Indiana State Federation of Colored Women's Clubs demanded federal protection "as Mothers, who are giving, our sons, husbands and fathers to our Country to fight for Democracy." A St. Louis defense worker and father of two, who received his draft notice days before the Shubuta lynchings, echoed this fear. "When I get on the battle front I am afraid I can't fight well for worrying about whether my sons are being linched," he pleaded. "Mr. president will you promise

FIGURE 4.2

Despite the failure of multiple antilynching bills since 1918, the fight against mob violence remained a top priority of civil rights activists during World War II. In this photograph, serviceman and St. Louis branch member Elmer Mosee holds a "Stop Lynchings" sign alongside NAACP field secretary Daisy Lampkin and Mississippi-born attorney and St. Louis NAACP leader Sidney R. Redmond. Visual Materials from the NAACP Records. LC-USZ62-119472. Courtesy of the Library of Congress Prints and Photographs Division and the National Association for the Advancement of Colored People.

me my sons will not be linched when I go in the army?" The president could make no such assurances of safety to Hilliard Lang, who reported for enlistment in December 1942. Lang went from repairing railroads in Mississippi to rebuilding railroads in Normandy as a member of the all-black 364th Engineering Regiment. While other black servicemen worried about their children back home, Hilliard Lang mourned a son lynched just two months before Uncle Sam called him up.[45]

While black parents feared for black children, activists pondered the impact of racist brutality on their white peers. In 1929, Walter White had opened his antilynching exposé *Rope and Faggot* with a story about the Florida children who, during one of his undercover investigations, recounted "the fun we had burning the niggers." Thirteen years later, the association reminded its members that lynching culture warped white minds even as it snuffed out black life. Of the scores of pages of reconnaissance compiled by Kennedy during her tour of Mississippi, only one snippet made it into the NAACP's annual report. In its synopsis of "the particularly atrocious lynching of two colored children," the association focused not on the Shubuta bridge but on that moment when the old logging truck carrying the bodies rumbled past the dusty schoolyard. White pupils "drawn by the air of excitement" rushed outside to view the uncovered corpses. The truck driver obliged and pulled to a stop. "Among the schoolyard crowd of onlookers was a seventh grader, a thirteen year old girl who had been a playmate to the boys," the summary continued. "She had not heard about the lynching until now."[46]

THE SWIFTEST AND MOST MILITANT STAND

Black activists recognized that lynching imagery could spur action. Yet unlike in 1918, they could do more than conjure gory scenes through prose. No outsider *saw* the corpses of the Clark brothers and the Howze sisters in 1918. In 1942, the boys' corpses, photographed by an opportunistic white tire dealer, laid bare the mob's brutality and sparked a furious reaction. Technological advances, racial politics, and world affairs mattered—the photograph, wired coast to coast, reached black and white journalists willing to print such images. After Victor Bernstein returned from his fact-finding trip to Mississippi, both *PM* and the *Pittsburgh Courier* ran the photograph alongside his report. "Ordinarily we don't print this kind of horror picture," Bernstein noted, "but this time we are trying to drive home a lesson—and we think this picture will help."[47]

The picture provoked strong emotions, and black activists hoped to put them to good use. The Mississippi lynching fueled the "Double V" rhetoric that drove the wartime civil rights campaign, but more than rhetoric was needed. In New Orleans, the NAACP branch put the boys' memory to work in a membership drive. During World War I, the New Orleans branch had set a goal of five thousand members. This time around, it aimed for ten thousand. Nationwide, an ambitious wartime drive netted nearly four hundred thousand new NAACP members—a 450 percent increase. In New Orleans, branch officers plastered the newswire photo of the boys' corpses on a recruitment leaflet. "THEY CAN NOT JOIN!" the flier announced, "BUT YOU CAN!" (fig. 4.3).[48]

The picture of lynched boys briefly focused black resentment, though the response by African Americans emphasized the broader patterns of discrimination and abuse they faced. The national outcry also revealed that, a generation removed from the Great Migration and in the midst of another wartime exodus, Mississippi-born blacks in the urban North had not forgotten their roots. The Natchez Social and Civil Club, one of dozens of similar organizations that had sprung up in Chicago to connect and support Mississippi migrants, petitioned the Justice Department to prosecute racial abuses in their native state. The club—named for the river-port town where its members grew up and where many of their relatives still lived—protested not only the "brutal lynching of two mere boys" but also school segregation, inadequate health facilities, employment discrimination in the defense industries, and the poor treatment of black soldiers on southern military bases. "We are willing that our Sons go over there and die," club members declared, "and we want Justice here." Across the nation, members of the Mississippi diaspora added their voices to the protest—a wealthy funeral director in Chicago, a War Department employee in Washington, the wife of a soldier stationed in Charleston. All invoked their Mississippi connections and demanded evidence "that democracy was meant for us also."[49]

News of the Mississippi lynching electrified Harlem, black America's political and cultural hub. While NAACP officials scrambled to mobilize their membership in support of a new antilynching bill, other groups adopted a more confrontational approach. "Two Dixie Youngsters Lynched by Crackers," announced the *People's Voice*, an upstart rival to the *Amsterdam Star-News*. Adam Clayton Powell, Jr., the paper's founder and New York's first black city councilman, was one of the

FIGURE 4.3

The New Orleans NAACP plastered the postmortem wire photograph of
Charlie Lang and Ernest Green on recruitment fliers during its wartime
drive for ten thousand members. Image of flier reproduced in Louisiana
Joint Legislative Committee, *Subversion in Racial Unrest: An Outline of
a Strategic Weapon to Destroy the Governments of Louisiana and the
United States*, part 2 (Baton Rouge, 1957), 265.

most outspoken and powerful civil rights leaders in wartime Harlem. A charismatic Baptist preacher and skillful organizer, Powell had engineered successful prewar campaigns against employment and housing discrimination in the city. After Pearl Harbor, he spurned the NAACP's strategy of litigation and lobbying and stepped up his calls for mass protest. "Maybe at some future date when the world returns to sanity we can return to educational processes, long-range planning, and the conference table," he wrote in his weekly "Soap Box" column, "but this day and hour demand direct action." Pressure through popular protest, he argued, was the only way for black people in New York and across the nation to achieve real and lasting gains.[50]

Through mass meetings, coordinating committees, and the *People's Voice*, Powell provided a gathering point for a diverse coalition of reformers, radicals, and ordinary New Yorkers. The black political establishment spurned socialists and Communists, but Powell embraced the politics of the Popular Front. This loose wartime coalition united leftists and liberals of varying stripes behind a common program of defeating fascists abroad and—like the "Double V" campaign—fighting their fellow travelers back home. For Popular Front activists like Benjamin Davis, a Georgia-born black Communist and candidate for New York's city council, lynching represented the ugliest expression of domestic fascism. "Lynchers must be ferreted out and put to death," Davis declared. "There is no difference between the crimes of a Berlin Hitler against occupied Europe and the crimes of these Mississippi Hitlers who brutally murder defenseless children." Blaming the poll tax system for perpetuating violence and discrimination, he argued that Jim Crow congressmen "should be impeached and prosecuted as enemies of the nation" and persons who defied the Fair Employment Practices Committee "should be jailed as pro-Nazi saboteurs." To drive home the link between fascists at home and abroad, Harlem Communists announced a series of street rallies whose aims were simultaneously to collect scrap "to beat the Axis" and to register protest against "the lynching of American children."[51]

Mob violence in Mississippi heightened cries for a war on race haters at home and abroad. NAACP officials, however, kept their distance from these street-protest theatrics. The organization had clashed with Communists and other leftist groups for years. In the early 1930s, the Communist-backed International Labor Defense had rushed to the aid of eight black Alabama youth sentenced to death for the alleged rape of two white women. The more cautious NAACP, initially reluctant to come to the aid of accused black rapists, attempted in vain to woo the boys' families with famed defense lawyer Clarence Darrow. Ultimately, the NAACP joined forces with the International Labor Defense and several other legal aid groups to support the Scottsboro Boys, as they came to be known, through years of appeals and suits. Nevertheless, resentment and mistrust persisted. Despite their outspoken and sincere support for black equality, NAACP leaders like Walter White and Roy Wilkins regarded their rivals on the left as a political liability. Black radicals responded by portraying the NAACP as too moderate in its push for racial change.[52]

While the International Labor Defense had fallen on hard times by 1942, its nominal leader—Congressman Vito Marcantonio—remained a formidable figure in New York City politics and a figurehead of the Popular Front. First elected to Congress as a Republican in 1934, the unapologetic leftist ran under the banner of the American Labor Party from the late 1930s onward. Marcantonio's support for minorities, labor, and the poor earned him the loyalty of his Harlem constituents even as it marginalized him in Congress. When Marcantonio threw his support behind the antilynching drive, civil rights advocates and New York politicians took notice. The day of the Shubuta lynching, Marcantonio fired off a telegram to Governor Johnson, who promptly replied that he was "opposed to mob violence as much as you are." Marcantonio then convened a meeting at Manhattan's Hotel Roosevelt to formulate "the swiftest and most militant stand against the evil of lynch law which is both a blot on our democracy and a powerful propaganda weapon for the Axis." Thirty people—clergy, labor leaders, newspapermen, and local politicians—showed up to found the National Emergency Committee to Stop Lynching. With Marcantonio at the helm, the interracial committee appointed Max Yergan of the leftist National Negro Congress and Ferdinand Smith, a Jamaican-born radical and America's highest-ranking black trade unionist, as his lieutenants.[53]

The committee organized a jam-packed rally at Harlem's Salem Methodist Episcopal Church that drew two thousand. The dais was as crowded as the pews. Nearly twenty speakers—including New York's lieutenant governor, congressmen, and members of the state assembly and city council—sat alongside trade unionists, black preachers, and civil rights militants. Several, including Davis, Yergan, and Harlem assemblyman W. T. Andrews, Jr., were southern born. Twenty-four years after his Baltimore newspaperman father had blasted Shubuta lynchers, Andrews echoed those calls for justice from a less lonely perch. Joseph Gavagan, the white New York congressman whose 1937 antilynching bill sparked a seven-week Senate filibuster, headlined the event. "Lynching," Gavagan thundered, "strikes against the divine law and against the natural law, destroying the soul of the lyncher." As ushers passed a collection plate, the secretary of the Negro Labor Victory Committee—a coalition of black trade unionists pledged to ending "jim crowism in all phases of American life"—announced that the money would be used to send delegations to the White House and the Mississippi governor's mansion. The speakers had kinder words for Governor Johnson—who had condemned the killings publicly—than for Roosevelt, who had remained mute. Speakers drew wild applause when they pledged to travel to Washington and to Mississippi to demand the prosecution of "native fascists."[54]

Not all of Harlem's top powerbrokers attended the meeting and rally. Noticeably absent were Brotherhood of Sleeping Car Porters president A. Philip Randolph, as well as NAACP executives White and Wilkins. Randolph, whose March on Washington Movement had helped force unprecedented, if limited, concessions from the federal government, had a long-standing ideological beef with the Communists. Rather than join hands with the radical National Negro Congress—an organization he had once headed—and the Communist Party, Randolph called on New York clergy to rally at City Hall. A few hundred showed up, men with black crepe armbands and women in funeral garb. No doubt some clergy and churchgoers attended both the Emergency Committee's mass meeting and the city hall prayer protest, but the lines separating leading black activists remained intact.[55]

As for the NAACP, no one could question the organization's anti-lynching credentials. "We protest this lynching, as we have protested all those that have gone before," Wilkins wired the White House, "but we are more shocked and outraged, as we are sure every decent American must be, at the thought that anywhere in our land in 1942 could be found a mob which would hang two boys barely in their teens." Wilkins, like White before him, implored the White House to publicly condemn the killings. Having handed off that task to Justice Department officials, Roosevelt remained silent. That exchange—or lack of one—underscored both the NAACP's stature and the limitations of its political strategy. Few black activists, and no other black organization, enjoyed the access to the White House and to Capitol Hill that the NAACP had fought so hard to gain. Yet that clout did not translate to legislative action or a successful federal prosecution, just as emergency committees and mass meetings a thousand miles from Mississippi would not bring lynchers to justice.[56]

Adam Clayton Powell proposed a more radical solution. Under a cartoon depicting Lady Liberty holding out Ernest Green, Charlie Lang, and Howard Wash, dangling from her clinched fist like the day's catch, Powell announced, "The hour has arrived for Mississippi to secede from the Union." Since the state had "given justice the double-cross, knifed liberty in the back and thumbed her nose at Christianity," Powell declared, "Mississippi from now on must be listed with the Axis Powers." He called on the federal government to declare war on the state and dispatch federal troops. Like southern white supremacists, Powell predicted a "race war" and warned that black Mississippians could only bear so much abuse. "If the Negro people of Mississippi resist this with force," Powell warned, "there can be no one to blame but the half-wit crackers themselves."[57]

AN UNFAMILIAR RACIAL JUNGLE

Lost in much of the uproar over the Shubuta lynchings were the voices of local black people. In 1918, Walter White infiltrated the town and slipped away having at least glimpsed grassroots resistance. Twenty-four years later, black courage again proved crucial to getting the truth out. If anything, a trip to Shubuta in 1942 proved more formidable a challenge than it had a generation before. The NAACP had dispatched a black female staffer to the scene, in tandem with Sara Craigen Kennedy, but Odette Harper encountered shuttered windows and cold stares when she ventured into Shubuta's bottoms. Shaken by the terror she encountered, Harper locked herself in the Quitman bus station's filthy "colored" restroom. Squatting on her suitcase—the toilet had no seat—and leaning her head against the sink, she waited for the first morning bus out of town.[58]

Several months later, as hopes of federal prosecution faded, a black man in a tattered suit and dirty shoes rolled into Shubuta. Enoc Waters still wanted the story. A reporter for the *Chicago Defender,* a self-proclaimed "militant" black paper that had enjoyed widespread circulation in the Deep South since the World War I era, Waters swung through Mississippi in the midst of a thirty-eight-state tour "to assess the state of the nation so far as Negroes were concerned." In his first dispatch from the Magnolia State, Waters announced, "The war is expected to have a greater effect upon the Negro in Mississippi than in any other state." Confident that wartime gains would benefit African Americans across the country, Waters predicted that these victories would mean even more in Mississippi. His rationale was simple: "His condition cannot be made worse."[59]

By his own admission, Waters was ill prepared for his venture into Mississippi. The son of Maryland migrants, the Philadelphia native had attended Virginia's Hampton University and started his career at the Norfolk *Journal and Guide.* Farther south—in what he deemed "the most vicious part"—Waters discovered a world quite different from his college days. "My awareness of law-enforced segregation was academic," he recalled, "and didn't prepare me for the gradual realization that it would inhibit my ability to perform my job." While critics blasted the black press for sensationalism, shoddy reporting, and a lack of patriotism, they overlooked the obstacles to Jim Crow journalism. Waters quickly discovered that he lacked access to the basic amenities—from hotels and restaurants to pay phones and public libraries—that he had come to expect in his years as a globetrotting reporter. If he refused the daily indignities of Jim Crow, like using the rear door and freight elevator of an office building to make an interview, his stories suffered. He envied Walter White, with whom he occasionally crossed paths on his travels, "because there were times when passing for white would have been very advantageous."[60]

Waters, like other black travelers, learned to rely on guest houses and college campuses for meals, lodging, and research. He carried a roll of toilet paper and a sandwich in his briefcase. And above all, he learned not to count on whites for anything. In four months spent below the Mason-Dixon Line, Waters noted, he "met only one or two southern white men who favor and are willing to work for full racial democracy for the Negro." The *Defender* still enjoyed wide readership and respect among black southerners—especially in Mississippi—but whites remained wary. Back in Chicago, the *Defender* often swapped files, photographs, and leads with white journalists. Down South, Waters discovered, white newspapers not only refused to help him but frequently tipped off police and city officials that he was in town. Despite these obstacles, Waters's dispatches—nearly two hundred stories in all—appeared in seventy-two straight weekly editions.[61]

Mississippi proved the toughest and most revealing leg of the tour. Waters started in Jackson, an oasis compared to the "little backwater town of Shubuta" that he hoped to infiltrate. On the campus of Tougaloo College, a black school founded by northern missionaries, he encountered his first Clarke County native. Eighty-two-year-old George Donald, born a slave, lived through Emancipation and Reconstruction before enrolling in Tougaloo College in 1884. "I used to vote," he told Waters. "I knew the time when almost every Negro in the South voted…and things were much better then, all around." Too many of Mississippi's black leaders, "tools of the white man" by Donald's estimation, had made peace with disenfranchisement and discrimination. "The most important thing for the Negro to fight for is the right to vote," he asserted, "and I don't think we can depend too much upon our old leaders to reach that goal."[62]

Percy Green, the outspoken black editor of the *Jackson Advocate*, understood as well as anyone the fine line that those leaders walked. The stocky, cautious newspaperman, who had conferenced with Governor Johnson and black leaders in the wake of the lynchings, believed the war crisis offered a glimmer of hope. His own self-assertion was as good a gauge as any to the small but significant opportunities presented by the war effort. Mississippi blacks, he informed Waters, were "much more militant" than in the past. Green printed wartime stories and editorials, Waters noted, "that Negroes have been chased out of town for writing in the past." The editor had blasted Mississippi's "reign of terror" and warned that Mississippi was lynching its way toward "a complete breakdown of Negro spirit and morale." Green also believed, as he informed Waters, that wartime turmoil and labor woes would force white Mississippians to yield to some black demands. Invoking the same rationale that had raised black hopes during World War I, Green believed that white elites realized that "unless the Negro has greater opportunities here he will continue to leave." As long as black Mississippians conceded to the "separation of the races in all things social," Green predicted that conditions would continue to improve.[63]

As Waters ventured east from Jackson, Greene's optimistic forecast quickly dimmed. The Chicago reporter, who followed his domestic tour with a stint in the South Pacific, later remarked that "an out-of-town black man trying to cover a lynching in Mississippi was like an American war correspondent trying to operate in Japan." Despite the risk, Waters wanted to get African Americans' take on an atrocity he considered unrivaled in its "cold, calculated barbarity." To get from Jackson to Shubuta, Waters relied on an "underground network" of black Mississippians who not only provided room and board to traveling reporters, but also quietly supported and protected their efforts to expose racial injustice. In some instances, these same contacts had helped to head off additional atrocities. For every lynch victim, Waters discovered, there were dozens of refugees who had been spirited away by this "Underground Railroad," and others like him who relied on that local network to navigate "through an unfamiliar racial jungle."[64]

Dr. Frank Zuber, Waters's contact in east Mississippi, typified the members of this underground network. A physician in the town of West Point, Zuber enjoyed relative economic independence and security.

He relied on other blacks, not whites, for his income, and his work put him in contact with dozens of colleagues across the state. His wife, employed by the Negro Rural School Fund to train black teachers, knew the state like the back of her hand. The doctor, a veteran of World War I and an NAACP member, embodied the spirit of resistance that decades of terror had failed to stamp out. Waters simultaneously admired and pitied his host, whose careful, well-schooled defiance of Jim Crow seemed decidedly less than militant. Still, Waters listened, and he complied.[65]

"Any little town that would lynch two 14 year old boys wouldn't hesitate to kill a newspaperman," Zuber cautioned, "especially a black one from Chicago." The doctor suggested hiring a car and driver, so that Waters would not be spotted lugging his portable typewriter through the bus station. "The crackers here have an alert system that operates with deadly—and I do mean deadly—efficiency," the doctor added. When Waters replied that no one had seemed to notice his presence, Zuber's shook his head. "You haven't been bothered because there has been no reason to interfere with you. But just because nothing has happened don't assume that your presence is not known."[66]

Zuber phoned ahead to Meridian. E. F. Young, Jr., his contact there, offered Waters the relative luxury and security of his small and tidy hotel. One of the wealthiest black men in the South, the farmer's son and former barber had started a thriving cosmetics business and bought up a sizable chunk of Meridian's bustling black business district. Like Zuber, Young had been an NAACP member for years, and along with a handful of fellow black professionals in the city, had been an active Black-and-Tan Republican. The vice president of Meridian's branch—his father was the president and his brother Roy the secretary—Young helped to enlist nearly one hundred dues-paying members by 1942. NAACP branch director William Pickens deemed Roy Young, who also edited a weekly newspaper, "our best leader in the savage state of Mississippi." However, that repressive atmosphere circumscribed the Young family's activism. Roy trod carefully in the wake of the Shubuta lynchings—he lamented the "disgraceful crime" in his *Weekly Echo* as a rebuke to "the great work that the Southern white christian women had done in curbing lynching." In an equally cautious follow-up editorial, Young used the word *children* nine times. "I wonder," he concluded, "if they called for mother?"[67]

A pair of editorials marked the zenith of public protest in Meridian, but the Youngs provided clandestine support for Waters's investigation. Their discretion represented more than mere self-preservation, as their guest faced greater danger than they did. "Any member of our group from the north or east or any section where colored people's privileges are greater than the privileges granted us in the south must be dealt with carefully, for their own protection more so than ours," Roy Young warned. "The white southerner readily looks upon new-comers with a critical eye." Nevertheless, Waters's hosts took him to see Thomas J. Harris, principal of Meridian's black high school, named after him, who in turn introduced the reporter to two students from Shubuta. Since Clarke County had, as noted, no high schools for blacks, a handful of families sent their children to Meridian to continue their studies. The teenagers, who had earlier funneled lynching details to the NAACP's Madison Jones, agreed to "adopt" Waters as a cousin and accompany him to Shubuta. The reporter's Meridian handlers found an "inconspic-uous" taxi—"a well-used Dodge in need of body work"—and driver to ferry the trio down to Shubuta and back for fifty cents a mile. Before leaving, the dapper Waters shed his fedora and tie, crumpled his re-cently pressed suit, and scuffed his shiny wingtips with a muddy rag. "As a final act of disguise," Waters recalled, he ripped all the labels from the lining of his suit jacket.[68]

On the ride down to Shubuta, the boys briefed Waters on their hometown—he had his story outlined by the time he stepped out of the car. As they passed through the tiny downtown, Waters glimpsed black children "playing happily about—in some cases with white chil-dren." Aside from its "impressive lynch record," he noted, nothing dis-tinguished Shubuta from dozens of sleepy southern towns that he had passed through on his tour. The chauffer drove his passengers straight to the home of a local pastor who also served as an agent of the local burial association. Once Waters entered the house, he did not leave. The pastor and the "cousins" brought the witnesses to him. Since people dropped by the house frequently to seek pastoral counsel or pay their association dues, no one noticed the quiet stream of visitors who came and went that day. Waters met the boys' relatives, neighbors, and others with stories to tell. All the while, the chauffer stood by for a quick getaway.[69]

Waters insisted he was "no detective," and he certainly had no aspirations of reopening the Feds' dead-end lynching investigation. He wanted to find out—and wanted his readers to understand—the "forces at work in the community" that led to the double lynching. From his conversations with local blacks—none of whom he named in his stories—Waters concluded that "ignorance and war hysteria" killed the boys. "Charles Lang and Ernest Green were lynched," he wrote, "not for what they had done, but rather as a warning to other Negroes that the whites are still in control of this town." Waters sketched a narrative of the killings that filled in the yawning gaps left by white reporters, federal agents, and defensive locals. More important, he gave voice to the town's black residents, and even a taste of divine justice.[70]

"A curious story of retribution," the *Defender* reported, "which transcended 'Southern justice' and the inability of the Department of Justice to obtain convictions in any lynching case in the South, has leaked out." According to Waters's local informants, Shubuta's deputy sheriff had died—strapped to his bed—just a few weeks after the lynchings. In his delirium, Ed McLendon screamed the boys' names and "breathlessly blabbered out a confession…naming many names." Accounts of the deathbed scene varied. Some said that McLendon saw visions of Charlie and Ernest, and that he yelled for someone to "get them off of me!" Others claimed that he clutched his own throat and gasped, "Take that rope away!" The town's white doctor and McLendon's black nurse, Waters added, "were pledged to secrecy." Nevertheless, the details of the deathbed confession slipped out of town in a battered sedan, tucked away in Waters's rumpled suit jacket. In "writhing agony," a Mississippi lyncher had finally confessed. "And so," the *Defender* concluded, "a law higher" had defied the southern custom of "'unable to recognize the guilty parties.'"[71]

The Slow but Rising New Spirit

Symbolic justice mattered. So too did signs that rural black southerners were ready to fight back. On the last count, black elites and activists seemed divided in the wake of the lynchings. Several decades later, in his memoirs, Waters expressed admiration for the black Mississippians who quietly resisted abuse and discrimination. "At the time," he wrote, "no Negro could be taken at face value. Often the stereotypical Southern darkey, smiling, respectful, and unlearned was a dedicated and active foe of white dominance." Over the course of his southern travels, Waters relied on hundreds who risked lives and livelihoods to help him get the story. Yet while Waters venerated these "unsung heroes of a necessarily secret operation" in later years, his on-the-ground assessment proved much grimmer.[72]

With a critical attitude that somewhat belied his own experiences there, Waters lamented that Shubuta's "Negro community has no cohesiveness" and that no effort had been made to "harness indignation." The churches were "one-day" institutions, and the schools were ill-equipped to serve as gathering places. Waters blasted "Negro Turncoats," like the black maid who witnessed the deputy sheriff's deathbed confession. Black locals had "information which would bring the boys' killers to justice" but chose to remain silent—except, of course, to serve as Waters's informants. "For even Shubuta," he reported, "has that despicable type of Negro willing to make any sacrifice of other Negroes to win the doubtful favor of whites." In later years, Waters attributed such behavior to "fear and despair born of unrelieved intimidation." In the moment, in the midst of a wartime campaign for equality, Waters saw little reason to think that rural blacks would rally to the cause. In southern cities like Mobile and Little Rock, Waters had documented protests against police brutality and discrimination. In Shubuta, he lamented, "not one Negro uttered a word of protest."[73]

While southern roots and common dreams connected northern activists with rural folk in the Deep South, their reactions to wartime atrocities revealed a gulf between them. "Waters Finds Rural Areas Lag behind Cities in Race Militancy," the *Chicago Defender* announced as Waters wrapped up his southern tour. The protest activity he witnessed in southern cities convinced the reporter that urban dwellers "tend to act concertedly on matters, whereas their brothers in Shubuta, Sikeston, and other rural communities are individualists." While "the rural Negro must not be forgotten," Waters concluded, southern cities provided the only base for any future mass movement.[74]

Despite such pessimism about rural protest, some African Americans read into the Shubuta stories signs of resistance that Waters failed to appreciate. Citing "reliable" reports—most likely the NAACP dispatch from Meridian—a few lynching accounts claimed the boys had been castrated and tortured. While the newswire photograph provided no conclusive proof, some interpreted sadistic acts as signs that the boys had fought back. In a story reprinted in a handful of black newspapers, a columnist cited reports that one of the boys had sustained a bullet wound in his back. When the boy "steadfastly refused to help in his own death" by jumping from the bridge, the report claimed, the lynchers shot him. Faced with certain death, the journalist concluded, "the helpless child displayed the slow but rising new spirit that is gripping the Mississippi Negro."[75]

If this seemed grasping at straws, other stories of individual and collective resistance appeared in black coverage of the lynchings. As in 1918, outside observers noted the relatives' refusal to claim the victims' bodies. While the boys' parents cited fear and poverty as their reasons for failing to claim the bodies, those observers cheered this "defiant refusal" as a protest against "Hitlerian savagery." The editor of the *Houston Informer* praised a black employee of Patton's Undertaking Establishment who reportedly vowed to "quit or die" before he would retrieve the bodies from the bridge. "Assuming an 'it was your dirty work, now remove it' attitude," the newspaperman announced, Shubuta's "mill workers, soil tillers, and railroad employees mustered up courage…and vehemently declined permission to bury the boys in a colored cemetery." Such stories had enormous symbolic significance for outsiders looking for signs that rural black southerners were ready to fight back. "They're learning to be proud," claimed the *Chicago Defender*. "They refused to bury their dead."[76]

Symbolic acts—real, exaggerated, or imagined—held immense power. So did the symbolism of the bridge itself. "A monument to 'Judge Lynch,'" as one black journalist branded the "rickety old span'" in 1942, stood for all that the wartime civil rights campaign sought to destroy. Few captured the mood of despair and defiance that the bridge evoked as effectively as the poet Langston Hughes. And few wartime events captured the poet's hopes and apprehensions as dramatically as the lynching of two black children in Mississippi. Protest verse was old hat to Hughes, the Harlem Renaissance pioneer who had drifted from radical politics in his younger days toward a more measured stance. Yet as the unofficial poet laureate of the wartime civil rights campaign, Hughes challenged Jim Crow and championed racial democracy in writings that resonated across the black political spectrum. From the NAACP to the more radical National Negro Congress, black activists embraced and applauded the poet's two-pronged attack on Fascism and Jim Crow. Hughes, who had included an antisegregation statement in his Selective Service questionnaire, was anticipating a hearing before a Manhattan draft board when the Mississippi lynchings hit the headlines. In addition, the poet had recently accepted an invitation to write a weekly column for the *Chicago Defender*. Through poetry and prose, Hughes encapsulated the "Double V" campaign in personal and profound ways. "You tell me that hitler / Is a mighty bad man," Hughes wrote. "I guess he took lessons / From the Ku Klux Klan."[77]

In the same late October issue that announced the third Mississippi lynching in a week, the Baltimore *Afro-American* published "Jim Crow's Last Stand," the title poem of Hughes's coming collection of wartime protest verse. "Pearl Harbor put Jim Crow on the run," Hughes warned, "That Crow can't fight for democracy / And be the same old Crow he used to be." Invoking the antifascist lingo of the Harlem Left, he rhymed: "If you want to get old Hitler's goat / Abolish poll tax so folks can vote!" And like civil rights advocates of various stripes, Hughes argued that millions of nonwhite Allies demanded racial justice:

"India and China and Harlem, too / Have made up their minds Jim Crow is through."[78]

Reeling from the Mississippi lynchings, Hughes maintained his position that racial violence portended a crisis both domestic and diplomatic. "Two 14-year-old boys are lynched at Shubuta Bridge," Hughes warned in his new *Defender* column, "and Harlem shudders—also Chungking." But the boys' death—and the bridge's meaning—struck a deeper chord with Hughes. In "The Bitter River," a poem he dedicated to the memory of Ernest Green and Charlie Lang, Hughes evoked the muddy Chickasawhay flowing below the bridge. The murky water, "tasting of blood and clay," reflected no stars—only the "bars" from the bridge's long shadow. Behind those bars, Hughes saw the Scottsboro boys, union organizers, "the voteless share-cropper," and a "soldier thrown from a Jim Crow bus." The bars evoked imagery culled not only from wartime headlines but from generations of racial abuse. Hughes, like Wilkins and Waters the grandson of slaves, saw in the shadowy bars "my grandfather's back with its ladder of scars."[79]

The lynchings tapped into a deep well. In the short term, the killings seemed to do little else. Like the reflections in "The Bitter River," the bridge and its victims provided a symbolic rallying cry for those anticipating an imminent revolution. Yet the case—and the sundry causes linked to it—stalled as another wartime round of white backlash and race riots swept the country. In Washington, southern Democrats derailed Vito Marcantonio's appointment to the House Judiciary Committee, which reviewed anti-poll-tax and antilynching bills, on the grounds that he would "sabotage the white people of the South." With "Poll Taxers Riding High in Congress," as the *Defender* gloomily announced, civil rights legislation stalled. In Mobile, where Enoc Waters predicted that hard-fought gains by black activists would lead the way for rural folks in Clarke County, white shipyard workers rioted in 1943 after their company promoted twelve black men to welding jobs. Turmoil in Detroit and dozens of other cities proved more deadly. And white Mississippians, anticipating the return of black veterans no longer content with second-class citizenship, mobilized a campaign of harassment and violence against prospective black voters that sent Theodore Bilbo back to Washington in 1946.[80]

As civil rights controversies mounted, the violence continued. Just as he had invoked egalitarian war rhetoric a decade earlier, Hughes linked postwar racial reform to the Cold War struggle for hearts and minds. "If the long-time lynch customs of the South are not un-American," Hughes declared, "I don't know what is." Yet white supremacists also exploited the rivalry with the Soviet Union, just as they had flipped the "Double V" rhetoric of wartime civil rights activists on its head. Hitching their political fortunes to the postwar anti-Communist crusade, segregationists attacked their most outspoken critics as sympathizers and subversives. An outspoken leftist in his younger days, Langston Hughes appeared before a congressional committee to answer for his political past. Dozens of black activists and artists endured these inquisitions— many convened by the same poll-tax politicians they had fought during World War II. "It would seem to me sort of nice," Hughes declared, "if the white politicians in Washington would now repay those distinguished colored Americans who have sworn and double-sworn their allegiance to American ideals, by investigating JUST A FEW of the white folks who hang 14 year old boys to bridges and throw them in rivers." Mississippi senator James Eastland, who brought his Internal Security Subcommittee hearings to New Orleans in 1954, showed more interest in grilling racial liberals than racial terrorists. "It ought to be even easier to catch lynchers than Communists," Hughes responded, "especially in Mississippi."[81]

Lynching may have gone "underground"—with vigilantes abducting and murdering under cover of night—but they relied more than ever on community complicity and political cover. When Mississippi vigilantes murdered another fourteen-year-old boy in 1955, two hundred miles from Shubuta in Tallahatchie County, Roy Wilkins and Langston Hughes turned again to the bridge over the Chickasawhay. Wilkins's family history had taught him how far the lynch rope could reach. Two months into his lengthy tenure at the helm of the NAACP—antilynching stalwart Walter White had died two months before white Mississippians abducted and murdered Emmett Till—Wilkins declared that Mississippi would continue "to maintain white supremacy by murdering children" (fig. 4.4). Like Wilkins, Langston Hughes reminded America that the Chicago teen was not the first child victim—and likely would not be the last. "Charlie Lang and Ernest Green were young Negro boys like Emmett Till, too," Hughes wrote. "Their adolescent bodies were hanged from the Shubuta bridge."[82]

FIGURE 4.4

With the 1955 lynching of Emmett Till—a black youth the same age as Ernest Green and Charlie Lang—Mississippi maintained its reputation as the nation's lynching capital and a symbol of violent white supremacy. In this photograph, NAACP executive secretary Roy Wilkins (second from left) holds a new recruitment poster with director of public relations Henry Lee Moon, labor director Herbert Hill, and special counsel Thurgood Marshall. Photograph by Al Ravenna, 1956, New York World-Telegram and the Sun Newspaper Photograph Collection. LC-USZ62-122432. Courtesy of the Library of Congress Prints and Photographs Division.

In Clarke County, the future of the freedom struggle fell to those raised on stories of lynched children. The cornerstones of that campaign—protection from violence, voting rights, desegregation, and economic opportunity—had been laid through Jim Crow decades when rural Mississippi seemed all but impermeable to racial change. Through those years, in the face of exploitation and abuse, local people and some of the most influential civil rights figures in modern America crossed paths. Violence had brought them together, and the violence had not yet come to an end.

PART III

1966

CHAPTER FIVE

THE FORMATION OF AN UGLY WHITE CROWD

NIGGER'S BEWARE!
All niggers will be shot and killed if any demonstrations
accure in Mississippi, All kinky headed darkies better stay on
your guard, and kut out all this smart allic demonstration.
You have got the civil law passed, what more do you want?
If you think that we'll lick your but, you got another thing
coming. If you think we'll take all this foolishness your crazy.
If you find your car windows dash in and it burn up, or your
wife hanging on a light pole, or kids strung up in the outdoor
toilet, it will be alright.
    —Mimeographed flier, Clarke County, summer 1966

Eula Mae McCarty Buxton was a small child when a Shubuta mob first lynched at the bridge in 1918. Twenty-four years later, Buxton was working as a schoolteacher. She taught at Liberty Hill, a country church just north of Shubuta that doubled as a one-room schoolhouse. Every day, she crossed over the Chickasawhay on her four-mile trek to work. On a Monday morning in October, she spotted a crowd as she neared the bridge. The bodies of Ernest Green and Charlie Lang had just been hauled up and tossed in the truck bed.[1]

In January 1966, Buxton awoke to flaming crosses on her front lawn. Her twenty-two-year-old son Warner had recently become the first full-time civil rights worker in Clarke County. A year before, from a small office in Quitman, Warner Buxton and other local youth had worked with a handful of northern volunteers to organize a voter-registration drive and a few small demonstrations. Late in 1965, Buxton composed a "Call to Action" in the local movement newsletter. "It is time that we arose to action and stood up for our rights," it announced. "I am sure that you do not want your children to grow up in the same fear that you and I grew up in," Buxton continued, "ready to tremble [every] time you hear the word 'Whiteman.'" In retaliation, nightriders burned crosses in front of the Buxtons' Shubuta home.[2]

At the height of the civil rights movement in Mississippi, the home of the bridge over the Chickasawhay remained a foreboding and seemingly impenetrable place. When a few civil rights organizers ventured into Clarke County in the mid-1960s, they invariably encountered stories of past killings. Asked to explain their neighbors' fear of registering to vote or joining up with anything smacking of civil rights, local African Americans returned again and again to the county's violent history. "I asked the group what people were afraid of," recalled a white antipoverty organizer who first visited the county in 1965. "Oh, you know how they is," a black woman explained. "They remembers things." Other women chimed in with stories of the 1918 and 1942 lynchings. "They still call that place in Shubuta the hanging bridge."[3]

Even those too young to remember the lynchings understood their lingering power. White supremacists killed "to keep the black community in line," recalled John Otis Sumrall, a local civil rights worker. "When black folks would talk about these things, they would speak about them with a trembling voice." For young men like Buxton and Sumrall, who grew up hearing stories of local lynchings and who counted among their earliest civil rights memories the magazine images of Emmett Till's battered corpse, racial violence shaped their understanding of freedom and equality. The killing did not stop with Till—a spate of assassinations and lynchings in the months following the teen's death prompted the NAACP to publish a pamphlet entitled *M Is for Mississippi and Murder*. While several of the attacks focused on black activists, the 1959 abduction and lynching of Mack Charles Parker—a young black man accused of raping a white woman—reminded black Mississippians that racial terrorism remained volatile, unpredictable, and sexually charged on the eve of a civil rights revolution. Yet even from the far side of a half decade of iconic campaigns and legislative victories, the memory of the Hanging Bridge loomed over racial politics in Clarke County. Perhaps this is why Sumrall and other locals drove white summer volunteers out to the spot, a foreboding initiation to the county's bloody but unfinished freedom struggle.[4]

Stories and images could only keep the local movement at bay for so long, but few African Americans in Clarke County considered the Hanging Bridge off-limits in the 1960s. The crude flier that arrived at the county's civil rights office in the summer of 1966 confirmed that whites would likely launch another round of violence to maintain the status quo. Just two summers before, county officials had boasted that they had the "racial situation" under control. Indeed, Clarke County seemed a remarkably quiet corner of a state in the midst of a revolution. White officials took pride in their ability to tamp down discontent and disorder. Even as Supreme Court decisions, civil rights bills, and grass-roots protest campaigns chipped away at Jim Crow in the late 1950s and early 1960s, local authorities reported no civil rights activity, no civil-rights-related arrests, and—as of 1960—not a single black registered voter. While the threat of violence remained, whites continued to rely on other tactics to maintain control. Of course, they always had. As local African Americans—young and old, men and women, the privileged and the poor—challenged the status quo, they forced whites to concede that the old order was under attack. The only question was how they would respond.

No Apparent Unrest among the Negroes

In 1958, Sylvester McRee and Samuel Owens strode into the registrar's office at the Clarke County Courthouse. McRee, the Quitman plumber who had attempted to charter a local NAACP branch in the 1930s, had tried to register to vote each time a new registrar came into office. Owens, a veteran school principal well into his seventies, had been one of the last black men to cast a ballot in Clarke County. Sometime around World War I, he recalled, the registrar had informed him that Mississippi's primary election "was for white Democrats only." Soon after, local officials scratched his name from the rolls. Four decades later, McRee, Owens, and a few allies went to see "Judge" A. L. Ramsey.[5]

Clarke County's elderly registrar, a retired electrician and former justice of the peace, hardly cut an imposing figure, but he guarded the voter rolls fiercely. When Owens, McRee, and three companions entered his office in 1958, the "Judge" calmly turned them away. "Everything was peaceful," Ramsey recalled, "but it looked like someone was trying to start trouble." The registrar asked the men to go home, "think it over," and come back some other time. "That was when we were having a lot of trouble over the country, especially in Little Rock," Ramsey later testified in federal court. So he told the men "that we folks here in Mississippi, white and colored, were getting along together and…we weren't going to have any trouble either way, and then I just suggested to them that they go back home and consider this matter." When the men returned, he noted, "I would still have a little talk with them about it, and ask them to still consider."[6]

For his visits, each no more successful than the previous, "Vester" McRee received death threats and an occasional brick through his living room window. He took to sitting up nights, a shotgun in his lap, lest the next missile be more deadly. Yet the white man who showed up at his door in early 1961 was not a vigilante but a lawyer from the Justice Department's Civil Rights Division. McRee, the de facto "president" of the county's small circle of dues-paying NAACP members, figured it was about time. "I'd been reading the '57 and '60 Civil Rights Bills," McRee told him matter-of-factly, "and I thought you'd soon be coming to find out about us."[7]

The registration attempts had yet to pay off locally, but Clarke County's lily-white voter rolls had attracted the outside attention that state officials had worked hard to avoid. The 1960 Civil Rights Act of 1960, a follow-up to a 1957 bill that had been stripped of its strongest provisions by segregationist southern senators, expanded the ability of the Civil Rights Division to investigate and prosecute voter discrimination. While the outgoing Eisenhower administration had soft-pedaled civil rights after the 1957 desegregation standoff in Little Rock, President John F. Kennedy's new appointees dispatched FBI agents and division attorneys into a handful of southern counties to investigate complaints. Hoping to crack Mississippi, the division sent Gerald Stern, a Memphis native and recent Harvard Law graduate, to Clarke County.[8]

An investigator from the Mississippi State Sovereignty Commission arrived fast on Stern's heels. The commission, established in 1956 by act of the legislature and funded with state tax dollars, monitored civil rights activity and suppressed news of racial incidents that would lead to negative publicity and federal intervention. By 1960, the commission used most of its quarter-million-dollar annual budget to spy on civil rights advocates and sabotage any racially progressive activity in the state. Before Stern's visit, an investigator rolled through Clarke County once or twice a year to check for "subversive" activity. Despite a few black voter registration attempts in the late 1950s, an agent reported "no apparent unrest among the negroes." After speaking with a white county official, the investigator concluded that "some fine new negro schools, which appeared to be very much appreciated...undoubtedly served to keep the negroes from becoming too antagonistic and restless."[9]

Across Mississippi, black school improvements became a key tactic in the fight to avoid integration. Since the early 1950s, as desegregation lawsuits made their way through the courts, Mississippi lawmakers argued that throwing more money at black education would convince federal judges that separate could finally be equal. From the outset, "equalization" was more political theater than public policy. In a state where local districts had traditionally spent ten dollars or more on white schools for every dollar spent on black schools, the costs of making up for decades of neglect proved more than Mississippi could pay. School surveyors estimated that it would take $144 million in school construction alone—and millions more in increased teacher salaries and operating costs—to bring black schools up to par with white schools. That was more than twice Mississippi's entire annual budget and five times what it spent per year on black and white schools combined.[10]

The state's small but growing NAACP rejected the equalization scheme and called instead for an end to Mississippi's "vicious system of segregation." Yet even in the wake of the Supreme Court's 1954 decision in *Brown v. Board of Education*, Mississippi segregationists clung to the belief that they could placate federal authorities and African Americans alike. A statewide school survey, completed just eighteen months after the Supreme Court decision, revealed both the desperation and delusion behind the equalization effort. In Clarke County, officials had shut down 75 percent of the county's black schools—many of them crumbling one-room cabins and country churches—and reassigned pupils to "attendance centers." With state funds, the county built its first two black high schools. Yet those campuses still lagged behind white schools in classroom space, equipment, and transportation. A year after *Brown*, the county spent $168 per white pupil but $91 per black pupil. After noting the discrepancies, and requesting another $600,000 for repairs and renovations to black schools, the surveyors maintained that "a continuation of segregation is not only possible but necessary for the best development of each group."[11]

State and county officials joined in the collective act of denial. With black high schools "newer and nicer than white school buildings," a Sovereignty Commission investigator argued after a visit to Clarke County, local authorities "anticipated no trouble in the near future." Whites believed they had bought the allegiance of black educators, whom they recruited as informants and spokesmen. They praised Shubuta's C. W. Falconer, a retired black educator who defended segregation as a divinely ordained plan "to maintain peace and order between the races." Falconer spent the better part of the 1950s fighting integration. In an introduction to one of Falconer's segregationist editorials, an East Mississippi newspaperman argued that "his wise viewpoint represents the thinking of the majority of Negro citizens in Mississippi." By the end of the decade, a penniless and ailing Falconer begged the governor and the Sovereignty Commission for help with his medical expenses. "I shall always fight the forcing of integration," he pledged.[12]

White officials considered Falconer the quintessential "good negro," but not all of Clarke County's black educators played the part. Samuel Owens's determination to register to vote certainly irked local officials, who had named the county's first black high school after him. After the

Sovereignty Commission informed county officials that federal "Civil Rights Investigators" might initiate legal action, Judge Ramsey finally handed over a registration form to Owens—on his seventh visit to the registrar's office in four years. To satisfy what was known as the "understanding clause"—an intentionally vague disenfranchisement tactic created to disqualify black registrants—Ramsey picked a particularly lengthy and complicated section of the Mississippi constitution for Owens to interpret. To satisfy the "literacy test"—another roadblock aimed at black applicants—Ramsey required Owens to write down his answer, which Owens did. Ramsey glanced it over, admitted it looked "OK," and asked Owens to come back in two weeks. When he returned, Owens became the first black man to register to vote in Clarke County in at least two generations. Days later, the Justice Department sued A. L. Ramsey and Theron C. Lynd, the registrar in nearby Forrest County, for "a clear-cut pattern of discrimination"—the federal government's first such action against voter suppression in Mississippi. The same week, Martin Luther King, Jr. made a rare public visit to the state. "In our quest for full citizenship rights," King told a Jackson crowd, "we must be willing fill the jails, or even die, if necessary."[13]

Back in Clarke County, the government's witnesses simply hoped to make it to their court date. Gerald Stern had recruited six black men in Clarke County, each of whom had attempted to register during Ramsey's term in office, to testify in federal district court. Judge Harold Cox, the most unabashedly racist judge on the federal bench and a law school roommate of Mississippi senator and Senate Judiciary chairman James Eastland, delayed the trial for sixteen months. Cox denied that the imbalance in registration in Clarke County and across the state had anything to do with discrimination. "Negroes have not been interested in registering to vote," Cox argued, "and very few have bothered to apply."[14]

The Justice Department's investigation revealed the obstacles that black registrants faced. Ramsey had refused to accept a single black applicant before federal agents showed up in 1961. He also claimed to have personally registered nearly 80 percent of the county's voting-age whites during eight years in office. In one case, he drove up to

Stonewall and set up a card table outside the denim plant so that mill workers could register during shift changes. Ramsey subjected black applicants to a barrage of tests and delays, but he did not even require whites to show up at his office. An FBI handwriting expert testified in federal court that Ramsey allowed whites to register spouses, relatives, and even employees by proxy. After examining the voter rolls, the agent discovered that fifteen hundred whites had signed up at least one other person during a trip to the registrar's office. One man signed up fourteen others at once. While Ramsey had started to administer literacy tests to white applicants after he learned of the pending federal investigation, two white witnesses admitted that the registrar had allowed them to copy Samuel Owens's written response to satisfy the requirement.[15]

The irony of two semiliterate white men copying a black man's literacy test response to register to vote proved too much even for Judge Cox. Forced to concede that Ramsey had "deliberately and improperly" denied blacks access to the ballot, Cox nonetheless maintained that the prosecution had failed to demonstrate a "pattern or practice" of discrimination. He ordered Ramsey to administer the literacy tests to each new applicant, which addressed neither the problem of improperly registered whites nor the discriminatory nature of literacy tests. Having preserved a key obstacle to black voter registration, Cox turned the tables on two of the black witnesses with a perjury charge. Pouncing on an immaterial error in their testimony, Cox declared Andrew Kendrick and W. C. Goff "fit subjects for the penitentiary" and placed them under $3,000 bond. When the district attorney refused to prosecute the men, Cox ordered him thrown in jail as well. An intervention by Attorney General Robert F. Kennedy forced the judge to back down, but Cox succeeded in miring Mississippi's first federal voting rights suit in more delays and litigation. He exposed black witnesses to local harassment, preserved the state's disenfranchisement tactics, and threatened future black registrants with legal retaliation. By 1964, African Americans in Clarke County remained wary of the registrar's office, and white authorities seemed no less confident than they had three years before.[16]

While the county's vanguard voting suit did not open the flood-gates to black voter registration, the campaign drew a handful of local people into the orbit of civil rights activity in Meridian. In January 1964, the Congress of Racial Equality (CORE) set up shop in east Mississippi's largest town. Formed in Chicago during World War II, CORE first cracked Mississippi in 1961, when Mississippi officials jailed several hundred Freedom Riders for challenging segregation in interstate transportation. The Freedom Rides established CORE as a force in the Mississippi civil rights movement and accelerated the rise of nonviolent direct action campaigns across the state. In their wake, CORE joined with the NAACP, the King-led Southern Christian Leadership Conference, and the Student Nonviolent Coordinating Committee (SNCC) to form a united front—the Council of Federated Organizations (COFO)—that would coordinate civil rights activity in Mississippi. Although CORE was strapped for cash and short of field staff, it demanded and received its own territory to organize—Mississippi's Fourth Congressional District.[17]

Initially, activities in the district's eastern half, a rectangular cluster of six counties that included Clarke, radiated out from CORE's Meridian headquarters. Michael Schwerner, a New Yorker who arrived in early 1964 to coordinate civil rights activities in the Fourth's eastern half, believed that the rural counties surrounding Meridian contained untapped potential. Yet when he called for representatives from the surrounding counties to meet in Meridian, only three people showed up—all from Clarke County. Their "unofficial leader," Schwerner reported, was a Methodist preacher with a three-inch cross dangling from his neck. Jesse Charles Killingsworth, a native of southwest Mississippi, had moved to northern Clarke County in the early 1960s to serve a small country church. While he had relatively little prior experience with the civil rights movement, he warmed quickly to the COFO campaign. "I just recognized the fact that I was a Negro and I was involved," he explained later, "as a minister and as a race man." Killingsworth invited CORE staff to his church, where they encountered thirty-two attendees and a "fair amount of enthusiasm." Buoyed by the federal lawsuit against the country registrar, a nucleus of local ministers, farmers, and teachers had formed a voters' league to encourage black registration.[18]

By the summer of 1964, the Clarke County Voters' League had merged with the Mississippi Freedom Democratic Party (MFDP), a statewide coalition that registered thousands of black voters and challenged the all-white state party delegation to the Democratic National Convention. In late July, the Clarke County's MFDP chapter convened to elect officers and delegates to the district convention in Meridian. The following month, county party leaders from across Mississippi traveled to Atlantic City, New Jersey, to rally with the MFDP delegation at the Democratic National Convention. The Freedom Democrats hoped to convince the credentials committee to seat them as the only party in the state loyal to the national ticket. Meanwhile, the FBI spied on the delegation and kept President Lyndon Johnson, who regarded the MFDP challenge as a divisive and embarrassing sideshow, informed about their plans. Johnson twisted arms and doled out political favors to keep the Freedom Democrats off the floor of the convention. When the credentials committee refused to seat the delegation—instead offering them two seats as at-large observers—the MFDP rejected the compromise. Movement leaders in Mississippi regarded the deal as a betrayal by the liberal establishment, and local activists returned home convinced that black Mississippians could not rely on national politicians and federal officials to turn the political tide. "Quit getting down on your knees," a Clarke County delegate declared at an MFDP district caucus. "Help *yourself*."[19]

The local MFDP registration campaign suffered from limited resources and hasty planning. Of the nearly 65,000 black Mississippians registered by the MFDP, only 158 resided in Clarke County. Plans to set up polling places for a parallel "Freedom Election" in November fell apart. The "mock elections," Clarke County's sheriff reported to the Sovereignty Commission, proved "very unsuccessful." A more promising political insurgency was taking place among local whites, nearly all registered Democrats, who had voted overwhelmingly for Republican presidential candidate Barry Goldwater. The Arizona senator received the GOP nomination just two weeks after voting against the 1964

Civil Rights Act, and Mississippi segregationists rewarded him with 87 percent of the statewide vote. In Clarke County, the Arizona senator received 93 percent of ballots cast. "Goldwater Fever" ran so high in the Fourth Congressional District that a Smith County poultry farmer rode the candidate's coattails into office. Prentiss Walker, who bested the Democratic incumbent by six hundred votes in Clarke County, became the first Republican congressman elected in Mississippi since Reconstruction.[20]

Despite signs of what was now being acknowledged in Clarke County as "unrest among the Negroes"—accompanied by heightened white anxiety—the most iconic year of the Mississippi civil rights movement had come and gone with little perceptible change. The COFO Summer Project had mostly passed over Clarke County—no freedom schools, no demonstrations, and only a few dozen local blacks registered to vote. A new county registrar continued to delay and disqualify black registrants at her whim, and policemen routinely harassed and detained the few CORE workers who ventured down from Meridian. Yet while local officials continued to boast that they had the "racial situation" in hand, a handful of so-called agitators made them nervous. "The authorities," a state investigator conceded in November, "are looking for more trouble after the election than they have had for quite some time." They needed look no further than Reverend J. C. Killingsworth, whose experience with the MFDP had convinced him that political organization alone would not bring change. Clarke County, like the rest of Mississippi, needed a dose of direct action to "test" new civil rights laws and rally the black community. In the home of the Hanging Bridge, that proved a formidable challenge.[21]

PLEASED TO TAKE THE RISK

In late March 1965, Reverend Killingsworth headed down Alabama's Highway 80 toward home. He had spent the better part of the previous two months in Alabama, where he witnessed firsthand the power of mass protest and prophetic witness. The reverend and thousands of fellow civil rights supporters had descended on Selma, in the heart of Alabama's

Black Belt, to rally support for a massive voter registration drive and a renewed push for a federal voting rights bill. Throughout January and February, Killingsworth attended mass meetings, marched, and joined the round-the-clock vigil at the clothesline barricade erected to keep protesters out of the Dallas County Courthouse. In March, Killingsworth joined the long-delayed march to the state capitol in Montgomery. "I feel like being in Selma meant more than helping to bring a new voting law," he remarked a few months later. "It also had a tendency to help convert men, giving them to know that God still lives." He traveled back to Clarke County determined to put that power to work—a "soul-saving" crusade to liberate black and white alike from the sinfulness of segregation.[22]

As he drove down Highway 80, Killingsworth spotted a few men huddled around a wrecked car in a ditch. The driver, a white woman and mother of five from Detroit, had joined the march after Alabama policemen attacked marchers at Selma's Edmund Pettus Bridge. Viola Liuzzo was returning to Selma after shuttling fellow marchers to the Montgomery Airport when a carload of Klansmen pulled alongside and killed her with a single shotgun blast. Back in Clarke County, Killingsworth led thirty-eight marchers to the courthouse lawn to "deplore the fact that it takes death to get the U.S. government to move on civil rights." In front of Quitman's only "federal" building—the post office—the reverend laid a wreath and led a prayer in the light rain.[23]

While he was not a Clarke County native, Killingsworth discovered quickly that violence hovered over any discussion of race and rights. He understood the county's bloody past and, like a local, would recount stories of lynchings and disappearances to explain Clarke County to outsiders. From his home in the county's northern reaches, Killingsworth heard of that "blue hole" where white vigilantes had dumped "many, many" black bodies. "Down the road here," he warned a northern visitor in 1965, "there's been the hanging place for a long time." After an MFDP newsletter reported that white nightriders had abducted a black man in Clarke County, the reverend assumed they were headed for "the same hanging place" where others had died before. Had he not escaped his captors, Killingsworth predicted, "they would have kept up this thing, and he would have gone into the blue hole."[24]

Killingsworth's encounters with mass protest and violent resistance convinced him that the future of the local movement lay not in the hands of a small circle of MFDP supporters but in an aggressive grassroots campaign. Based in the northern end of Clarke County and relatively prosperous compared to African Americans in the southern half, the county's black registered voters represented a privileged elite. In the southern part lay the vast majority of the county's black residents—poorer, less educated, and more vulnerable to white pressure. Among his relatively well-off congregation, the reverend encountered little enthusiasm for direct action. "You don't find too many people...in the heart of the church who think in terms of freedom or are working towards this cause in any sense," he lamented. "Singing and praying and preaching" mattered, he argued, "but you've got to recognize that if you want your prayer answered, you've got to get up and hustle....We want everybody on the ball-rolling side." With the establishment of a county COFO headquarters in early 1965, Killingsworth seized the opportunity to inject some youth and energy into the local movement.[25]

Since few men and women of Killingsworth's generation joined in public demonstrations, the local movement rested on a foundation laid by trailblazers of a different sort. In early 1965, COFO set up shop in the back of a small brick hotel that had served as a hub of Quitman's black community for two decades. Rufus McRee, son of the county's first NAACP member and one of its earliest registered voters, had built the hotel in the late 1940s. McRee, who had learned the plumbing trade from his father, Sylvester, convinced town officials to approve a pipeline that ran from the town water tower to his hotel. The first black-owned building in Quitman with running water, the McRee Hotel housed a restaurant, grocery, and beauty salon. From early 1965 through the next few summers, it housed a civil rights headquarters as well (fig. 5.1). Greg Kaslo, a white University of Chicago student and CORE field worker, operated the office on a shoestring budget and little community support. "There is no money," Kaslo reported, "and folks will not risk the slightest."[26]

Short on funds and friends, the county civil rights office became a magnet for a few young people. Like Killingsworth, they understood

FIGURE 5.1

The McRee Hotel, built and operated by the son of Clarke County's
first NAACP member, became a hub of Quitman's black community and,
in the mid-1960s, the headquarters of the local civil rights movement.
Courtesy of the Historic Preservation Division, Mississippi Department
of Archives and History.

the risks but had less to lose. John Otis Sumrall, who graduated from
high school in 1964, grew up in a small brick house next door to the
McRee Hotel. While he was raised with stories of lynchings and news
footage of anti-civil-rights violence, Sumrall and his friends took different lessons from a revolution that was increasingly televised. "We
all used to sit around talking about what was going on in the news,"
he later recalled, "and if we were going to join the movement or not."
Sumrall's friend Warner Buxton, who lived in Shubuta but attended
high school in Quitman, shared a desire to join a movement he first witnessed on a 1963 news broadcast. "I saw a lot of people in Birmingham
on television," he remembered, "a lot of Negroes getting beat up by
local rednecks...and I was struck very deeply by what was going on,
and it left within me a yearning to do something about it." By the time

COFO arrived in Clarke County the following year, Buxton recalled, "I'd chanced to do something."[27]

Like Killingsworth, Sumrall and Buxton shared a "militant" outlook. "When I say militant, I mean, direct action," Buxton explained to an interviewer. "If something is not as it should be, you get right on it, you really press it till something happens." Even before COFO set up shop in his hometown, Sumrall participated in sit-ins and boycotts in Meridian after the passage of the Civil Rights Act of 1964. Killingsworth led the county's first sit-in at a bus-station lunch counter in Stonewall. With the establishment of the COFO office in Quitman, Killingsworth, Sumrall, and Buxton launched actions to "test" the Civil Rights Act's desegregation provisions—first at the local state park's swimming beach, then Quitman's Majestic Theater and a couple of local restaurants. They faced hostility and harassment but little overt violence. Still, reports of young people engaging in improvisational protests finally forced the authorities to acknowledge that Clarke County had a problem on its hands. The sit-in campaign, a Sovereignty Commission investigator warned, "appears to have set off a chain reaction which could be dangerous in the near future."[28]

Direct action also connected Clarke County activists to a statewide movement. Jackson police twice arrested Killingsworth and his young lieutenants—first for protesting Selma sheriff Jim Clark's keynote at a Mississippi police convention and later for joining an MFDP protest against a summer legislative session called by Governor Paul B. Johnson, Jr. In anticipation of a pending federal voting rights bill, Mississippi legislators convened to devise a plan to circumvent mass black voter registration. When hundreds showed up to protest the legally questionable session, Jackson police crammed them into cattle pens at the state fairgrounds. By participating in protests beyond the county line, Killingsworth, Sumrall, and Buxton made contacts with activists across in Mississippi. When the MFDP organized a voter registration campaign for the summer of 1965, party leaders assigned six white volunteers to operate out of Quitman's civil rights office.[29]

Despite the white supremacist scheming in Jackson, the Voting Rights Act finally provided the leverage that earlier actions had lacked.

If the earlier voting suit had given black registrants a foot in the door, the threat of federal officials descending on Clarke County kicked it wide open. "Things sort of snow-balled after a slow start," a white summer volunteer reported. Killingsworth marveled at seeing blacks lining up "more than two hundred at a time" in front of the courthouse. Ramsey's successor in the registrar's office "hasn't been nasty or anything," another MFDP volunteer noted, because she knew "there will be a Federal Registrar if she swerves off the path." By summer's end, MFDP legal advisors estimated that a third of the county's voting-age blacks had registered (fig. 5.2).[30]

The dramatic turnaround was heartening for a local movement hampered by a lack of resources and community support. But direct action protests and voter registration campaigns did not address the poverty that plagued rural counties like Clarke. Most of the county's poor blacks—particularly women—remained outside the movement's

FIGURE 5.2

John Otis Sumrall (in front, hat and neckerchief) canvasses for voter registration with a group of local black youth. Rural Clarke County, summer 1966. Photograph by John Cumbler. Courtesy of John Cumbler.

reach. The civil rights bills of 1964 and 1965 did little to address the most powerful weapon in white supremacists' arsenal, economic power. While the registrar no longer withheld registration paperwork from black applicants, the forms still required them to list their employer. In addition to facing the threat of losing their jobs, African Americans knew that white county officials held the purse strings to everything from school budgets to welfare payments.[31]

Local activists recognized this fundamental problem. Warner Buxton, the county's only full-time civil rights worker, emphasized the need for black economic power and independence. Inspired by the Poor People's Corporation, a grassroots initiative that organized economic cooperatives to produce and sell handmade goods, Buxton promoted the establishment of a sewing co-op to help local people "get out of white...kitchens and earn a decent living." Black apathy and fear, Buxton believed, was at its core economic—"putting up with anything he does or wants to do because he lets you have a few groceries or are on the welfare and if you don't stay right with Mr. Charlie he will have you took off."[32]

Without an educational and economic agenda to offer poor blacks, local activists could not expand their campaign. Even as the civil rights movement nationwide reached a climax of legislation and demonstrations, rural people still awoke to grinding poverty. And while a year of mounting activity had passed with surprisingly little violence, whites feared both the militancy that younger activists embraced and the broader economic agenda they advocated. "We're just ready to rebel," Buxton declared in the summer of 1965. "I don't mean a revolution in terms of physical warfare....I mean a revolution for revolution's sake." By the end of the year, that insurrection had arrived in an unlikely form.[33]

THERE IS A REVOLUTION IN MISSISSIPPI TODAY

Jimana Sumrall did not march. By the end of 1965, her son John Otis had walked from Selma to Montgomery and been jailed during demonstrations in Jackson. Mrs. Sumrall had sheltered civil rights workers—before and after the local movement had set up shop next door to her home. From her front stoop, she watched the flurry of activity at the McRee Hotel with apprehension and bemusement. Beyond registering to vote, there seemed little for a middle-aged mother of twelve to do for the movement. "I've followed civil rights in the past, and I've let civil rights workers sleep here," she said, "but I had read a lot about being nonviolent and getting knocked around in a march, or something. I wasn't interested in that." Intelligent, engaged, and respected, all she lacked was a project that suited her. Early that summer, her son returned from a civil rights conference with just such a proposal. "When I had a chance to do something peaceful for progress, this Head Start thing," she recalled, "I was pleased to take the risk."[34]

Head Start programs entered Clarke and twenty-three other counties that summer under the auspices of the Child Development Group of Mississippi (CDGM), an agency created by activist educators to provide preschool classes, medical care, and hot meals to poor children. A linchpin in Lyndon Johnson's War on Poverty, Head Start and other federal Community Action Program initiatives called for local leadership and "maximum feasible participation of the poor in the solutions of their own problems." The Office of Economic Opportunity, established by Congress to oversee these antipoverty initiatives, aimed to make CDGM a model for Head Start programs across the country. With an initial outlay of $1.5 million—the largest Head Start grant to a single agency—the Office of Economic Opportunity funded a seven-week summer program for Mississippi children. Just weeks from their July start date, CDGM organizers fanned out across the state to organize local committees and centers.[35]

Like others who gravitated to the Child Development Group, Jimana Sumrall knew all too well what black women in Mississippi endured. She also understood, like Mississippi migrants spread from coast to coast, the broad reach of racial discrimination and abuse. Her family had migrated to East St. Louis, the site of one of the worst race riots in the World War I era, in search of opportunity and security. Sumrall finished seventh grade before her family returned to Mississippi on the eve of the Great Depression. In Quitman, she finished her eighth year of school—the highest level of public education offered to black students in Clarke County until well after World War II—and spent the next thirty years raising a family.[36]

The wife of a skilled tradesman, who belonged to an integrated cement masons' union and worked mostly on out-of-state jobs, Jimana Sumrall enjoyed a measure of freedom and flexibility that many of her neighbors lacked. When CDGM came to Clarke County, she considered herself "just another housewife." In a town where the threat of economic retaliation deterred black activism, she seized the moment. Her husband's economic independence proved a valuable asset, especially when she stepped up to chair Quitman's Head Start program. "Some whites here asked where he worked, I suppose to fire him for my goings on," she chuckled. "But nobody seemed to know where he worked."[37]

The prospect of poor, undereducated black women running preschools offended local administrators. When Sumrall went looking for classroom space, the local school superintendent refused to host Head Start. "They say we're not good for much," she remarked, "but we're good for taking risks when they won't....If there's going to be a Head Start here for the little children, we'll have to organize it." She started next door, at the McRee Hotel, where she secured ten rooms and space for nearly one hundred children. Organizing a local Head Start committee proved more difficult. "They're afraid they'll be cut off welfare for stepping out like that," Sumrall explained. But for some local women, particularly those who recognized the educational opportunities being denied them and their children, the program's promise outweighed the risk. By the time a CDGM organizer visited Quitman in late summer, Sumrall had recruited twenty-three black women. Nearly all cleaned, cooked, or did laundry for a living. For most, a Head Start salary would triple or quadruple their income. While many of the women played leadership roles in their neighborhoods and churches, the Child Development Group put them in direct control over federal dollars—a role previously reserved solely for whites. In a few weeks, they had rounded up classroom space, transportation contracts, and dozens of students for an untested and controversial program.[38]

Mississippi officials did not wait for the start of school to attack the Child Development Group as a haven for "extremists and agitators." John C. Stennis, an influential member of the Senate Committee on Appropriations, worked feverishly to cut off the program's funding. CDGM critics vilified the program's creator, Tom Levin, a self-described "New York Jewish radical" who had organized medical support teams during the 1964 Freedom Summer project. A psychologist by training, Levin argued that the Head Start program involved far more than early childhood education: "It can act as a focus to organize a community around all their social aspirations." Building on the example of the Freedom Schools, which designed a curriculum that emphasized black dignity and social engagement, the Child Development Group did not hide its commitment to organizing and empowering poor people. In rural counties like Clarke, where civil rights activists and antipoverty organizers lacked an institutional base, the line was blurred from the start. At Quitman's McRee Hotel, civil rights meetings and Head Start classes took place under one roof.[39]

When Mississippi's most powerful politicians, including Stennis, attacked CDGM, local organizers fought back. Jimana Sumrall wrote directly to President Johnson. "I'm very proud and pleased to be a part of this wonderful program," she declared. "It has done great for my community and my people. It has brought us closer together as a team—not as *your* program but *our* program." In her letter to the White House— reprinted in the Child Development Group's newsletter—Sumrall denounced Senator Stennis as a liar and a hypocrite. Invoking the book of Matthew, where Jesus denounced the scribes and Pharisees for choosing legalism over justice and mercy, Mrs. Sumrall declared, "Mr. Stennis is gagging at a gnat while swallowing a camel." Via CDGM, a black woman from Clarke County with an eighth-grade education tangled openly with one of the most powerful men in Washington.[40]

As Sumrall and her colleagues worked feverishly to train teachers, distribute supplies, and pay workers on time, Mississippi's Sovereignty Commission investigators spied on Head Start centers for evidence of fraud and graft. Instead, they found a chaotic but surprisingly viable grassroots program. With little advance preparation, the Child

Development Group had organized eighty-four centers that employed over one thousand adults and educated six thousand children. According to a federal evaluation, a few were "excellent" and most were "astonishingly adequate." All provided hot meals and medical exams to some of the state's poorest children. As the initial seven-week session came to a close in September 1965, Clarke County's Head Start workers kept their centers open with no federal funds for salaries, transportation, food, or supplies. Mamie Jones, a Head Start worker from Shubuta, shuttled fifteen preschoolers to school in her two-door coupe. "If the government isn't ready in January," Jones pledged, "we will be willing to continue on a volunteer basis."[41]

While Mississippi politicians and Office of Economic Opportunity bureaucrats haggled over the Child Development Group's grant renewal, Jones planned to expand Head Start operations into Shubuta. In January 1966, she demanded that Sargent Shriver, head of the Office of Economic Opportunity, explain the "holdup" in funds. "We have gone too far now, to fall by the wayside," she warned Shriver. "We aren't tired, we're broke. We don't want to let our little ones down." A few weeks later, after two busloads of Mississippi Head Start teachers and preschoolers staged a sit-in on Capitol Hill, federal officials awarded CDGM $6 million to run 120 centers for six months. In Clarke County, Head Start workers had already laid plans to open several new centers and enroll scores of new students. Allie Jones, a retired Shubuta schoolteacher who had worked in the original Child Development Group program in Quitman, signed up over two hundred preschoolers—more than countywide enrollment during the previous summer. The registration forms revealed the extent of poverty in and around Shubuta. Twenty percent of preschoolers' parents reported no income other than welfare checks. The remaining 80 percent's household income averaged forty dollars a week—about half the national poverty threshold.[42]

Within months of its establishment, Clarke County's Head Start program had achieved what civil rights workers had failed to accomplish. With War on Poverty funds, the Child Development Group established a beachhead in the county's only black-majority town. Head Start offered impoverished families a free preschool program but also a chance to earn a decent wage and achieve a measure of economic independence from local whites. "They are really trying to hire poor people," a CDGM administrator reported after a February visit to Shubuta. Allie Jones did not have to look hard to find them. The thirty-three workers she recruited had earned an average of twenty-five dollars a week in their previous jobs. Childhood Development Group salaries averaged twice that amount. In a town where white employers controlled access and dictated wages for nearly all work, a federally funded and black-controlled job program shook the status quo to its core. As in previous generations, when whites complained that military service and defense jobs were luring away cheap and tractable black labor, CDGM provoked white hostility.[43]

The inhospitable climate made it hard to find shelter. An abandoned white high school sat empty across town, but town officials refused to open any public buildings to Head Start. Allie Jones set up classrooms in an old Masonic hall next door to her home and in the Mt. Zion Methodist Church across the street. Workers hung sliding curtains in the two-story lodge and the church sanctuary to create a dozen classrooms for two hundred preschoolers. Because neither building had indoor plumbing, Jones's home served as the Head Start kitchen, office, and storage area. When Child Development Group supervisors visited shortly after the start of the school session, they found preschoolers and workers crammed into a space suitable for half the students enrolled. Amid the crowding, chaos, and shortage of supplies, a CDGM staffer reported, "The staff is very proud."[44]

In addition to lessons, hot meals, and medical exams for children, the program provided economic and civic benefits for parents. Shubuta Head Start workers embraced the War on Poverty's stated goal of empowering poor people through community action. "The parents and citizens of Shubuta are doing meaningful things on their own for their children," Allie Jones reported. "The important part of it all is that people are feeling that if they want things like this for their children they can not sit and wait, but must think and act for themselves." A local Head Start teacher asserted that "the parents...are learning to participate in their community welfare more abundantly." Head Start parents reported that the program served as a gathering point for the community, a direct source of jobs, and a child-care option that allowed them to work while their children attended school. For a mother on welfare whose children attended the Shubuta Hall center, Head Start represented the fulfillment of President Johnson's lofty crusade to spread economic opportunity to the margins. Asked what CDGM meant to her, she replied, "It means that our children will get an early start in entering into this 'Great Society.'"[45]

More than any previous federal action, antipoverty programs provided an avenue for civic engagement in white-dominated, black-majority rural communities like Shubuta. In the short run, voting lawsuits and civil rights bills had little tangible impact on locals' daily lives, but an infusion of federal dollars suggested that someone in Washington acknowledged their citizenship. Entrusted with federal funds and employed under federal fiat, local Head Start leaders spoke and acted as "tax-paying citizens." The Child Development Group's critics blasted the program as a "front" for racial agitators, but Head Start organizers regarded political involvement as a civic duty. In Clarke County, CDGM's paid community organizer, Garlee Johnson, demanded that all Head Start employees register to vote or lose their jobs. "Her tactics are a bit rough," a civil rights worker admitted, "but she gets things done" (fig. 5.3).[46]

Segregationist politicians circulated similar stories as proof of the program's "subversive" mission. CDGM's defenders countered that federal employees, like state and local officials, had every right to engage in the rights and duties of citizens. "Was it civil rights," a movement journalist wrote after visiting Shubuta, "or just good citizenship when 24 Clarke County [Head Start] teachers were loaded into cars and taken down to register to vote?" Furthermore, supporters noted, white officials frequently used their control over welfare disbursements and poverty programs to keep potential troublemakers in line. Mississippi had floated on a sea of federal assistance since the New Deal, and local powerbrokers had become quite adept at using government aid to shore up the status quo. "Compared to the way powerful whites manipulate their own county 'community action agencies,' CDGM centers

FIGURE 5.3

John Otis Sumrall (background) and Mrs. Garlee Johnson, a local
administrator in the Child Development Group of Mississippi Head
Start program, Clarke County, 1966. Photograph by John Cumbler,
courtesy of John Cumbler.

were paragons of democracy and honesty," a sympathetic journalist argued in the *New Republic*. "But that didn't seem to be the point."[47]

The charge that the Child Development Group was a front for "political" activity was not only hypocritical—it also oversimplified the interaction between Head Start and so-called movement people. In Clarke County and elsewhere, Head Start employees—like civil rights workers—were risk takers. Taking a job with a controversial program like CDGM was a political statement in and of itself, so it is unsurprising that employees registered to vote and engaged with civil rights issues more than the average person. Not all activists embraced antipoverty workers as natural allies. Some—particularly younger SNCC and CORE members—spurned CDGM and other War on Poverty programs because they mistrusted the federal government. In Clarke County, civil rights workers welcomed the program but quietly grumbled about the strong-arm tactics and squabbling of the CDGM staff. At a statewide MFDP meeting, John Otis Sumrall worried that Garlee Johnson and other authoritarian staffers would "mess up the whole area for organizing." Unschooled in the consensus-building style and organizing strategies favored by civil rights workers, Head Start leaders could seem bossy, bureaucratic, and "out of contact with the people and the movement."[48]

Clarke County's Head Start leaders may not have hewed to "movement" tactics and language, but the programs did provide a gathering place for engaged and outspoken people who were shut out of nearly every other civic space. Before the Child Development Group came to Shubuta, a visiting civil rights worker noted, "Negroes had never cooperated on anything but church programs. This spring they discovered that poor black people working together could run a better program for their children than the white school officials ever had." The political implications, she continued, had white supremacists on edge. "The Klan isn't worried about Head Start children getting a wading pool," she observed. "It's worried that parents who discover they can work together to build a wading pool will discover they can work together in a political campaign as well."[49]

Even more alarming and explosive than Head Start's "political" nature was its economic challenge to white power. While its outspoken critics preferred to demonize the program's politics, the controversy boiled down to a question of money and who controlled it. In small towns like Shubuta, CDGM administrators contracted with white merchants for thousands of dollars in food and supplies, and Head Start employees cashed their paychecks with local bankers and storekeepers. Whites had long used their control of jobs and credit to keep black people in line, but government contracts and federal paychecks threatened to disrupt that relationship. As criticism of the Child Development Group mounted in 1966, federal investigators reported that white anxiety—not black corruption—fueled hostility toward Head Start. "The implications of the control of this amount of money by the Negroes and the life changes that can take place," the investigators concluded, "account for the reason why there is a revolution in Mississippi today." The authors of the investigative report, one of several authorized by the Office of Economic Opportunity in response to complaints from Mississippi officials, contended that the controversy was at root "a class struggle...wherein the 'haves' are concerned that the 'have nots' are moving up the economic ladder....The whites are terribly concerned about this and wish it to be stopped immediately."[50]

In Shubuta, whites felt the tremors of this revolution every time Head Start workers deposited government paychecks or placed their weekly food and supply orders with local merchants. Head Start administrators did not beg for a credit line or curry favor—they wielded the leverage of contractors who could take their considerable accounts elsewhere. That combination of confidence and independence proved unsettling to whites who had never dealt with black women in such a position. Whites may not have liked CDGM's politics, but they resented its power even more. As black Mississippians demanded more of that power—and the freedom that came with it—that resentment turned violent.

WE'RE NOT THE OLD BLACK JOE NOW

Head Start's quiet revolution collided with a louder insurrection in June 1966. On the first Sunday of that month, James Meredith headed south from Memphis on his "March against Fear." Meredith, who just four years earlier had integrated the University of Mississippi, intended to walk to Jackson "to challenge the all-pervasive and overriding fear" that still kept most black Mississippians from seizing on opportunities created by the previous summers' bills and breakthroughs. On the second day of Meredith's walk, just sixteen miles south of the Tennessee border, a white man unloaded three loads of number 4 birdshot into Meredith's head, neck, and back. As Meredith recuperated in a Memphis hospital, civil rights leaders and supporters descended on the city to march in his stead.[51]

From the outset, the Meredith march revealed the tension between the "big five" civil rights organizations and the increasingly militant mood of many younger activists. NAACP head Roy Wilkins and the Urban League's Whitney Young stormed out of a planning meeting when Student Nonviolent Coordinating Committee chairman Stokely Carmichael argued that the march should "serve as an indictment" of President Johnson's reluctance to enforce federal civil rights laws. He also demanded that the gun-toting Deacons for Defense, a Louisiana-based protective group, join the march as a security detail. Carmichael and new Congress of Racial Equality leader Floyd McKissick contrasted sharply with Martin Luther King, who threw the Southern Christian Leadership Conference's support behind the march despite concerns about the militant rhetoric of SNCC and CORE. The marchers' manifesto demanded that the federal government enforce civil rights laws, dispatch registrars to every Deep South county, and expand antipoverty programs, but the media focused instead on sound bites. "We're going to go through Mississippi like a tornado and a hurricane," McKissick warned. "And when we leave it's going to be a little different than the Mississippi in which James Meredith was shot."[52]

Civil rights activists from across the state joined the demonstration. When the march reached Batesville, the seat of black-majority Panola County, Reverend Killingsworth and the local Mississippi Freedom Democratic Party chairman led a detachment of marchers to the courthouse for a voting rights rally (fig. 5.4). In perhaps the march's most poignant and hopeful moment, a formerly enslaved man—over a hundred

FIGURE 5.4

Rev. J. C. Killingsworth, center with fedora and jacket, walks with
Student Nonviolent Coordinating Committee leader Stokely Carmichael,
sweater over shoulder, Congress of Racial Equality national director
Floyd McKissick, far right, and Southern Christian Leadership
Conference executive Rev. Ralph Abernathy, second from left, in the
March against Fear. Later that day, Killingsworth co-led a voting rights
march into Batesville, Mississippi, that resulted in the registration of a
formerly enslaved 106-year-old man. Como, Mississippi, June 10, 1966.
Courtesy of the Associated Press.

years old—joined the fifty-plus local people who registered on the spot. When El Fondren emerged from the courthouse, two marchers hoisted him onto their shoulders and carried him through the cheering throng. Whites mostly avoided the spectacle—even the Klan distributed leaflets discouraging violence and harassment. Governor Johnson dispatched twenty highway patrol cars to flank the column as it crept down Highway 51. But as the march continued and more African Americans went to their local registrars' offices, police protection fell off and white hostility increased. "The only way to get freedom is to take it," McKissick declared. "No one is going to give it to you."[53]

Carmichael contended that pleas for freedom fell on deaf ears. "*Power* is the only thing that is respected in the world," he argued, "and we must get it at any cost." After white police in Greenwood arrested him for pitching tents on city property, Carmichael took the cry for *power* to the people. His advance man, Willie Ricks, had been priming activists and local people for the new slogan at nightly rallies and meetings along the march route. "This is the twenty-seventh time I have been arrested—and I ain't going to jail no more!" Carmichael declared to a crowd of three thousand in Greenwood. "We been saying freedom for six years and we ain't got nothin'. What we gonna start saying now is Black Power!" He repeated the phrase five times, and then the crowd joined in.[54]

For most journalists covering the march, and most who followed the news from Mississippi, the phrase "Black Power" overshadowed everything that happened from that moment. Asked yet again what he meant by the phrase, Carmichael told a reporter that black Mississippians would stop being "shot down like dogs" only "when they get the power where they constitute a majority in counties to institute justice." While he had no qualms about armed self-defense, as his alliance with the Deacons made clear, Carmichael emphasized political challenges aimed at elected officials who refused to protect blacks and prosecute their attackers. Likewise, Carmichael's Black Power call resonated with Child Development Group organizers and civil rights workers who were committed to creating economic opportunity. When the SNCC chairman argued that "we gotta take over the community where we outnumber people so we can have decent jobs," he evoked the economic plight of impoverished blacks in Deep South towns like Shubuta as well as urban ghettoes nationwide.[55]

For John Otis Sumrall, who marched with his comrades from CORE and SNCC, the new slogan highlighted the importance of "economic power." Sumrall liked the idea, as he put it, of being "treated fair at the financial institutions...getting loans and developing our community." While he cheered the speeches by Carmichael and Ricks, Sumrall had his own take on the slogan. Joyce Ladner, a marcher from southeastern Mississippi, later interviewed several dozen Black Power supporters and noted a split between *cosmopolitan* and *local* understandings of the term. The former tended to be young, middle-class, and college-educated civil rights workers from elsewhere, while the latter tended to be homegrown activists like Sumrall. "The great difference between the cosmopolitans and locals," Ladner concluded, "is that the locals are committed to concrete economic and political programs." Local activists advocated strategies that would address poverty wages, substandard housing, and other problems perpetuated by segregation and discrimination. Political setbacks—the MFDP's failed challenges to the state Democratic Party, the attacks on CDGM—and mounting white backlash had primed them for a more aggressive stance. "Negroes are tired of being without power," Ladner concluded, "and want to share in it."[56]

Racial violence shaped grassroots understandings of Black Power. Sumrall and other civil rights workers, after all, had answered the call to march after a white man gunned down a black man in broad daylight. Such brazen violence convinced many, Ladner argued, that only Black Power could protect them from unchecked racial terrorism. Certainly, Black Power supporters embraced armed self-defense, but Sumrall stopped well short of advocating a suicidal "black uprising." Given the state and federal firepower arrayed against would-be grassroots guerrillas, Sumrall scoffed at white fears that "if a bunch of black people got together you had another Nat Turner on your hands." Although journalists covering the march focused on Black Power's supposedly violent connotation, rural blacks did not need Carmichael to school them on armed self-defense. Sumrall had learned from CORE the tactics of nonviolent direct action, but admitted he "was never non-violent, personally." Sumrall believed that while nonviolence could make a point, a loaded gun within easy reach made an even stronger impression on would-be nightriders. Back in Clarke County, Sumrall and his comrades stashed loaded revolvers in desk drawers and glove boxes. "Everybody is carrying a gun or has a gun loaded back home," a white volunteer reported. "People carrying guns in their cars and everything it is amazing."[57]

Like his younger lieutenants, Killingsworth embraced the ethos of self-defense long before Black Power hit the headlines. He boasted that he had laid out a dozen men who attacked him when he attempted to integrate Clarke County's largest white church. When several shouting and cursing parishioners surrounded him, Killingsworth said, "I realized that I would have to practice my religion actively." He bragged that he kept them at bay with "an uppercut, a bolo, and...a foot." While many men of Killingsworth's generation shared his attitude toward self-defense, the reverend proved more receptive to Black Power than most of his peers. As Ladner noted in her survey, local Mississippi Freedom Democratic Party leaders embraced the term because they viewed it in conventional political terms. "When they refer to developing black-power programs," she noted, "they speak of registering to vote, running for political office, and building independent political parties."[58]

The Meredith march revealed a widening rift between national civil rights leaders—personified in the split between King and Carmichael over Black Power. It also sparked grassroots insurgencies in towns along the march route and beyond. Those campaigns, from a voter registration drive in Belzoni to a summer-long boycott of white businesses in Canton, reflected both Killingsworth's emphasis on *political* power and Sumrall's emphasis on *economic* leverage. The local protest campaigns that gathered momentum in the march's wake revealed both a continuity in tactics—voter registration, boycotts, and cooperative economics—and a more confrontational tone. The Meredith march, which had skirted the eastern edge of the black-majority Delta region, inspired protests in towns across the state where political and economic power

197

rested in the hands of a white minority. In southern Clarke County, black-majority Shubuta most closely resembled this mix of unrelenting white power and unrealized black potential. After the Meredith march, the focus of the local movement turned toward the town with the Hanging Bridge.[59]

While on the march, Sumrall had recruited white volunteers to help with a follow-up summer project. Days after the march ended, a rising sophomore at the University of Wisconsin stepped off a Greyhound bus in Quitman. Sumrall met him at the bus station and took him on a quick tour that included the Shubuta bridge. "People in the rural areas are very scared," John Cumbler wrote in a letter to his fiancée back in Wisconsin. "There is a great difference between here and where we were on the March." Racial fear made an impression, but so too did the abject poverty in Clarke County's black communities. "You wouldn't believe the living conditions down here," he wrote. Cumbler snapped photos of the sagging cardboard and newspaper that insulated plank walls and ceilings. An indoor toilet or faucet, he discovered, was a mark of prosperity. Most families made do with an outdoor pump and an outhouse.[60]

To an outsider, the link between poverty and discrimination remained as clear as day. In the towns, street paving and sidewalks stopped where black neighborhoods started. Parts of each town, Cumbler noted, "look beautiful"—just not the sections set aside for African Americans. In Shubuta, where more blacks than whites paid municipal taxes, the discrepancy in infrastructure and services was most pronounced. The town's economy floated on black labor and black dollars, and the small amount that whites doled out in wages came right back to them with interest. "The trouble with the town," Cumbler concluded, "is that the whites own all the stores, and the negroes have all their money taken from them." Head Start helped, but like black laborers and domestics, Child Development Group employees traded their paychecks for credit at white-owned stores. "The white people charge the hell out of these people," Cumbler complained. "What they need is a store where they can get cheap food." The cooperative project—"a type of country store," he explained, except one that would be owned by black people—seemed an answer to the white monopoly in Shubuta.[61]

Plans for a cooperative proceeded apace with a campaign to pressure local officials and businesses to take black grievances seriously. Across the state, a streak of "blackouts" had turned downtowns into ghost towns. Successful boycotts in Natchez and other southwest Mississippi towns in 1965 ran some recalcitrant white merchants out of business and forced others to hire and promote black employees. By bringing business districts to a standstill—particularly in black-majority towns and cities—local activists hoped to force white officials to concede to municipal improvements as well. The Shubuta boycott was particularly daring, given the town's small size and the hostility toward civil rights. In larger towns, boycott campaigns inspired by the Meredith march took months or years to materialize. Clarke County activists gave themselves less than six weeks (fig. 5.5).[62]

FIGURE 5.5
Civil rights meeting, Clarke County, summer 1966. Photo by John Cumbler. Courtesy of John Cumbler.

On their first day canvassing for the boycott, civil rights workers saw what they were up against. Out of two hundred people contacted, about fifty showed up for a meeting. Cumbler estimated that only half of those "seemed willing to do anything." Most of the enthusiasm for the boycott came from women and youth. "The women are the only ones who do anything," Cumbler noted, "except for a few men and some young people who want to be in the action." What youth lacked in buying power, they made up for in energy. In towns across the state, black youth served as the muscle behind boycott campaigns. They marched to rally support and, once the boycotts started, confronted neighbors who refused to take part. "I have a feeling if anything is going to do something," Cumbler noted, "it will have to come from the younger people, because they are the ones who can't see the excuse of being afraid." After a series of youth meetings, Sumrall and Cumbler had recruited a couple dozen marchers. Something had lit a fire. No doubt the Black Power buzz had something to do with it. Someone suggested a name for Shubuta's new vanguard—"The Black and Brave Coordinating Committee." The name certainly summed up the summer's mood.[63]

Black Power inspired a different sort of boldness in local whites. Local police stepped up their harassment of civil rights workers and sympathizers. White youth assaulted staffers and volunteers in broad daylight, and nightriders circled menacingly around meeting places and CDGM centers. The previous summer, black locals and white volunteers had "integrated" the local theater, state park, and a few cafes without violence. But in Cumbler's first couple weeks in Clarke County, white toughs attacked integrated groups that ventured downtown to Quitman's movie theater and cafe. "I thought for sure I was going to get killed," he wrote his fiancée. "To say that the Civil Rights bill has accomplished much in Miss. is ridiculous."[64]

Local activists attributed the spike in threats, harassment, and assaults to "the Klan"—a blanket term for white supremacists who favored terrorism over more refined tactics. The organization remained largely in the shadows, but civil rights supporters recognized that Clarke County lay squarely between two nerve centers of Klan activity. Forty miles southwest, in the lumber-industry hub of Laurel, a vending-machine company owner named Sam Bowers lorded over his secretive White Knights of the Ku Klux Klan. To the northeast, from its headquarters in Tuscaloosa, Alabama, Robert Shelton's United Klans of America organized public rallies and massive recruiting drives across the South.[65]

Situated between the region's major Klan hubs, Clarke and surrounding counties witnessed a surge in violence and harassment. The White Knights earned a brutal reputation due in large part to their involvement in the 1964 slaying of civil rights workers Michael Schwerner, Andrew Goodman, and James Cheney in Neshoba County. Shortly thereafter, the White Knights established a klavern in nearby Clarke County. The competing factions proved highly unstable, but Klan-related activity in and around the county persisted. By 1966, FBI agents had identified three United Klans of America klaverns operating in the county. By mid-summer, agents reported, "the Shubuta situation" had spurred the moribund and disorganized units to action. Affiliation and organizational distinctions mattered little to local African Americans, who recognized that the Klan's violent spirit loomed over Clarke County and extended beyond card-carrying members.[66]

In Shubuta, lawmen and vigilantes alike targeted Head Start workers. Allie Jones became a prime target. Jones had "spread food money around evenly at stores in town," a Child Development Group report noted, but few whites seemed grateful. Instead, lawmen circled her home and repeatedly arrested houseguests for "disturbing the peace." As word spread that Jones and her young allies were planning something big, vigilantes joined in the harassment. In mid-July, the Quitman office received a call that nightriders were circling the Jones house and threatening to blow it up. "We had about 10 loaded guns and about three guards up all night," John Cumbler reported. "During the last few days I have begun to realize what the West must have been like."[67]

The mounting harassment did not derail the planned boycott. In late July, the "Community Planning and Improvement Committee" drew up a list of demands, signed by Jones and three other members of the local Head Start committee. Jones hand-delivered the petition to the town marshal, a local grocer, and Mayor George Busby's appliance store. "We have been trading in this town all of our life," the letter began. "We feel that we deserve respect and courtesy...as tax-paying citizens." The list of demands included basic improvements—stop signs, street lamps, paving, sidewalks, a sewage system—that municipal authorities routinely denied black neighborhoods. The committee called for an integrated jobs committee and African American police officers. Other demands—a dentist office, drug store, theater, and "new factories"—reflected the decline of a town a half-century past its prime. More pointed, the committee called for an end to black exclusion from public facilities and demanded that the old white high school be reopened as a Head Start and community recreation center. "We will not accept promises," the letter concluded. "Action is our acceptance. Should you fail to comply, we will have to take our trading elsewhere."[68]

The ultimatum would have overwhelmed any small-town mayor. A municipal sewage system alone—even Shubuta's white residents relied on septic tanks—would have cost about ten times the town's annual budget. But Busby focused less on the demands and more on the "arrogant" demanders. In a defiant reply, the mayor refused "to be influenced by or have anything to do with outside pressure groups" and their "unreasonable demands and threats." Meanwhile, the harassment around the Jones house and the CDGM buildings escalated. "Shubuta center has had quite a bit of trouble from whites intimidating and threatening," a visiting CDGM staffer reported the following week. "Cars speed by... 5 or 6 times per day....Police came and demanded to see applications of out-of-state whites working there." Unfazed, Jones canceled her weekly orders with local merchants and traveled to Meridian and Laurel to contract with wholesalers. She instructed Head Start workers not to cash paychecks or shop in town. On August 1, 1966, the boycott began in earnest. Five days later, the town witnessed its first civil rights march.[69]

That morning of the march, the *Meridian Star* carried a front-page photo of Martin Luther King, Jr. clutching the back of his head. A Chicago mob, shouting "white power" and "nigger go home," had pelted King and several hundred demonstrators with bricks and bottles as they marched in protest of residential segregation and housing discrimination. "Chicago Whites 'Stone' King," Mississippi's "Voice of the New

South" crowed. "Feel That Lump?" The same morning, Gail Falk headed south from Meridian to cover a march that the *Star* failed to mention. A civil rights worker and reporter for the *Southern Courier*—a movement paper—Falk had never had a reason to visit Shubuta. The "dusty little one-street town," she recalled, seemed "really far back in time compared to Meridian.... *Way* out there." She noticed a small fleet of highway patrol cars—an impressive show of force for a town with only one salaried policeman. Local authorities had planned response and, as state officials reported, asked for "as much help from the MHP as they could get."[70]

FIGURE 5.6

Rev. J. C. Killingsworth (center) and Congress of Racial Equality regional project director George Smith, Jr., of Meridian (right) lead marchers through the streets of Shubuta. August 6, 1966. Clipping from *Southern Courier*, July 8–9 1967: 1.

The police detail seemed excessive when Falk spotted the marchers. About sixty of them, mostly teenagers, wound their way through several black neighborhoods on their way downtown (fig. 5.6). The chairman of the Black and Brave Coordinating Committee—"a new young people's organization," Falk noted—led the way. The march passed near the home of Mintora Green, mother of the 1942 lynching victim Ernest Green, who remained in Shubuta following the killing. She died a few years later, in 1971. Perhaps she was home that day—most black townspeople ducked inside when they saw the marchers headed down their street. Falk saw a man wave from his porch. When the marchers reached the center of Shubuta, they stopped in front of the tiny town hall for a rally. Scores of bystanders, mostly white, watched silently.[71]

A state investigator summed up forty minutes of oratory as "mostly degrading the white people," but the speakers summed up the new mood of the Mississippi movement. "We're not the Old Black Joe now," shouted George Smith, a Meridian CORE worker. "We're not going to hang our heads any longer." Reverend Killingsworth blended the militant rhetoric of power with the familiar language of the prophet. Like King, who had responded to the "Black Power" call by arguing that blacks should organize into "units of power" to elect black officials and appoint black policemen, Killingsworth emphasized the ballot. "Blacks outnumber the whites two to one in Shubuta," he argued. "We're going to pick our own candidates for office. The first shall be last and the last shall be first." Unlike King and others in the Southern Christian Leadership Conference, the reverend did not shy away from the controversial new slogan. A blend of the Bible and Black Power suited him just fine, and he reminded white onlookers that the wages of sin had not changed. "We are going to have Black Power in Clarke County," he shouted, "and if you don't like it you can go to Hell. If you believe things are going to be the same as they have been, you are crazy for thinking it and a fool for believing it."[72]

By the time John Otis Sumrall stepped up "to make some closing remarks," Mayor Busby felt the white crowd simmering behind him. "This has got to stop," someone hissed, "and we are going to stop it." Sumrall knew good and well that some of the onlookers would like to tear his head off, but he declared that Clarke County blacks faced bigger obstacles than white toughs. Paternalistic officials and merchants played their part as well. White powerbrokers spoke "with cake in their mouths and cornbread in their hearts"—a line Sumrall was especially proud of—and the "blackout" would teach them to trifle with black demands. As for the Klansmen and the hecklers, Sumrall warned, "if you come by night, you will find us waiting with guns."[73]

White and black onlookers differed on what exactly the speakers said, but everyone agreed that the rally ended the moment Sumrall mentioned *guns*. Two highway patrolmen grabbed him by his elbows. "All right you've talked long enough," one of them barked. "I thought I was being arrested," Sumrall recalled, but the patrolmen shoved him into the crowd. The rest of the patrolmen formed a ring around the marchers and started pushing them away from the town hall. A couple of troopers snatched walking sticks and canes from marchers and used them as prods. Fred Mittleman, a white summer volunteer, snapped a shot of patrolmen pushing and kicking the marchers. Instantly, he felt a yank on his camera strap. As two patrolmen grabbed for his camera, Mittleman tossed it toward another white CORE worker. "When I picked up the camera," Joe Morse remembered, "one of the patrolmen hit me very hard on the head with a walking stick." Two more troopers pinned down Mittleman while a third beat him with a cane. By the time they dragged him to a patrol car, Gail Falk reported, "he was bleeding so heavily that I believed him to be seriously wounded."[74]

After a quick trip to the town doctor, who patched up Mittleman, the highway patrolmen tossed the prisoner in the county jail's "colored cell." When he asked what he was charged with, a patrolman chuckled. "We'll think of something." Pretty soon another prisoner from Shubuta joined Mittleman. It was the man who had waved at the marchers. He'd been arrested for public drunkenness and locked up on $150 bond.[75]

A VICIOUS MOOD

The following morning, the *Meridian Star* failed to mention the Shubuta march. A snapshot from a different protest graced the front page. In response to John Lennon's quip that his band was "bigger than Jesus," a hundred white teenagers in Jackson tossed records onto a "Ban the Beatles Bonfire." Back in Clarke County, white authorities' show of force had slowed the boycott's momentum. A visiting civil rights lawyer doubted that future protests would yield better results. "There was not much popular response to the first march," he reported, and the boycott was meeting with "only fair results." While Reverend Killingsworth and his young comrades had no plans of folding, the lawyer conceded, "the police harassment at the march has frightened some Negro parents so much that they may not allow their children to go on the later marches."[76]

Locals had more to fear than nightriders and police beatings. The fallout from the August 6 march proved less violent than the buildup, but no less frightening. When marchers returned to work on Monday, several discovered they no longer had a job. The Scott Paper Company fired Peter Blakely, a pulpwood hauler and the designated "chairman" of the Black and Brave. A local mill owner told a white pulpwood hauler that he wouldn't buy another load from him until he fired a marcher's father from his crew. A town "bigshot" fired his maid for marching, and town officials dismissed John Heard from his job "cleaning out ditches." He had not marched, but his mother had.[77]

Local black boycotters also used intimidation. "Civil rights workers were stationed in front of every business in town," an investigator reported, "in an attempt to keep local Negroes from buying." Young enforcers confronted black shoppers, blocked store entrances, and even tossed grocery bags in trash cans. Some fell in line, and others simply steered clear of downtown to avoid the hassle. "I am not too afraid to come to town, but I don't like to go too much," an elderly black woman admitted. "I don't want any part of this mess."[78]

Two weeks of retaliation cast a pall over the town. Then, on Saturday, August 20, a small crowd gathered at a black elementary school just before noon. The marchers had backup—two observers from the Jackson-based Lawyers' Committee for Civil Rights under the Law—but thinner ranks. Forty people—mostly teenagers—showed up. Mayor Busby and Sheriff Riley rolled by in a patrol car. They had backup too. District Attorney George Warner had rolled in from Meridian, and most of the county's lawmen had driven down to reinforce the highway patrol detachment. The group could march, the sheriff informed Killingsworth, but they could not stop downtown. "A march without a speech is meaningless," the reverend shot back. He asked for ten minutes at town hall. Busby replied that the group could hold a meeting in a vacant lot or a field, but not downtown. His people were not cattle, Killingsworth replied, and they would not hold their meetings in pastures. They had a constitutional right to rally where they pleased. He could forget about the Constitution, the mayor replied: "We have our own laws and regulations, and you will have to abide by them."[79]

The marchers set out on their roundabout walk to the town hall. Reverend Killingsworth and John Otis Sumrall, in his characteristic straw hat, led the way. A highway patrol car crept along behind them. The black neighborhoods they passed through were even quieter than two weeks before, but parked pickup trucks and patrol cars choked the town's main street. Joseph Gelb and Jack Joyce, the civil rights lawyers who had driven over from Jackson, walked twenty feet behind the marchers. They noticed a crowd of whites milling about near town hall. Most of them appeared to be in their teens and early twenties. A patrolman estimated that more than two hundred whites had gathered downtown. The mayor noticed a number of out-of-town plates and unfamiliar faces.[80]

When the marchers reached the town hall, they halted for a rally. Before the line could close in around the building, a gauntlet of highway patrolmen turned them toward the opposite side of the street. As the marchers spilled into a vacant lot across from the town hall, Gelb and Joyce heard someone shout, "That's right, you all go get them." Instantly, white men with bats and ax handles poured into the lot. Together with policemen, they swung at any marcher within reach. Walter Pickett, a sixteen-year-old from Quitman, blacked out after the sheriff clubbed him in the back of the head. A blow from a blackjack laid out Ann Miller, a Shubuta teenager, who staggered to her feet and outran the mob. Two marchers scrambled over a fence. Another hid in an outhouse.[81]

Killingsworth, who towered above the fleeing teenagers, caught the brunt of the attack. The reverend saw dozens of whites coming at him "like a flying wedge," and then felt the first of many blows land on his head. He had been a thorn in the side of local lawmen for several years, and few missed their chance to take a swing at him. A highway patrolman clubbed him so hard with a baton that it broke in half. The blow left a gash, as the doctor's report later stated, "deep and gaping with skull bone exposed." A black bystander put it more bluntly—"he looked like a butchered hog." The mob kicked him in the ribs and stomped on his back.[82]

Patricia James, a Meridian teenager whom Gail Falk had sent to cover the march for the *Southern Courier*, snapped shots of the beatings until Shubuta's town marshal knocked the camera from her hands. When James stooped to pull the film roll from the smashed camera, a highway patrolman smacked her arm with his billy club. With her other hand, she flipped open her notepad and started scribbling furiously. The patrolmen jabbed her in the ribs and snatched the pad. "I'm not scared of you," she shot back. When a white man in plainclothes started beating her with a club, James finally fled the scene.[83]

Like James, the notepad-wielding lawyers were prime targets. As they followed the mob into the vacant lot, patrolmen snatched their pads. A red-haired teenager laid out Jack Joyce with a roundhouse punch and pounced on him. Someone hit Joe Gelb in the face with a club, and a gang of men rained blows and kicks on him as he crawled away. When he scrambled to his feet, someone grabbed him by his jacket collar. Gelb slipped free of his suit jacket and ran toward a patrolman. "They want to kill me," he sputtered. The patrolman pointed toward "Niggertown," and told him to start running.[84]

Joyce stumbled into Barlow's, a black-owned greasy spoon across the vacant lot from Eucutta Street. Several marchers, including an unscathed Sumrall, were hiding inside. Through the café window, a black teenager spotted a lingering crowd of whites still "in a vicious mood." A gauntlet of young toughs taunted the marchers to come out, Sumrall remembered, like a "Soul Train line" of buzz cuts and axe handles. After a few minutes, Sheriff Riley entered the café. "I'll get you out so you won't be killed," he announced dryly, and Sumrall, Joyce, and two Quitman marchers piled into his patrol car.[85]

By the time the sheriff dropped them off at the McRee Hotel, word of the free-for-all had spread to Quitman. A few black teenagers milled around the building, while a few carloads of whites circled menacingly. A white Chevy sedan roared to a halt across the street, and two white teenagers stepped out. One carried a billy club, and the other brandished a pair of brass knuckles. John Brown, one of the marchers who had ridden back to Quitman with Sumrall, chucked a bottle in their direction. The boys jumped back in the car and, spotting town marshal Billy Kemp at the Dixie Gas Station, headed over to report the incident. Five minutes later, Kemp and two deputy sheriffs converged on the McRee Hotel. Kemp asked who had thrown the bottle. Jimana Sumrall, drawn from her stoop by the commotion next door, stepped between the policemen and the small crowd of black teenagers. "Why is it you always see what we do," she asked, "but never see what the white boys do?"[86]

"When I said this," Jimana Sumrall testified later, "[Deputy James] Parker told me to shut my mouth and slapped me. After he slapped me, I hit him with my fist." When the deputy raised his billy club to strike her, John Otis punched him. As Parker and Sumrall scuffled, Deputy C. H. Culpepper reached for his blackjack. "The next thing I knew," Mrs. Sumrall remembered, "Culpepper was hitting me on the head, and I was fighting back at him as hard as I could." If she could have reached a blunt object, she later told the FBI, she would have used that too. Even without a weapon, mother and son did six stiches worth of damage to the deputy's chin. "She stated she was not mad at anyone," the FBI agent noted, "except she felt she had a right to strike the officers after she was slapped." Otto Sumrall hurried over and pulled his wife away. Bleeding from her head and nose, she stumbled back to her house while the officers subdued her son. At gunpoint, the policemen loaded him into a patrol car. Culpepper walked over to the Sumrall's doorstep and called for his mother. "You come out. You're going, too."[87]

After locking up the Sumralls, Kemp and Parker went looking for Solomon Marshall—a bystander who had tried to snatch Deputy

Parker's billy club during the scuffle. They found him walking to the courthouse to inquire about charges against the others. "Get in the damn car," Parker snapped. Charged with assault, Marshall joined Brown and Sumrall in the cell block. The police charged Brown with "bottle throwing"—technically, malicious mischief—and held him on $100 bond. Sumrall faced a list of charges—profanity, resisting arrest, assault and battery.[88]

Mrs. Sumrall sat in the women's cell, charged with obstruction of justice and assault. A few hours later, her husband posted her $200 bond. "As we left," she remembered, "I did notice a large crowd of whites near the jail." Word had already reached the Jackson FBI office, where an agent advised that "a white mob...was forming around the Clarke County Jail." With the sundown and the crowd showing no signs of dispersing, the sheriff phoned the highway patrol. Around eleven o'clock, the police loaded Sumrall, Brown, and Marshall into a patrol car and drove them to Meridian. In decades past, newspapers would report that an inmate had been "transferred for safekeeping." Such transfers were an old antilynching tactic intended to deter mob violence and the outside condemnation that came with it. In Clarke County, local authorities had never bothered before, and they had the grim record to prove it. But they did that day. Sumrall and his friends spent the night in the Lauderdale County jail, the local authorities explained, "to assure their safety."[89]

CHAPTER SIX

THE *REAL* BATTLE FOR FREEDOM

Paul Johnson is my Shepard
I am in want.
He maketh me lie down on a empty stomach
He restoreth my doubt in the old faith
He leadeth me in the path of starvation for his Segregations
　sake
Yea though I walk through the Alley in Mississippi I am yet
　hungry as hell
I do fear evil for thou are against me though anointest my
　income with outcome
Surely poverty and hard living have followed me all the days of
　your administration.
But I shall live until I have nourishment to say freedom.
　　　　　—Warner Buxton, "The Negroe's Psalm" (1965)

"The real story of a demonstration," Gail Falk wrote after a return visit to Shubuta, "is what happens when it's over." The civil rights worker and *Southern Courier* reporter had catalogued the police harassment and economic reprisals that had preceded the violence on August 20. When she returned to Shubuta in September, an eerie quiet had settled over the town. White resentment had boiled over in a spate of beatings and arrests, but local authorities had other weapons at their disposal. Two letters, mailed in the wake of the disturbance, did more to undermine the local movement than mobs and billy clubs ever would.[1]

First, George Busby sent Allie Jones's boycott letter straight to Washington, where it landed on the desk of Sargent Shriver, head of the Office of Economic Opportunity (OEO) and President Johnson's top general in the War on Poverty. The mayor also funneled copies to Mississippi officials. The battle over the Child Development Group's refunding was nearing a crescendo, and the program's critics wanted all the ammunition they could get. Shubuta's black activists, Mississippi officials believed, had handed them a silver bullet. The letter itself announced that a newly formed "Planning and Improvement Committee" had called for the boycott, but the attached list of demands carried a different letterhead—"Shubuta Head Start Committee." For months, Mississippi politicians had accused CDGM workers of funneling Head Start resources into civil rights activity. The "Head Start" letterhead, they hoped, would be their smoking gun.[2]

Quitman mayor Edgar Harris had his own letter to mail. Local officials had settled on a strategy for getting rid of John Otis Sumrall, who had been a thorn in their side for months. After a scuffle with a police officer, the young activist had every reason to expect the authorities to throw the book at him. "It seemed to me," a visiting civil rights lawyer noted, "that the local law enforcement officers would like nothing better than to get something big on Sumrall." However, when they finally had that something—assault and battery on a police officer—they threw it out. Then Quitman's mayor contacted the local draft board. "It is my understanding that John Otis Sumrall is scheduled for induction into the Armed Services of the United States within the very near future," he wrote. As Quitman's police judge, the mayor offered to throw out the pending charge "upon the induction of this man into the service.... You are at liberty to take action accordingly as if this charge were already dismissed."[3]

In the span of a few years, a black family and a grassroots movement found themselves caught between two wars. Jimana Sumrall fought to keep the War on Poverty alive in Clarke County, and her son refused to fight in an overseas war he deemed unjust and hypocritical. While his mother and her colleagues faced off against hostile white politicians, John Otis Sumrall challenged the state's all-white draft boards in court.

Along with Reverend Killingsworth and Warner Buxton, the Sumralls argued that civil rights laws meant little as long as poverty and repression plagued Mississippi. Even as national attention drifted away from the civil rights movement toward other domestic and diplomatic controversies, rural people reminded the world that the black freedom struggle could not be separated from conflicts over Vietnam and the War on Poverty. Such talk made them militants and subversives in the eyes of Mississippi politicians, but these local people reminded the world that the *real* fight for freedom was far from finished.

THE END OF THE SECOND RECONSTRUCTION

No sooner had John Otis Sumrall made bail than he and Reverend Killingsworth filed an injunction in federal court. They demanded the right to march, with police protection, in the future. Stories of beatings in a backwater town hit the newswire, and the *New York Times* reported allegations that Mississippi policemen "broke up the march with billy clubs, fists, flailing feet, and the assistance of young white toughs." Mississippi authorities responded with a carefully worded denial. District Attorney George Warner, who had driven down for the August 20 demonstration, claimed that "not one soul was hit by anybody on the main street of Shubuta." The qualification—*on the main street*—mattered, since the police deliberately forced the marchers off that street and into a vacant lot before turning the mob loose (fig. 6.1). "Any marchers attacked or complaining of being attacked," a state investigator concluded, "had apparently gone to areas out of sight of the officers present."[4]

Local white authorities did more than deny. They launched a counterattack. First, they sued to stop any demonstrations that might "interfere with businesses" on downtown streets. "Even under the Civil Rights Act," the district attorney argued, "merchants have some civil rights, too." Then officials scrambled to gather intelligence on the local Head Start program. Two days after the march, a Mississippi Department of Public Safety official forwarded a copy of the boycott letter and list of demands to the governor's office. Noting the "interrelation and open tie

FIGURE 6.1

Eucutta Street, Shubuta, 1966. After the beating of civil rights marchers
in August 1966, the defense team for the Mississippi Highway Patrol and
local law enforcement officers snapped photographs of the march route
for an injunction hearing. This photograph, facing west, shows Shubuta's
tiny town hall, with striped awning, on the left-hand side of the street.
A line of police forced marchers to turn down an alley, slightly farther up
the street and on the right-hand side, where marchers testified that most
of the attacks took place. Photograph M313-300, Charles Marx Papers,
Special Collections. Courtesy of William McCain Library and Archives,
University of Southern Mississippi.

with CDGM," the investigator pointed out that the boycott planners
shared letterhead and a post office address with the local Head Start
committee. A week after filing an injunction against Mississippi authorities, the tables turned on the marchers. "Is Great Society money financing
racial agitation in this small Clarke County town?" the *Meridian Star*
announced, "Local officials say it is." Even the *New York Times* changed
its tune—"Poverty Unit's Link to Boycott Studied."[5]

The "study" was in fact a smear campaign, carried out by Sovereignty Commission investigators with enthusiastic assistance from local authorities. Black townspeople spotted Mayor Busby snapping pictures of Allie Jones's home and both Head Start centers. Local police stepped up surveillance and harassment of the chairwoman as well. Before the boycott, police had arrested Jones's houseguests for disturbing the peace, reckless driving, and "using profanity." After the boycott and marches, local authorities swore out affidavits that claimed visitors to the Jones home had engaged in sex trafficking and attempted murder. Even the deputy town marshal's wife got involved, using binoculars to spy on the Head Start centers from her kitchen window.[6]

By the time a Sovereignty Commission investigator arrived, local whites had done the bulk of the work for him. L. E. Cole simply cataloged their charges against Head Start and collected statements from black "informants" lined up by local officials. The Sovereignty Commission had long relied on counterintelligence from black Mississippians, many of them public employees or others dependent on the state's good graces. In Shubuta, black informants proved particularly vulnerable to white coercion. All four received checks through the county welfare office. Two were disabled. A crippled World War II veteran who supported five children scribbled out a statement that white civil rights workers had threatened to burn down his house if he did not support the boycott. Mamie and Lester McFarland gave similar statements, but the father of eleven betrayed an ulterior motive. "I have been pronounced totally disabled by doctors," he noted, "and I can't lose my welfare." Only one informant had any direct connection to Head Start. Mamie Heard, who supplemented her county welfare checks with a job in the Head Start kitchen, claimed that Jones and other CDGM leaders demanded kickbacks from employees and held boycott planning meetings during the school day.[7]

Like most Sovereignty Commission investigations, the Shubuta probe relied heavily on rumors and innuendo. As in many anti-civil-rights investigations, those allegations revolved around sex. Civil rights workers had reported that both white Head Start volunteers had fled town in response to white harassment and threats. However, the investigator claimed that a black man had run Fred Mittleman out of town after he caught him "loving on his daughter." Through her binoculars, the deputy marshal's wife claimed that she spotted another white volunteer "kissing and feeling around all over a Negro girl inside the church." Local lawmen alleged that both men "would kiss and hug on the children" in their classes, and the town's unpaid deputy marshal reported that Head Start workers taught the children sexually suggestive songs and exposed themselves in public. Shortly before the boycott started, the deputy claimed, a Head Start worker had taunted him by pulling up her dress and warning that the marchers would be "moaning and groaning" once they reached the town hall.[8]

Whites played up Head Start workers' "immorality," but they downplayed the impact of the boycott. Some quietly admitted that local grocers were struggling and that a dry-cleaning business almost closed. Nevertheless, white officials refused to acknowledge that anyone other than Head Start workers had participated voluntarily. "There is no actual boycott by most of the Negro citizens of Shubuta," the Sovereignty Commission investigator concluded. "The average Negro does not do much shopping in town because they are afraid of these people and the consequences."[9]

Gail Falk attributed the faltering boycott to a white "counter-attack." The bank had stopped cashing CDGM checks, she reported, and most Head Start workers were "now very cool towards anything that sounds like civil rights. They are afraid Busby's attacks will destroy any hopes for CDGM being re-funded." The federal grant would expire in mid-September, and neither the group's supporters nor opponents believed the boycott would survive without that leverage. "All local Negroes are buying as usual," the Sovereignty Commission reported in late September. "Since Head Start has no money to buy with, things are back to normal again."[10]

As they had the previous summer, Head Start workers in Clarke County kept school running after federal funds ran out. With food donated from local people and students transported by volunteers, the Shubuta centers stayed open through September. Allie Jones promised that funds would arrive soon, but the political tide had turned hard against the Child Development Group. Mississippi politicians had been flaying the agency in the media and lobbying the OEO to defund it since before the first Head Start centers had even opened. After the June Meredith March, and the subsequent national obsession with "Black Power," charges that CDGM harbored and supported "subversive" civil rights activity further eroded support for Lyndon Johnson's War on Poverty. Throughout the summer, Mississippi politicians had publicized charges that Head Start workers had provided transportation, food, and meeting space to participants in the March against Fear. Even worse, CDGM critics alleged, "Black Power" posters were popping up in Head Start centers across the state.[11]

In the eyes of CDGM's enemies, the Shubuta boycott capped off a summer of federally funded subversion. Nationally, conservative critics seized on the provocative allegations to settle their own scores with the Office of Economic Opportunity. Shirley Scheibla, a Washington-based financial journalist who specialized in War on Poverty exposés, published her "Story of the Child Development Group of Mississippi" just days after the Sovereignty Commission submitted its Shubuta report. Scheibla led with the story of the "militant civil rights leader" Allie Jones, whose Head Start committee had used CDGM funds "to finance civil rights violence." With claims lifted straight from the Sovereignty Commission investigation, Scheibla embellished local officials' charges against Jones and her allies. "The Shubuta classes are just one example of scandalous Head Start operations...by the Child Development Group of Mississippi," Scheibla claimed, "an unincorporated organization controlled by leftist militant civil rights workers." The journalist even reprinted verbatim the police affidavits against Jones, and concluded with a damning rhetorical question: "Who wants Head Start money to be used to incite riots?"[12]

The day after Scheibla's article ran in *Barron's*, a sister publication of the *Wall Street Journal*, Mississippi congressman John Bell Williams read excerpts from the floor of the House of Representatives. He presented the hit piece as proof of the Child Development Group's ties to "the militant black power movement." Scheibla's revelations, he announced, were "extremely timely this week when we are being asked to authorize $1.750 billion to continue the poverty program." Williams, Mississippi's most outspoken segregationist congressman and an aspiring gubernatorial candidate, alleged that civil rights activists had used antipoverty dollars to incite racial turmoil. The "scandalous situation" in Shubuta, Williams declared, proved that federal antipoverty programs should be run "by responsible local citizens rather than irresponsible outside elements." Williams's tirade previewed the anticipated CDGM showdown in the Senate. Noting that Shubuta's mayor had been "passing ammunition" to his congressional delegation, a black Capitol Hill correspondent predicted that Stennis would "stage a fight" either before his Subcommittee on Appropriations or on the Senate floor itself.[13]

The OEO had no desire to cave to Mississippi segregationists. Nevertheless, months of attacks had transformed the Child Development Group from the agency's star program into a political liability. CDGM had been an end run around the state's white supremacist officials; now War on Poverty officials scrambled to create an alternative agency in order to save Head Start in Mississippi. "Either we shut it down," Sargent Shriver reasoned, "or we start a new organization" to run the preschool program. Anticipating a politically damaging showdown on Capitol Hill, Shriver called moderate white newspaperman Hodding Carter III and state NAACP president Aaron Henry to Washington. "I need somebody to get my ass out of this sling," Shriver reportedly told them. He had to "dump" CDGM, and he appealed to Mississippi moderates to create a rival agency that could administer the Head Start grants in the state. Carter recruited two fellow white moderates, Delta landowner Leroy Percy and Yazoo City industrialist Owen Cooper, to charter Mississippi Action for Progress, Inc. (MAP). Governor Johnson signed MAP into existence with no press coverage. By the time the agency's existence leaked to the press over two weeks later, MAP had already submitted its grant application to OEO.[14]

Federal officials had already rejected the Child Development Group's ambitious request for $41 million, which would have expanded Head Start to serve thirty thousand children. Instead, OEO had offered a quarter of that amount to maintain the centers already in operation.

At a jam-packed August meeting at Jackson's Masonic Temple, CDGM workers and supporters reluctantly whittled down their grant to just over $20 million. Many of the two thousand attendees—the largest gathering at the Masonic Temple since Medgar Evers's 1963 funeral— had not come to compromise. "I'm asking for the whole thing," Jimana Sumrall declared. "It's nothing but taxes you've paid over the years and ain't got nothing back for." The crowd roared approval. Nonetheless, the delegates ultimately jettisoned three-year-olds from the program and scaled back their expansion plans in order to cut their budget in half. Federal poverty workers in Mississippi warned that ditching the Child Development Group could spark a "complete revolt" against OEO and any rival Head Start agencies.[15]

After news of MAP's founding leaked to the press, an even larger crowd converged on Jackson to "save" CDGM. MAP board members ignored invitations to attend. A flier for the meeting warned that if OEO transferred control of Head Start to the new agency, "we may as well get ready for the third era of slavery. The structure is set. We have the plantation owner, the field overseer, the house nigger, and the field niggers. And we ain't gonna get no freedom—i.e. a right and means to determine our own lives, and be productive, creative, and economically secure human beings." The pro-CDGM crowd, three thousand strong, showed how much support the agency enjoyed among poor black Mississippians. The agency had also provided a political and economic anchor for rural blacks, and supporters perceived an impending "takeover" of Head Start as an attempt to put them back in their place. "Around CDGM" Gail Falk wrote after the meeting, "people are talking about the end of the second reconstruction—saying the MAP board represents the same union of big business, plantation interests and middle class Negroes that defeated reconstruction the first time around."[16]

Mississippi politicians made their own Reconstruction analogies. Three days after the rally, when OEO awarded $3 million to MAP, Governor Johnson danced on what appeared to be CDGM's grave. "Not since the days when Mississippi was occupied by scalawags after the War Between the States have we been subjected to such an obnoxious group as those who operated the Child Development Group of Mississippi," the governor announced. Invoking the sexual and economic anxieties that boiled over in Shubuta, the governor claimed that CDGM "promoted immorality and used its vast supply of taxpayers' money in agitation in the counties, civil right activities and boycotts." Glossing over the widespread distrust of federal programs among SNCC and CORE militants, Johnson claimed that CDGM "coined 'black power'" and promoted the ideology with federal funds.[17]

Office of Economic Opportunity officials took their jabs as well and promoted MAP as a professional, integrated, and apolitical alternative to the Child Development Group. "In most centers," an OEO attorney announced, "CDGM amounts at best to custodial day-care by persons untrained and unskilled, under conditions of inadequate facilities." Not only were its poor black employees untrained, he continued, they were untrainable. Justifying OEO's abandonment of the agency, the spokesman declared that Child Development Group's employees "have shown themselves unable to benefit either from experience or assistance."[18]

The charge that CDGM was a "segregated" preschool program galled local organizers who had tried to recruit white board members, employees, and children. Months before he spurned the boycotters' demands, Mayor Busby had refused to join the local Head Start committee or offer them classroom space. As in CDGM counties across the state, Clarke County organizers canvassed poor whites. Some feared sending their children to schools that might be bombed, and others chaffed at the prospects of mingling with black students and teachers. Killingsworth recalled a recruiting visit to a poor white family's "rundown" cabin. "It's true I need a job," a young woman told him, "but I'd starve before I'd work with old niggers."[19]

Given the widespread hostility to integrated antipoverty programs, dissenters at the Office of Economic Opportunity doubted the wisdom of MAP's reliance on "moderate" white leadership. "In Mississippi," an OEO official and Child Development Group supporter reported, "counties exist that do not have moderate whites." In rural areas where membership in the arch-segregationist Citizens' Council made one a *moderate*, another OEO official reported, county poverty boards "do not offer the Negroes of Mississippi anything more than paternalism at best." Furthermore, antipoverty workers in Mississippi questioned the OEO's obsession with placating hostile white critics. Washington saw MAP as an agency that would "rock the political boat the least," but observers on the ground warned that "the Negro reaction to such a decision would in the long run rock the boat quite a bit more." The Child Development Group's most vocal defenders agreed. The Delta Ministry—the agency that had first introduced John Otis Sumrall and Clarke County to CDGM—warned, "The arbitrary decision to kill off the Child Development Group of Mississippi and replace it with a hand-picked board is producing a wave of bitterness and cynicism among the poor people of Mississippi." The agency's "unforgiveable crime," the Delta Ministry argued, was taking seriously "the Constitutional idea of representative democracy" and OEO's stated goal of "maximum feasible participation" by poor people in the War on Poverty. "When you destroy hope, you are sowing the seeds of bitterness and hatred," the Delta Ministry concluded. "And the men of power are doing that; they are trampling a dream."[20]

War on Poverty officials needed look no further than Clarke County to see these predictions play out. The "moderate" tapped to head the county MAP board was George Busby, the mayor known for his prominent role in the anti-CDGM propaganda campaign. His primary qualification, indeed his most moderate credential, was his willingness to serve on the board at all. But the Shubuta mayor's flat refusal to cooperate with any "CDGM people" pointed to another consequence of MAP's creation—women who had quit low-paying jobs to work for Head Start now faced a new form of economic retaliation. Unqualified for teaching positions in the new MAP centers and black-listed by white employers, they found themselves unemployed with few options, federal or otherwise. In other counties, a CDGM supporter noted, former employees were making plans to flee the state "for economic reasons." In Clarke County, Head Start workers decided to stand and fight.[21]

The Great Toy Robbery

After MAP put George Busby in charge of Head Start, the Shubuta mayor went looking for Jesse Allen. He had heard the man was working on a building.

Since the Shubuta Head Start opened the previous spring, Allen had ferried preschoolers from the rural St. Mary community into town. He grew tired of the daily fifty-five-mile round trip, and saw that the crowded in-town centers could not keep up with the demand. So with funds cobbled together from neighbors, and a white merchant willing to sell them materials on three years credit, Allen built a ten-room cinder block school for St. Mary. Community members cleared the land, laid the foundation, and put up the walls. Unlike the makeshift Head Start centers in Shubuta, the new building featured indoor plumbing, two toilets, and a kitchen. By the time the Office of Economic Opportunity's funding decision came down, the St. Mary center lacked only a roof and a well. Jesse Allen, who had financed and built the center without a dime of taxpayer funds, forged ahead with roofing plans.[22]

Child Development Group supporters pointed to St. Mary as an example of the enthusiasm and initiative that the Head Start agency had sparked. The agency's defenders noted that by the time the Head Start grant ran out, nearly fifty such centers had sprung up across Mississippi with "no Federal funding which have nonetheless been christened 'CDGM' centers by the community." When organizers lobbied for increased appropriations, they pointed to the unfunded centers popping up every week across the state. When the Office of Economic Opportunity cut off funds in October, sympathetic journalists published pictures of Jesse Allen and local children standing in front of the roofless, bare-block St. Mary center. Overnight, the monument to grassroots initiative became a concrete-block memorial.[23]

The St. Mary center also became, to quote a *Washington Post* reporter, "a strategic fort in the final skirmishes of Mississippi's epic battle over anti-poverty Headstart school funds." Mayor Busby offered to rent the building for the new Mississippi Action for Progress preschool, but he offered credit instead of cash. "He said I'd have to spend the rent money in Shubuta," Allen recalled, "and I told him I'd spend it where I wanted to." Busby also demanded that any building rented by MAP could be used only for Head Start. "He said he'd have to have the keys seven days a week," Allen remembered, "and I told him it wouldn't be a community center then."[24]

Busby's demands, clearly intended to prevent Head Start workers from exerting economic pressure on merchants or sheltering "agitators," only increased black distrust of MAP. The agency's secrecy and un-willingness to work with former Child Development Group employees and supporters deepened the divide. Just weeks after the Office of Economic Opportunity transferred its Head Start funding to the new agency, federal officials in Mississippi blamed MAP's disorganization and "lack-luster" progress on its apparent disdain for the dispossessed CDGM. "This attitude—or its image," an OEO staffer advised, "will hardly dispel the fears of those vocal and organized poor who tasted the heady wine of 'running their own show.'"[25]

From the moment they learned of MAP, Clarke County's Head Start workers feared for the worst. "The first we knew about MAP, we read in the paper," Child Development Group organizer Garlee Johnson recalled. "We thought, oops! There we go, back to the cotton patch!" MAP's lack of transparency disturbed CDGM workers, and the composition of the local board angered them even more. Mayor Busby had tapped two more whites—the school superintendent and the county welfare agent—as well as three black professionals to ad-minister the local Head Start program. CDGM workers dismissed the black board members—a minister and two high school principals—as "Uncle Toms." The same men had ignored invitations to join the Child Development Group advisory boards, a local organizer complained, or "put up the white civil rights kids" and Head Start volunteers. Busby's appointment as chairman only heightened the distrust. "MAP people, before this, I don't say they were Klansmen," a local CDGM worker claimed, "but I say they sat silent and *watched* the Klansmen."[26]

In Washington, War on Poverty officials claimed that Mississippi Action for Progress would honor the precedent of electing local leader-ship and including the poor in decision making. Unlike the Child

Development Group, which placed its operations largely in the hands of everyday people, MAP aimed to strike a balance between "skilled" professionals and the "unskilled" poor. But in former CDGM counties like Clarke, where white officials handpicked their boards and refused to hold elections for poor representation, MAP staffers worried the entire Head Start program would "be junked" for lack of participation. When Busby finally called a meeting at Quitman's black high school, the MAP director drove over from Jackson to referee. When fifty CDGM supporters showed up, the school's principal—one of Busby's appointees—shuffled them into the school library and disappeared into a closed-door meeting. They heard plenty of shouting, but no one emerged for three hours. Busby, who claimed he had "picked the three best Negroes in the county" and did not have to "fool around with elections," refused to speak with the CDGM delegation. "If I have to work with those people," he threatened, "I'll quit."[27]

The next day, Busby's wife phoned the Jackson MAP office to report that "known Communists" had attempted to hijack the board meeting. She also castigated the black principal, who had run interference between CDGM supporters and white board members, for "talking to FDP and CDGM radicals." The situation in Clarke was so volatile that MAP's director returned two days later to preside over the election of an "advisory board" of local poor people. MAP believed its balance of elite leadership and poor involvement would increase Head Start's access to community resources and "bring the poor into the mainstream of the county." As MAP's director argued, "If they stay back in the bushes, they will never get anywhere." This top-down approach worked quite well in "hard-core counties," where the poor had never been invited to participate in anything. But in CDGM strongholds like Clarke, where the poor had led their own programs for two years, locals dismissed MAP's advisory board as token representation. "Truth is, CDGM *little* people had more information and federal know-how than MAP *leadership* people," a Head Start veteran argued. In MAP's world, she argued, the inexperienced but educated elites would "rule the roost." As for the "unskilled" former teachers and trainees, she argued, "we'll say *yassir*, obey the dictates, and wipes the babies' bottoms."[28]

The election meeting revealed that Child Development Group supporters were hardly ready to roll over. They did not want to hold elections. They did not want MAP. Black MAP board members announced they had "finalized" plans for two centers and 105 students—a fraction of the number previously served by CDGM. An elderly woman in a green gingham dress spoke up. "All of us black folks need this program. And you're goin' to pick up my child and leave his child at home," she said. "I would tell the highest man in the United States—I just don't think it's fair and I don't like it." When MAP officials asked for nominations for representatives from various sections of the county, CDGM backers walked out.[29]

By December, the political fallout from the MAP "takeover" forced the Office of Economic Opportunity to partially re-fund the Child Development Group in select counties. The $8 million grant was the largest yet, but Clarke and four other former CDGM counties were excluded so as not to create competition for MAP. Undaunted, CDGM workers in Clarke kept their centers open. A MAP organizer complained that the county's CDGM–civil rights coalition hijacked her meetings. Allie Jones "took the floor saying that MAP wasn't any good," she reported, and Reverend Killingsworth denounced MAP supporters as "Uncle Toms." When she asked for volunteers to recruit employees and students, Warner Buxton appealed instead for delegates to attend a grant-writing workshop in Jackson. If the federal government refused to fund CDGM in Clarke and other MAP counties, then the existing centers would lobby philanthropists. In the meantime, they would stay open on a volunteer basis.[30]

By the winter, the Child Development Group had more centers open than when its federal grant expired. When Head Start could no longer pay the rent at Pearlie Grove Baptist Church, Jimana Sumrall convinced her pastor at the nearby Church of God to host the program. In addition to the St. Mary center, two other communities had organized preschool programs that were not part of the original CDGM grant. Some centers closed sporadically, and others scaled back their hours and meal plans, but the former CDGM workers showed no signs of giving in to MAP. "They got the money," a CDGM stalwart boasted, "but we got the children."[31]

Like Jesse Allen's cinder-block community center, Clarke County's revolt against MAP attracted outside attention. As former CDGM centers struggled to stay open through the winter, stockpiles of school supplies sat unused in a warehouse. On the cover of *Jet*, above a photograph of Massachusetts Republican Edward Brooke, the first black United States senator elected since Reconstruction, a headline announced, "Headstart Agency Takes Toys Back from Negro Kids in Mississippi." Full-page spreads depicted unopened school supplies and tricycles piled head high. A young girl stared longingly at the unused toys through a cracked warehouse door, while preschoolers in Clarke County made do with trains made of milk cartoons and tambourines fashioned out of Prince Albert tobacco cans. Amid the images of the "Great Toy Robbery," *Jet* printed a shot of Jimana Sumrall sifting through receipts in the CDGM office. The bills were piling up, but she showed no signs of backing down. "We don't want MAP here," she said. She had 167 children in Quitman's defunded CDGM program, far more than MAP had recruited to its lone center in the county. "If they get one of my children, I'll go right up there in my car and take him out by his hand," she warned. "I'll go to jail before I give them to MAP."[32]

I Would Be Just Like the KKK over There

Jimana Sumrall's trip to jail, in the aftermath of the August 20 march in Shubuta, lasted only a few hours. Perhaps local authorities wanted to avoid a courtroom confrontation or to avoid defending publicly the practice of slapping black women. Even many local whites "didn't like that," her son remembered. "Especially for no reason at all." Local authorities likely reasoned that locking up a black mother of twelve was hardly worth the trouble. With the Child Development Group defunded and her Quitman center fighting for its life, Jimana Sumrall seemed a neutralized threat. Her son was a different story. Although he too did not face any significant jail time for his role in the scuffle with local deputies, the authorities had a different plan for him. They were anxious to send him off to the front lines of another war.[33]

To white officials' dismay, Sumrall's rap sheet kept getting in the way. "Sumrall always manages to get himself arrested on a misdemeanor charge just about the time he is due to be inducted into the army," a Sovereignty Commission investigator complained. Selective Service officials had twice ordered Sumrall to report for induction, and both times they rejected him due to pending charges stemming from civil rights activity. "The Quitman officials have been in touch for months with their local draft board and with Col. Sanders, Recruiting Officer in Jackson," the Sovereignty Commission investigator reported, "in an effort to get this man out of Quitman and in the service." When authorities locked up Sumrall after the August 20 march, local authorities decided to wipe the slate clean as quickly as possible.[34]

Mississippi officials knew they could have a fight on their hands. In addition to his being "a militant Negro...who publicly advocates Black Power," state investigators noted that Sumrall "is said to be against the draft." They were right. As soon as he received his induction notice, Sumrall filed suit against Mississippi governor Paul Johnson and local, state, and national Selective Service officials. The suit accused Mississippi officials of conspiring "to terminate his civil rights activities." Sumrall's attorneys, provided by the Lawyers' Committee for Civil Rights under the Law, argued that Selective Service officials had intervened to have him drafted out of turn, despite a criminal record that "would ordinarily disqualify him from induction." But the Sumrall suit had a higher objective—to protest white Mississippians' total control of the Selective Service system. A few southern states had already taken steps to preempt such criticisms by appointing a handful of blacks or quietly removing racial extremists from draft boards. In 1966, for example, Louisiana officials removed the chairman of a Baton Rouge draft board because he was also the Grand Dragon of the state's Ku Klux Klan. By making notable replacements and token appointments, officials in other southern states hoped to avoid anti draft spectacles.[35]

With characteristic defiance, Mississippi's draft boards remained lily white. Since blacks had been "purposely and systematically excluded" from the process, Sumrall's lawyers requested that the federal courts suspend induction of black Mississippians until state officials granted them proportional representation on local draft boards. All-white draft boards, like all-white juries, became yet another weapon to wield against racial agitators. In southwest Mississippi, a local draft board had targeted the twenty-four-year-old Wilkinson County NAACP president James Joliff. Despite the fact that the young man struggled with epilepsy, the local draft board reclassified Joliff from 4-F—unfit for military service—to immediate eligibility. He was nowhere near fit for active duty. After suffering seizures during basic training, Joliff spent a month recuperating in a hospital before the military released him.[36]

Before the first black bodies started returning home, civil rights activists questioned American involvement in Vietnam. John D. Shaw, one of the first black Mississippians killed in Vietnam, had participated in demonstrations in his hometown of McComb—an early hotbed of civil rights protest in the southwestern corner of the state. Four years later, after Shaw was killed in action, McComb civil rights workers distributed leaflets that listed "five reasons why Negroes should not be in any war fighting for America." The anonymous manifesto urged black youth to refuse induction, black servicemen to stage hunger strikes, and black mothers to "encourage their sons not to go." In January 1966, after an Alabama gas station attendant murdered navy veteran and civil rights activist Sammy Younge for attempting to use a whites-only bathroom, the Student Nonviolent Coordinating Committee released an antiwar statement that linked the black freedom movement with the anticolonial struggle, equated racist repression in the South with American military actions against nonwhites, and advocated draft resistance. Instead of sending black men to Southeast Asia, the SNCC statement proposed "a draft for the Freedom fight in the United States."[37]

In Clarke County, local activists echoed these sentiments. "When I think of the Movement, I associate the Movement—yes—with the war in Vietnam," Warner Buxton told a northern visitor, "I mean, all this must go hand-in-hand." Buxton wondered why blacks should fight abroad "for freedom," when back home "there's a good chance that we could walk into a white café and get our head cut off." Buxton claimed that "everybody else down here" felt the same way. Grassroots organizations and local activists increasingly denounced the war as a distraction from problems at home. Patricia James, the teenage reporter attacked at the Shubuta marches, editorialized, "There is a war going on in the United States—a war against poverty.... The U.S. should just get the hell out of Viet Nam." Even before John Otis received his draft notice, Jimana Sumrall brought down the house at a "save CDGM" rally when she blasted the federal government along similar lines. "If they can spend $2 billion a day to fight a war in Viet Nam," she announced in a packed Jackson auditorium, "surely they can give you $41,000,000 to run schools for a year."[38]

White officials dismissed such rhetoric as a byproduct of summertime "invasions" by northern college students, but Mississippians black and white had their own reasons to resent the war effort. When US defense secretary Robert McNamara flew to Jackson for a rally and visits with state leaders, Reverend Killingsworth joined the integrated picket line outside the Mississippi Coliseum (fig. 6.2). McNamara's winter visit, which included a meal hosted by Senator Stennis, suggested that pro war patriotism might help smooth the White House's rocky relationship with Mississippi segregationists. Earlier that day, students from Millsaps College distributed antiwar pamphlets in white neighborhoods. Leaflets distributed by black protesters, the *Southern Courier* reported, "had an extra section which compared the bombing of Vietnamese children with the bombing of Negro children by racists." Outside the coliseum, Killingsworth paced solemnly with a sign: "Stennis Dinner A Toast to Racism & War-Making."[39]

John Otis Sumrall's exposure to northern college students did not predetermine his stance on Vietnam, but his involvement with civil rights organizing connected him to the antiwar ferment on campus. The young activist had visited college campuses across the Midwest to fund-raise and collect donations for the struggling movement back home. Speeches in Chicago, Minneapolis, and Madison paid off. Sumrall bought a used one-ton Chevy pickup, loaded it with food and clothing, and headed home. A few months later, as Sumrall fought his induction and antiwar protests broke out on each of those campuses, student activists called him back. At the University of Chicago, where Greg

FIGURE 6.2

Some of Clarke County's most prominent civil rights activists were also vocal critics of the war in Vietnam. While John Otis Sumrall awaited a verdict in his draft resistance case, Rev. J. C. Killingsworth and an integrated group of picketers protested US secretary of defense Robert McNamara's meeting with powerful Mississippi senator John C. Stennis in Jackson. Photograph 99-185-0-5-1-1-1ph, Mississippi State Sovereignty Commission Records. Courtesy of the Mississippi Department of Archives and History.

Kaslo—Clarke County's former COFO project director—went to school, students staged a three-day sit-in in the spring of 1966 to protest the administration's practice of disclosing class ranks to draft boards. The following semester, the "Students against the Rank" organized a draft resistance conference to coincide with a university-sponsored, reform-minded draft conference. While the university conference featured senators, congressmen, academics, and military experts, the "We Won't Go" meeting attracted two hundred of the country's most outspoken antiwar activists. As a radical pacifist later reported, the meeting "provided the opportunity for many attendees to see for the first time real live 'draft-dodgers,' as the papers call them." It also brought Mississippi's most outspoken resister back to Chicago.[40]

Sumrall's Chicago appearance dramatized the connections between the southern civil rights movement and student activism. However, his speech also revealed the gulf that separated his grassroots reality from campus rebellion. Sumrall, a rural organizer with a high school education, shared the stage with University of Chicago student activists, college professors, and full-time antiwar organizers. The only other scheduled black speaker, Mississippi-born Baptist preacher and Southern Christian Leadership Conference lieutenant James Bevel, had coordinated the Selma voting rights campaign and the Chicago Open Housing movement for Martin Luther King, Jr. A seminary-trained pacifist, Bevel invoked theology, political philosophy, history, and Gandhian nonviolence. Antiwar arguments that focused on winnability, cost, or politics missed the point, Bevel argued. Vietnam represented more than a distraction from domestic problems or a betrayal by Lyndon Johnson—it was genocide, plain and simple. Draft resisters, Bevel thundered, should unite behind the message that "mass murder of people does not solve human problems."[41]

Bevel's speech lasted four times as long as the soft-spoken twenty-year-old from Quitman, but Sumrall's plain talk was no less revolutionary. "There are more black people now being inducted in the Armed Services in the South," he argued, "simply because they are now starting to take hold, to look up and fight for what is rightfully theirs. The white people there are afraid of this." Back home, he argued, civil rights opponents had many weapons at their disposal. When he dodged "their old method—the lynch rope," white supremacists turned to newer tactics. "If they can't shoot them or do something like that," Sumrall argued, "then they use the legal way and draft them into the Army." Back in Clarke County, the civil rights worker drove northern college students out to see the Hanging Bridge. In Chicago, he connected the legacy of lynching to the suppression of dissent. In a "soft and pleasant manner," the radical pacifist journal *Liberation* later reported, Sumrall placed Mississippi's all-white Selective Service system on a continuum of racist oppression: "When the lynch rope and other means of intimidation fail,...there is always the draft."[42]

Sumrall's comments also reflected the mounting disillusionment of Mississippi activists over three tumultuous summers. "In 1964, when the Mississippi Freedom Democratic Party was denied the seats to rightfully represent the whole people of Mississippi, not just a group of white folks, it was made clear to me that I am not a citizen of the United States," Sumrall said. "I don't have a country so I don't know of any reason to go over in Vietnam and fight." While the government claimed that its soldiers would bring freedom and democracy with them, Sumrall argued that America had exported its racial baggage. He had heard that white soldiers had formed Klan klaverns on military bases. "They got segregated restaurants and segregated bars over there also, you know," he argued. "Negroes walk into a place and then get kicked out, the same as it is over here."[43]

Fears of spreading racial conflict and repression resonated in Chicago, where civil rights activists faced off against white mobs and, increasingly, hostile authorities. As soon as Sumrall finished his speech, a conference organizer announced that Chicago police had raided the local SNCC secretary's apartment on a trumped-up narcotics charge. Once there, they showed more interest in Black Power pamphlets and posters than in dope. They confiscated "subversive literature" and jailed the activist on $1,500 bond. Two Chicago SNCC members took to the podium to read a prepared statement of support and pass the hat for bail money. Their antiwar remarks echoed and expanded the arguments of southern civil rights workers. The Chicago SNCC statement likened the killing of Vietnamese peasants to the murder of black activists and blasted the federal government's refusal to enforce civil rights laws with "power and sincerity." Since "elections in this country, in the North as well as the South, are not free," the statement continued, "we question...the ability, and even the desire, of the United States government to guarantee free elections abroad." SNCC dismissed the government's call to defend freedom abroad as "a hypocritical mask" that obscured the government's hostility toward national liberation movements that did not abide by the terms of American Cold War diplomacy.[44]

At the Chicago conference, neat distinctions—between Vietnam and civil rights, global and grassroots, North and South—blurred. Before heading home, Sumrall joined some white picketers outside a Chicago induction center. A white enlistee asked him why he opposed the war. "Because of the color of my skin," he answered. "I am going to stay here and fight the *real* battle for freedom." That theme—Freedom at Home—captured the imagination of Alice Lynd, an antiwar activist who recorded the conference and compiled draft resister testimonies for an antiwar anthology. When she sent Sumrall a transcript of his speech, he scribbled three pages of additional thoughts. "I'd much rather chance a jail sentence here than a possible death sentence, or even more [be] part of a machine that stomps out people lives," he wrote. "For me personally, I would be just like the KKK over there."[45]

Back in Mississippi, Sumrall informed Lynd, he hoped to start a "draft resistance league," but his primary focus remained on civil rights and antipoverty work. As his mother and her colleagues kept their Clarke County centers running without government funds, Sumrall ventured into neighboring counties. In previous summers, civil rights and Child Development Group activity had spilled over into neighboring Jasper County. Together, Clarke and Jasper formed a CDGM administrative area. A rural, black-majority county, Jasper had lagged behind Clarke in civil rights activity. However, when the Office of Economic Opportunity approved a new CDGM grant in late 1966, it re-funded the program in Jasper County and neighboring Smith County. For the first time, John Otis Sumrall went to work for the Child Development Group of Mississippi.[46]

When Sumrall headed west into Smith County, he felt like he was stepping back in time. CDGM provided no car, so he and a fellow organizer canvassed by foot and hitchhiked from community to community. Sumrall encountered locals frightened by the backlash against CDGM. "It has been confused with Civil Rights," Sumrall reported, "and people were afraid to participate." In an adjoining county, nightriders had torched a Head Start center and shot into the house of a white CDGM employee. Nevertheless, after a series of mass meetings, a coalition of eight communities organized two local centers. By April 1967, Smith County's Head Start centers were ready to open, and Sumrall remained on staff as a payroll clerk for the two-county area. A few weeks later, Mississippi officials ordered him to report to Jackson's Army Induction Center.[47]

On May 10, Sumrall refused to take the symbolic "step forward" that signified enlistment. Faced with a maximum jail sentence of five years and several thousand dollars in fines, Sumrall staged a press conference before returning home to await trial. Flanked by lawyers and visibly deflated by the day's events, Sumrall defended his decision. Reporters peppered Sumrall with questions about his "strong feelings against the war." He repeatedly returned to the problem of all-white draft boards. While he reiterated his desire "to get a lotta more people, especially Negroes, to … refuse induction," Sumrall conceded that his pending prosecution would make that nearly impossible. "As for organizing an anti-draft movement right now," he conceded, "I don't think I can." He would return home and go back to work for CDGM, he announced, and canvass for voter registration in his "spare time."[48]

As he awaited a criminal trial, Sumrall did just that. Despite calls from Mississippi politicians to suspend Sumrall, Sargent Shriver replied that he could keep his CDGM job until convicted of a crime. Sumrall's congressman, G. V. "Sonny" Montgomery, blasted the federal government for "condoning and rewarding Sumerall [sic] for refusing to be drafted in the United States Army." Along with Senators Stennis and Eastland, Montgomery called for his suspension and speedy prosecution. Sumrall's supporters and critics alike expected Judge Harold Cox to throw the book at a "black power" draft dodger. As Sumrall awaited trial, local activists entered a summer of discontent. If the previous summer's struggle made the local movement a symbol of grassroots protest and rural militancy, Clarke County reemerged a year later as a reminder of the poverty and repression that persisted after the marching stopped.[49]

I GUESS THAT'S WHAT THE WHITE POWER
STRUCTURE WANTS

On a stifling summer afternoon in 1967, Etha Mae Nelson welcomed a white reporter into her home. Nelson, her husband, and their ten children lived in a four-room frame house just a few miles north of Shubuta. They owned a refrigerator and a television, but no window fans. Four children slept in a double bed, and the rest slept on the floor to escape the summer heat. On a good week, Mr. Nelson could make sixty dollars cutting pulpwood. Mrs. Nelson worked three days a week as a housekeeper for a white family. She earned two dollars per day. With ten children aged two to sixteen, money disappeared quickly. The Nelsons could not send their children to the doctor, the mother explained, "because I didn't have the money and the doctor didn't want to credit them." With no mule to plow their garden plot—it "got killed" the previous winter—the Nelsons survived mostly on bread and grits. "We ain't starving," Mrs. Nelson admitted, "but the children ain't getting the right kind of food." The glow from a television set in the otherwise threadbare cabin provided a distraction from gnawing hunger. "Sometimes I get to looking at TV," Mrs Nelson explained, "[and] I quit thinking about it.... When I turn it off, my stomach goes back to growling." Days later, a smattering of newspapers nationwide carried journalist William Vaughn's dispatch from rural Mississippi: "When Family Is Hungry: 'We Watch Television.'"[50]

In Quitman, Vaughn encountered more stories of poverty, hunger, and repression. Sarah Price raised six children in a three-room house, and her husband earned $1.40 an hour at a local cotton gin. Doctors had declared Joe McLindon, thirty-two, "permanently disabled" due to asthma. To support their eight children, the McLindons drew sixty dollars a month in welfare. After McLindon's wife went to work for Quitman's independent Head Start center, the county welfare agent cut their payments in half. Local officials justified the cut because Mrs. McLindon "was employed," even though the defunded Child Development Group centers paid their workers sporadically. "If she quits," McLindon told the reporter, "they said they would raise it back."[51]

By the summer of 1967, the former CDGM centers were running on fumes. One of the last holdouts against the Mississippi Action for Progress "takeover," Clarke County Head Start workers remained defiant but weary. Early in 1967, the five former CDGM counties banded together to form the Friends of Children of Mississippi, Inc., a privately funded network of former Head Start centers. The new agency brought Greene County, just two counties south of Clarke, into the fold as well. With a grant from the Field Foundation and donations from northern allies, the Friends of Children preschools received enough funds to make it through the summer. For months, the centers had survived on community offerings, volunteer workers, and donated food. Through the colder months, the hot meals in the centers consisted mostly of soup and cornbread. "They get more here than they do at home where they only get cornbread," a Clarke County worker reasoned.[52]

Even with the Field Foundation's infusion of cash, the Friends of Children centers struggled to keep up. Quitman's MAP Head Start center enrolled only forty children, compared to several hundred enrolled in the rival Friends centers, but benefited from federal dollars and relatively cooperative whites. Mississippi officials had worked relentlessly to kill the Child Development Group, but the state welfare department requested that county officers make commodity foods available to MAP centers, state health officials urged doctors to participate in MAP clinics, and even some local newspapers ran MAP job ads and announcements. Meanwhile, Friends of Children centers supplemented their meager budget with produce from local gardens and proceeds from selling barbecue plates. In Clarke County, the MAP Head Start center operated out of a local school building—an arrangement that would have been unthinkable with CDGM. Whereas MAP spent fifty cents per day to feed each child, the Friends of Children centers could only afford to spend twenty.[53]

Journalists characterized the rivalry between the preschool programs as "a deep philosophical quarrel over how the poor should be involved in antipoverty projects." Mississippi's "poverty wars" also reflected a broader crisis over the federal government's efforts to extend economic opportunity to the margins. In April, four members of the Senate

FIGURE 6.3

Rev. J. C. Killingsworth testifies with Mississippi Freedom
Democratic Party leader Fannie Lou Hamer at a hearing
of the US Senate Subcommittee on Employment, Manpower, and
Poverty in Jackson, Mississippi. Testimony focused on hunger,
malnutrition, and the fate of antipoverty programs like Head Start.
April 10, 1967. Photograph by Jim Peppler, Courtesy of the Alabama
Department of Archives and History.

Subcommittee on Employment, Manpower, and Poverty—including
New York senators Robert F. Kennedy and Jacob Javits—traveled to
Mississippi to assess the War on Poverty's progress. Sitting alongside
fellow Mississippi Freedom Democratic Party and CDGM stalwarts
Fannie Lou Hamer and Unita Blackwell, Reverend Killingsworth testified that white manipulation and coercion had undercut the antipoverty program's effectiveness (fig. 6.3). The only panelist from a *former*
CDGM county, Killingsworth declared that he had helped organized
the Friends of Children "to continue to struggle against great odds...for
the kind of program that the local people can have a voice in." As
for MAP, he argued, "they go to county officials and to schools...and
bypass the poor people."[54]

The poor were not just struggling, the panelists argued. They were starving. Attorney Marian Wright, a CDGM executive board member and the first black woman admitted to the Mississippi Bar Association, testified that "the poverty program has done nothing to change the basic economic structure, which needs to be changed." She challenged the senators to venture into the countryside "and just look at the empty cupboards...and the number of people who are going around begging just to feed their children." To her surprise, the senators took her up on the invitation. On their headline-grabbing tour through the Mississippi Delta, the senators reeled at the deplorable conditions they observed. Kennedy declared Mississippi's rural poverty "a condemnation of all of us" and expressed disbelief that such conditions "could exist in a prosperous nation like ours." Following the tour, the Senate subcommittee called on the president to flood the state with food aid. In Mississippi, the senators "observed, firsthand, conditions of malnutrition and widespread hunger that can only be described as shocking, and which we believe constitute an emergency."[55]

Following the senators' tour, others descended on Mississippi to confirm these reports. In May, a medical team—including physicians from MIT, Harvard, and Yale—toured Clarke and five other counties. Four of the counties—Neshoba, Clarke, Wayne, and Greene—lay along the state's eastern border, and two—Leflore and Humphreys—lay in the heart of the Mississippi Delta. Sponsored by the Field Foundation, which had also supported the Friends preschools in those six counties, the doctors examined children cut off from the federally funded Head Start program. The physicians, several of whom had extensive field experience in the rural South, Appalachia, and developing nations, expressed horror to find black Mississippians living "under such primitive conditions that we found it hard to believe we were examining American children of the Twentieth Century." After touring preschools and rural homes in the six Friends counties, the doctors held a Capitol Hill press conference. "We do not want to quibble over words," they warned, "but 'malnutrition' is not quite what we found; the boys and girls we saw...are suffering from chronic hunger and disease and directly or indirectly they are dying from them—which is exactly what 'starvation' means."[56]

The focus on hunger and malnutrition revealed that many grassroots activists continued to broaden their conception of "civil rights" in the wake of landmark, yet limited, legislation. The Civil Rights Act of 1964 and the Voting Rights Act of 1965 took aim at racial discrimination and disenfranchisement but did little to address urgent issues of poverty and public health. Charges of starvation, first from black activists and then from distinguished physicians, dramatized both the ongoing repression faced by a politically mobilized poor and the unrelieved desperation of the nation's most vulnerable citizens. The word itself— *starvation*—sparked a political firestorm that spread from Mississippi to Washington. The Senate subcommittee convened a special summer hearing on the state's hunger crisis, and papers nationwide carried reports of "children starving" in Mississippi. The US surgeon general, the secretary of agriculture, and a smattering of congressional liberals descended on Mississippi to see for themselves. Like Bill Vaughn, who toured Clarke and the other six counties after the "starvation" story broke, journalists confirmed the desperate conditions with a flurry of on-the-ground exposés.[57]

Mississippi officials responded with characteristic defiance and coordinated denial. Governor Paul Johnson, who claimed in a television interview that "the nigra women I see are so fat they shine," enlisted the state health department, the all-white Mississippi Medical Association, and, as always, the Mississippi State Sovereignty Commission to discredit the "invaders." State officials dispatched a rival medical team of white Mississippi physicians to two of the counties named in the report, with orders to find "the worst conditions known to exist in the area and the most destitute persons living there." While the Mississippi doctors admitted that many of the children observed "were obviously receiving sub-optimal diets" and "suffering from various degrees of undernutrition," they concluded that "no cases of 'starvation' could be found." The team's report consisted largely of its interviews with local white welfare agents, who blamed black malnutrition on parental ignorance and irresponsibility. A member of the team traveled to Washington to testify at the Senate hunger hearings, but the Field Foundation physicians dismissed the rival report as a political stunt. White North Carolina physician

Raymond Wheeler, whose daughter was spending the summer volunteering in Clarke County, declared that the governor's team had "substantiated…the tragic conditions in which the Negro Mississippian lives…though I hope, with a greater sense of horror and indignation than they have permitted themselves to express."[58]

The doctors took a back seat to the politicians, who pounced on the hunger controversy to discredit the civil rights–antipoverty coalition. The president of the Mississippi Press Association offered a $500 reward to anyone who could prove "ONE single case where a Negro has starved to death because of persecution or his inability to secure food because of the white man." The Mississippi Republican Party, still struggling for a foothold in the Democrat-dominated state, seized the opportunity to prove it could defend the state's honor. In a pamphlet, *Genocide…Are They Deliberately Starving Negroes in Mississippi?*, the state GOP compiled denials of starvation from prominent citizens "as a public service" but also, as the Republicans admitted privately, for its "public relations value." Not to be outdone, Democratic senator Stennis accused the Field Foundation medical team of "gross libel and slander" and, in an act of pure political theater, introduced a bill to provide $10 million annually "to provide food and medical services to *any* individual in *any* state" to prevent death by starvation. When a few constituents cried foul at another bleeding-heart poverty bill, the senator explained the stunt had undercut "the unwarranted and unfair criticism" and "taken Mississippi out of the spotlight as a place where people are starving."[59]

The spotlight did shift the following week, when an all-white jury took just twenty-seven minutes to find John Otis Sumrall guilty. True to form, Judge Cox had stacked the deck against the defense team. Sumrall's lawyers had less than two weeks to prepare for trial, and the judge threatened to hold them in contempt if they requested a postponement. Sumrall's supporters decried the hypocrisy of the judge's haste. "We can't help wondering," the Freedom Information Service declared, "why Judge Cox has taken *3 years* to get to a trial for [Neshoba County lawmen] Rainey and Price and their friends for murdering three civil rights workers." During the trial, the judge refused to admit any discussion or evidence of segregated draft boards, and Clarke County officials made no secret of their desire to get Sumrall out of the area. As Quitman city attorney Tally Riddell admitted in court, he and his clients wished "to see him gone." Asked about dropping the charges stemming from Sumrall's brawl with the police, Quitman's mayor replied, "I didn't want any little old misdemeanor to keep him out of the service."[60]

Judge Cox sentenced Sumrall to five years in prison and a $2,500 fine. "His point for the maximum sentence," Sumrall later reported to his antiwar contacts, "was to set an example for future guys who refuse the draft." A fellow black draft resister from Jackson, ordered to report for trial the same day, "changed his mind" and told Judge Cox he was ready to enlist. Sumrall did not waver. Asked if he had anything to say, he replied, "People such as me don't have freedom as provided by the Constitution of the United States." The judge and jury, he added, had made up their minds before the trial even started. "You have a misconception of the law," Judge Cox shot back. "That's un-American. I'm shocked to hear somebody make a statement like that." Sumrall returned home, out on bond and awaiting appeal.[61]

The day after the trial, an NAACP-backed boycott rocked nearby Hattiesburg. "No negroes have ridden the buses," a Jackson paper reported, "and there were very few Negro shoppers in the heart of the business district." Eighteen months after a Klan firebombing claimed the life of Vernon Dahmer, a prosperous local farmer and civil rights supporter, Hattiesburg blacks boycotted after white officials ignored their demands—hire more black policemen, appoint a black school board member, employ black clerks in city offices and downtown stores, and improve streets and lights in black neighborhoods. Back in Shubuta, where blacks had boycotted in support of similar demands, Gail Falk found little enthusiasm for another round of protests. A year after the Shubuta marches, the federal courts finally granted an injunction. Although the judge ordered the local authorities to protect marchers, he limited protests to daytime hours, prohibited singing or chanting, and forbade any demonstrations in front of the town hall.[62]

Neither the protections nor the prohibitions mattered much by midsummer. "Residents said they aren't thinking of marching anytime soon," Falk reported. Neither Sumrall nor Killingsworth, the original march leaders, could provide much help. While Sumrall awaited the outcome of his appeal, the reverend packed boxes. The Methodist Church had reappointed him to a church in Hattiesburg, where he continued his civil rights activism and emerged as a key leader of the city's protest campaigns. Back in Clarke County, a Sovereignty Commission investigator reported that local authorities had "the racial problem" well in hand. The investigator stopped at Clarkco State Park, a facility integrated two summers before by Killingsworth, Sumrall, and local youth. He noticed a group of African Americans eating lunch "as far away from other picnickers...as possible." The park superintendent predicted that blacks would stay away from the swimming beach, where a young man had drowned the previous summer during a "wade-in" protest, "because of their unusual suspicion." In Quitman, Sheriff Riley attributed the calm to "the fact that the Methodist Church had moved J.C. Killingsworth, a negro agitator and civil rights troublemaker...and the fact that Sumrall had received such a stiff sentence and fine."[63]

Racial tension seemed to have subsided, though the highly publicized "poverty war" in Clarke County pitted whites against whites and blacks against blacks. Diehard segregationists criticized Busby and the white MAP board members for cooperating with Head Start, just as Child Development Group partisans lashed out at blacks who participated in the new program. When a black minister joined the MAP board, Garlee Johnson called him a "Judas" and tried to convince his congregation to stop paying his salary. While the Friends of Children kept the former CDGM centers open through the summer, Jimana Sumrall and her colleagues saw more and more neighbors defecting to their well-funded rivals. "I'm wondering what would've happened if the Negroes of Clarke County would've stood together, that worked with CDGM in 1965 and 66," a weary Sumrall lamented in September. "I wonder if MAP would still be here now." The bitterness of the Head Start feud brimmed over as Sumrall faced another shoestring winter session. "If MAP is that good, why is there so much under-cover, underhanded backbiting, stealing, cheating, lying, and deceiving," she asked. "I guess that's what the white power structure program wants and will do anything to get.... And our poor little weak-minded, money-hungry Negroes will be under their feet as long as they live."[64]

AMERICA IS ONE BIG LIE

As his case made its way through the federal appeals process, John Otis Sumrall did not exactly lie low. "I'm in the process of trying to organize a voters league," he reported in October 1967. A convicted draft dodger was no more welcome in Clarke County than a Black Power militant, and Sumrall encountered harassment and threats wherever he went. "I was in a pretty bad way in terms of local opinion...people calling me a coward," he remembered. "I couldn't stop to get gas without somebody pouncing on me." Still, Sumrall refused to back down. After one man called him a coward, Sumrall recalled, "I told him, courage and fear had nothing do with it....I got to sleep every night with the KKK riding around in my front yard. It's a principle." Sumrall kept in touch with his antiwar contacts, and asked them to publicize his case. "I cannot fight this unjust war, when Black People have a war here at home," he wrote to Alice Lynd. "I cannot fight for the American Way of Life. A life that denies freedom, and upholds racism, poverty, and death."[65]

Domestic turmoil seemed only to mount as Sumrall waited for the United States Supreme Court to hear his case. In November, one thousand young men turned in their draft cards to the Justice Department. The Conscientious Resistance mobilized professionals, academics, artists, and college students—most with exemptions—to inspire and support other resisters. "So far, however," the *Southern Courier* lamented, "it is still a Northern movement. No students or professors came forward on behalf of John Otis Sumrall." By year's end, rural Mississippi's most notorious draft resister had gone underground, where he avoided a federal dragnet for several years before serving time in a California prison.[66]

An overlapping but distinct wave of protest swept black colleges, as anger over Vietnam collided with ongoing protests against racial discrimination. In April 1967, after Howard University disciplined four students for heckling Selective Service director Lewis Hershey during a campus visit, protestors hanged effigies of the nation's top-ranking draft official and two administrators they deemed "Uncle Toms." The scene took Roy Wilkins, for one, back to the Hanging Bridge. The NAACP executive secretary had spent the better half of the decade clashing with other activists over protest tactics, Black Power, and Vietnam. In his syndicated column, Wilkins blasted the Howard protest as "a throwback to the mind and the methods of long-ago Shubuta" and warned that "blind black-ism is becoming a cult as arrogant as any white-ism." The veteran NAACP official wondered how "a people, hanged at Shubuta and elsewhere in the lynching era, permit themselves to be a part of a hanging."[67]

The following winter, after state troopers in Orangeburg, South Carolina, opened fire on student protesters on February 8, 1968, it seemed like a new wave of killing might break out. Three students, two from historically black South Carolina State College and one from a local high school, lay dead. White leaders blamed the riot on "black power advocates" like Cleveland Sellers, a Howard graduate and SNCC's state coordinator for South Carolina. One of the thirty-seven wounded in the Orangeburg Massacre, Sellers had defied the draft. Like Sumrall, he argued that all-white southern draft boards were railroading civil rights activists into military service. With the scapegoated Sellers locked in the state penitentiary under $50,000 bond, Roy Wilkins spoke to a packed house on campus. As he had so many times before, he invoked "a lot of dead way back yonder" and wondered when the killing would stop.[68]

In Mississippi, campus killings overtook Klan bombings as the top threat to black youth. In May 1967, white police fired into a group of protesters after two days of protests at Jackson State College. Ben Brown, a truck driver with a history of civil rights activism, died from multiple bullet wounds to his back and head. When administrators from nearby Tougaloo College tried to rein in student participation in the demonstrations that followed, a new wave of campus activism swept Mississippi's capital. From state NAACP officials to SNCC activists, the speakers at Brown's packed funeral lamented how little Mississippi had changed and how high the stakes remained. "We must organize around one thing," announced Mississippi Freedom Democratic Party leader Lawrence Guyot, "*survival*." Like the Orangeburg killings, Ben Brown's death reminded black activists, as historian John Dittmer noted, "that, whatever their ideological differences, they still faced a common enemy." And like Roy Wilkins, Shubuta's own Warner Buxton discovered that the road from the Hanging Bridge to a campus massacre was short indeed.[69]

Buxton arrived at historically black Jackson State College the fall following Ben Brown's murder. With the Clarke County movement crippled by state surveillance, poverty wars, and targeted campaigns against local leaders, Buxton decided to go back to school. While he dreamed of leaving Mississippi for Madison, Berkeley, or Cambridge, Buxton ended up in Jackson. Back home, the cerebral and easygoing Buxton lacked the flair and bravado of his friend Sumrall. In Mississippi's capital, he put his movement experience and militant politics to work on campus. By the spring of his junior year, he was a force to be reckoned with, and his classmates elected him student body president. Jackson State did not have a reputation as a "political" campus, but Buxton's election suggested the mood was changing. The student government page in the college yearbook reflected the shift. Draped in a dashiki and raising a fist, Buxton presided over a cabinet of suit-wearing future mayors, legislators, and congressmen.[70]

Shortly after Buxton's election, and just three days past the third anniversary of Ben Brown's death, Mississippi police killed two and wounded twelve outside a Jackson State dormitory. The May 15 shootings occurred just eleven days after National Guardsmen gunned down four antiwar demonstrators at Ohio's Kent State University. "The students weren't too pleased about the Cambodia situation," Buxton remembered, referring to the bombing campaign that sparked protests at Kent State and across the country. Three days after Kent State, five hundred Jackson State students turned out for a protest rally that Buxton helped to organize. "The students were appalled by Kent State, I'm sure, but I don't think they ever thought at the time that it would happen to them." However, after a small riot broke out a week later, with students and neighborhood kids throwing bottles and bricks at passing cars, highway patrolmen unloaded 140 rounds into a crowd outside Alexander Hall. Buxton, who had attempted to calm down the crowd, witnessed the shootings. When the thirty-second barrage of gunfire ended, a college junior and a high school senior lay dead.[71]

As Jackson State mourned Phillip Lafayette Gibbs and James Earl Green, congressmen, civil rights leaders, and federal officials poured into the city. Archsegregationist governor John Bell Williams, who vehemently defended the officers' actions and decried the "political vultures" descending on the campus, dispatched thirteen hundred National Guardsmen and patrolmen to monitor the four thousand mourners who packed the Masonic Temple. On campus, the twenty-six-year-old student body president-elect, in plain clothes and an open collar, escorted United States senators around a bullet-riddled dormitory. "Do you think it would be fair to describe this [as] a lynching," Washington civil rights attorney Joseph Rauh asked. "Buxton," reporters noted, "said yes."[72]

The Shubuta native, whose schoolteacher mother had crossed the Hanging Bridge each morning on her way to Liberty Hill schoolhouse, knew the ravages of racial hatred. In the wake of the Gibbs-Green killings, Buxton sat atop a powder keg. "I was one of the soldiers," he remembered, who "tried to keep down disturbances." The week following the killings, he helped resolve a tense standoff in front of Alexander Hall that allowed workers to remove physical evidence, with the proviso that the state building commission turn it over to the FBI (fig. 6.4). The bullhorn-wielding president-elect spent the better part of the next month attempting to channel student anger into a coordinated protest campaign.[73]

Just two weeks after the shootings, Buxton's Committee of Concerned Students and Citizens called for a boycott of Jackson's white-owned businesses. The manifesto demanded that city merchants hire one black employee for every white one, promote blacks to management positions, and contract with black wholesalers and tradesmen. In protest of white newspapers' coverage of the campus killings, the committee demanded that the publishers fire two openly white supremacist columnists, hire black reporters, and eliminate segregated newspaper sections. A broader set of "Goals and Objectives" included increased

FIGURE 6.4

Student body president-elect and Shubuta native Warner Buxton, holding megaphone, helps to negotiate between students holding vigil at the scene of the Jackson State shootings and Mississippi State Building Commission officials waiting to remove bullet-riddled windows and doors from Alexander Hall. Courtesy of Special Collections and University Archives, Henry T. Sampson Library, Jackson State University.

funding to the state's black public colleges, greater campus autonomy, police reform, and integration in city government offices and recreational facilities. Student protesters called for a citywide strike and a statewide "day of mourning," and they encouraged seniors not to wear robes to graduation but instead "march in clothes which are common to your environment and that will show your real economic status."[74]

When students returned for summer classes after a month-long campus shutdown, Buxton plastered campus with a call to action. The flier, entitled "Jackson State College: Community or Genocide?," Buxton urged unity and calculated defiance. "We only hope," he wrote, "that as a part of the bereaved family, you haven't forgotten the injustices served us, that caused your sudden departure, and you have returned ready to take care of business." The student body president called on students to "show the world that we are not satisfied with the racist political and social structure of this state....If you are not part of the *solution*, you are part of the *problem*."[75]

For the next few months, Buxton served as the face of the Jackson State student body at events across the country—at a Washington fundraiser hosted by Senator Ted Kennedy, alongside Kent State's student body president at a national lawyers' conference, and at a Jackson hearing convened by President Richard Nixon's Commission on Campus Unrest. Buxton's testimony before the commission, part of a federal inquiry into the killings at Kent State and Jackson State, expressed the bitter disillusionment that had only grown since Buxton's "Call to Action" in Clarke County four years earlier. The intertwined concerns—violence, repression, and poverty—that pulled him into the movement still fueled his activism. "The fact that Blacks are more in proportion in Vietnam than they are in the country," he argued, "is a product of economic repression and...racism." As for reforms that would instill "confidence and hope," as a commission member put it, Buxton replied that "this Commission and five Commissions like it can do absolutely nothing." The high-profile inquiry, he noted, followed a similar initiative by President Johnson, the National Advisory Commission on Civil Disorders, after a wave of urban riots swept the nation two years earlier. That commission's report, which warned that the United States was "moving towards two societies, one black, one white—separate and unequal," was "shoved under the table," Buxton said, "and the thing continues to go on."[76]

"This is the big problem," he continued, "that America is one big lie....You go to class every day and you are taught about how great America is and the great American dream and about equality and fair treatment and equal justice under the law and all this crap, and you walk right out of the class room and you see just the opposite...there is the big lie staring you in the face." Black and white youth, he argued, desired not to destroy society but "to throw off the shackles of hypocrisy and move forward." If the federal government wanted to shift course, Buxton argued, it must "change this attitude about Black people and poor people and quit trying to make the nation a police state, and quit trying to ride hard on peaceful dissent."[77]

A commission member interrupted Buxton to ask him to differentiate between white policemen calling blacks *niggers* and blacks calling white policemen *pigs*. "Number one," Buxton replied calmly, "when a law enforcement officer calls you a nigger, most likely you don't shoot him." As for President Nixon's call for "law and order"—a wildly effective appeal to Americans angered by increasingly militant protests—Buxton dismissed the rhetoric as a throwback to "Hitler in 1932....[L]aw and order means killing people who disagree no matter how they do it." The failure to punish anyone involved in the Jackson State shooting, Buxton argued, gave the "green light" to Mississippi's law-and-order racists. In the wake of the shootings, the *Jackson Daily News* had printed an editorial cartoon depicting a white hand grabbing a brick-wielding black arm. "Anarchy," the white supremacist standard-bearer demanded, "Must Be Stopped!" For Buxton, the message was clear: "Kill up all the niggers you want."[78]

While Buxton's warnings of "genocide" never materialized, activists warned that black Mississippians faced a more sinister threat. As a coalition of antipoverty agencies announced in the wake of the Gibbs-Green killings, violence had always coexisted alongside—and frequently overshadowed—the "Daily Repressive Tragedies" of black life in Mississippi. Head Start and other antipoverty initiatives aimed to address decades of neglect in education, public health, and community development that rendered poverty "automatic and systematic" for most black Mississippians. The failure of white officials to address those glaring deficiencies, the antipoverty coalition announced, "can only mean a deliberate scheme to preserve and exploit conditions of poverty." As the violent clashes and racial killings of the civil rights era faded from the headlines, the violence of poverty persisted. "Mental and physical handicaps and deaths resulting from ignorance and poverty does [*sic*] not attract attention and indignation in the way of a senseless campus slaughter, but are far more deadly," the *Mississippi Press Forum* warned in the wake of the Jackson State killings; "only an aroused public can end the tragedy."[79]

EPILOGUE

Caroline Buxton Thomas was sixteen years old when she marched on Shubuta's town hall. When a white mob came at her with ax handles and baseball bats, she fled the scene. Thomas ran so fast, she recalled five decades later, that her shoes flew off. A younger sister of local activist Warner Buxton, she remembered her schoolteacher mother's stories of crossing the Hanging Bridge every day—including the morning after the 1942 lynching of Ernest Green and Charlie Lang—on her way to the Liberty Hill schoolhouse. Thomas recalled the crosses burned on her front lawn in January 1966 after her older brother released his "Call to Action." In 2010, forty years after her brother and his allies warned that the "Daily Repressive Tragedies" of poverty, malnutrition, and poor education would persist long after the Jackson State shootings faded from the headlines, Thomas reflected on her hometown's progress. "Things hasn't improved much along the line of racism," she concluded. "Without education, money, and jobs [it] will never come full circle."[1]

The decades following Mississippi's unfinished revolution unleashed a different kind of violence on Shubuta's most vulnerable citizens. Thomas never again faced off with club-wielding whites and burning crosses, but she watched as economic decline ravaged what had once been—for a privileged few at least—a prosperous and pleasant place to live. A stone's throw from her doorstep, shuttered storefronts line Eucutta Street. To the north, the ruins of lumber mills and small manufacturing plants dot the old state highway that leads past Shubuta's mostly abandoned business district. A highway bypass allows most passing motorists to avoid the scene entirely. Fewer and fewer have a reason to head into town— Shubuta's current population has declined in the past century from nearly twelve hundred to slightly more than four hundred. Since 2000 alone, the town's population has declined by a third.

The town's prosperity, from slavery through the last days of Jim Crow, had been built on the backs of a black majority that reaped few of its fruits. In the years following the fall of legalized segregation and electoral disfranchisement, those who had helped dismantle that old order struggled to build a new one. Approximately three-quarters of Shubuta's current residents are black, and the town suffers from poverty and unemployment as well as a disproportionately high rate of working adults living in poverty. In Mississippi, the nation's poorest state, nearly a quarter of the population lived below the poverty line at the dawn of the twenty-first century. In Shubuta, nearly half did.[2]

History, of course, did not end when the marching stopped. Even as the political tide turned against the War on Poverty, the Friends of Children of Mississippi soldiered on into the 1970s. In the wake of the Child Development Group of Mississippi controversy, congressional conservatives had transferred control for federally funded antipoverty programs—including approval of budgets, personnel, and programming—to local and state officials. With a staff made up almost entirely of native Mississippians and funds cobbled together from private donors, Friends of Children took pride in its "independence from the existing power structure." To its staff and supporters, the agency represented "something that offers self-respect, dignity, and opportunity...and a small advance toward economic equality."[3]

A flashpoint in the fight over the Child Development Group, Clarke County became a hub of Friends of Children activity. Only Wayne County, its southern neighbor, boasted more Friends-affiliated preschools. A 1971 grant proposal estimated an enrollment of four hundred children in Clarke County, with the largest centers clustered in and around black-majority Shubuta. A Friends of Children booklet, distributed to a national network of supporters, highlighted the mobile medical and dental clinic, passenger vans, and modular classroom buildings secured through private grants. Classroom pictures included a sprinkling of white students—something unimaginable just a few years before. Despite these accomplishments, several years of operating in survival mode had taken their toll. "The people, by their own admission, are very, very tired," Friends of Children organizers reported. "Things are a little better now," admitted Jimana Sumrall, who headed Quitman's Pearlie Grove Center. "Until people gave us donations, we used to have to clean out the cupboards to feed the children." Still, she added, "it just don't make sense to me why we have to crawl, scratch, and fight so....We've worked so long looks like we ought to be getting somewhere."[4]

Like the Child Development Group of Mississippi before it, Friends of Children strove "to mean more to the people in the community than simply a pre-school education program." To that end, Head Start workers continued to think big. And they continued to grapple with a past that civil rights legislation and grant money could not erase. At an FCM-sponsored workshop on "Black Awareness," Head Start workers were asked to define *freedom*. A legacy of violence and repression dictated their response. "We did come up with a list of what we wanted to have 'freedom from,'" the attendees reported. Their list could have been written five—or fifty—years before:

> Joblessness—inability to get work that allows a man to receive a living wage.
>
> Mis- or non-education—we want an educational system that will not cripple our children.
>
> The fear of being killed because of color.
>
> Being discriminated against because of our color.[5]

The list highlighted the forces—economic coercion, state-sponsored repression, and racial terrorism—that had propped up Jim Crow for nearly a century. That system of legalized discrimination cut off economic and educational opportunity, but laws alone could not keep African Americans in their prescribed place. Violence had always operated in tandem and in tension with other forms of repression, and black Mississippians recognized this uneasy balance. In the World War I era, black activists connected lynching to "debt slavery." During World War II, investigators discovered that white anxieties about outmigration and rising wages fueled mob violence. By the end of the 1960s, some civil rights activists had concluded that poverty and malnutrition constituted the latest attack on black Mississippians. Still more woke every day to the realization that civil rights legislation had not cleared a path to decent jobs, good schools, and reliable protections of life and liberty.

Violence had always shaped freedom dreams in the rural South, but the definition of what was *violent* proved broad and elastic. Mobs lynched, but segregation, poverty, and memory exacted a toll as well. Maggie and Alma Howze, Major and Andrew Clark, Ernest Green and Charlie Lang were all caught in a system that denied them a basic education and sent them scrounging for pennies. All six defied that system—intentionally, allegedly, or accidentally—at moments of crisis, and lost their lives to forces and fears larger than themselves and their actions. Despite the legal and social advances since the last lynching at the Hanging Bridge, the prospects for a black child born in Shubuta in the 1960s—or since— were still bleak. In 2010, forty years after the "movement" decade ended, half of the children in the town lived below the poverty line.[6]

If poverty persisted, so too did the energy and expectations unleashed by the civil rights movement. In early 1971, woodcutters in Clarke County chartered the Mississippi Gulf Coast Pulpwood Association, an interracial union that spread across the Piney Woods. Hundreds of cutters and haulers joined the association, which used strikes and pressure campaigns to fetch higher prices and enforce fair measuring standards at local paper mills and wood yards. The Mississippi State Sovereignty Commission, still on the lookout for subversives, attributed the campaign to "known Communists" who had been active in earlier civil rights campaigns. Nevertheless, white woodcutters and mill workers in Mississippi's Piney Woods, some of whom rode with the Klan and terrorized civil rights workers just a few years before, joined forces with black pulpwood haulers and veteran civil rights organizers. "While we were there [in 1964]," a former Freedom Summer volunteer and union attorney pointed out, "we found that not only were Black people discriminated against but the White as well as Black pulpwood worker was being pushed to the back of the bus." Another union supporter, a local black minister, agreed. "It is really not different from the Civil Rights Movement," he argued,

"It has the same foundation: people have to be given their human rights; they will not stand to be oppressed forever."[7]

While some invoked the movement's memory to draw attention to persistent social problems, others proved eager to forget the struggle entirely. That urge coexisted uneasily with Shubuta's healthy appetite— even by Mississippi standards—for history and its evil twin, heritage. From the earliest signs of Jim Crow's demise, the town's white elite began to memorialize a mythic past. Frank Walton, a son of Shubuta who headed up the War Production Board's textile division during World War II, penned a tribute for the town's memorial association in 1947. Like those of his father's generation who cheered on Woodrow Wilson's crusade to make the world "safe for democracy," Walton sensed no conflict between his country's soaring World War II–era rhetoric and his hometown's racially exclusive vision of citizenship. "We love freedom and democracy," Walton wrote, "the kind we know and understand." At a time just five years removed from the town's last lynching, Walton argued that a pilgrimage to the "Banks of the Chickasawhay" would bring a little sanity to a world gone mad. "A week in old haunts will bring back many memories and revivify the sound ideas taught earlier, most of which helped make our democracy work. Thinking will become easier and clearer as one re-lives the past."[8]

The civil rights movement ripped the veneer off such romantic remembrances and shone a light on another past. No longer could locals ignore their town's most historically significant landmark, even if their accounts confined the Hanging Bridge and all that it represented to a distant and murky era. In 2004, Dr. Robert C. Weems published *My Shubuta: Boyhood Recollections of a Great Small Southern Town*. Born in 1910 into one of the town's leading families, Weems conceded that his town was no racial paradise. When he was "very young," Weems witnessed thirty robed Klansmen march into a church service and hand one hundred dollars to the pastor. The Weemses, who owned the bank and had a hand in most of the town's business ventures, used a portion of their wealth to tamp down racial tension and disorder.[9]

Like his Aunt Mary, the town matriarch who unknowingly hosted an NAACP-sponsored investigator in 1942, Dr. Weems understood that he could not stop ugly truths from coming out. The best he could hope to do was to contain them. Just eight years old when a mob lynched four people two miles from his house, Weems omitted the incident from his "boyhood recollections." When he heard that another author, a Shubuta-born college professor at the University of Minnesota, was asking around about the Hanging Bridge's history, Weems tacked on a final chapter about his town's most infamous landmark. He found, reprinted in a previously published local history, an excerpt from a black Cincinnati newspaper that detailed the 1918 lynchings. Like a few of the dozens of papers that followed the killings, the *Union* omitted the "t" from the murdered dentist's last name. "I was rather relieved that the so-called Shubuta man, Johnson, was probably not a Shubutan," Weems reported. "The Johnstons—different spelling—were a prominent Shubuta family." While conceding that there was "some question whether it was a Johnson or Johnston, and this may never be adequately resolved," Weems was content to let sleeping dogs lie. As for the vigilantes, Weems concluded, "I knew practically all of the citizens of Shubuta, and couldn't imagine any of them being associated with the doings of a lynch mob."[10]

In the Shubuta town cemetery, history hides in plain sight, and what local whites choose to remember and forget can be measured in granite. A few paces from the Weems family plot, Everett Lavega Johnston's headstone—death date listed as December 10, 1918—sits alongside those of other members of his "prominent Shubuta family." A short walk away lies James Edward McLendon, the town marshal with the shaky alibi, whose passing just two months after the 1942 lynchings sparked legends of a deathbed confession and divine retribution. William J. Patton, the undertaker and rumored 1918 mob leader who supervised the hasty burial of all six lynch victims, is also interred nearby. Amid the headstones and family plots, a twelve-foot memorial "To Our Confederate Dead" towers over the final resting places of at least a few lynching accomplices. The monument appeared three decades after the Civil War, in the midst of a bloody white supremacy campaign that swept through Mississippi and the South. Like hundreds of similar monuments across the region, the expensive granite shaft represented local whites' devotion to their "sacred duty...to perpetuate the memory of the dead who gave their lives for what they believed was right."[11]

Those unrepentant Confederates and their white supremacist progeny felt no such compunction when it came to lynching victims. Twenty paces north of the cemetery fence, and not much farther from the banks of the Chickasawhay, the unmarked graves of Ernest Green and Charlie Lang lie within a small wrought-iron pen. For reasons we cannot know, Will Patton parted with a few dozen feet of waist-high cemetery fencing to mark the spot. Yet he declined to provide even the crudest of headstones, and the buried remain nameless and obscured in a lonely thicket. Today, the pen is choked with saplings and underbrush. Sections of the fencing have collapsed, and the unhinged gate leans against an iron fencepost nearly swallowed by a tree stump. The exact locations of the graves are no more perceptible than the final resting places, likely nearby, of Andrew and Major Clark and Maggie and Alma Howze (fig. E.1).

The most durable memorial to Shubuta's lynching victims still hovers over the Chickasawhay, two miles upriver from their unmarked graves. The Hanging Bridge, like so many of Mississippi's more bloodstained historical sites, enjoys no official recognition. The best way to forget, many have concluded, is to have nothing to remember. Indeed, the urge to glorify the past and gloss over its "ugly" moments has pervaded state politics and culture. In 1974, the white-majority state textbook board rejected *Mississippi: Conflict and Change*, a revolutionary and award-winning effort by authors James Loewen and Charles Sallis to incorporate the history of the black freedom struggle into the state's social studies curriculum. The screening board denounced the "inflammatory" book, which included a photograph of a lynching, as "too racially oriented" and preoccupied with "isolated incidences of mis-treatment of slaves and blacks by whites."[12]

The state of Mississippi spent the rest of the decade, and thousands of taxpayer dollars, defending the screening board against the authors' lawsuit. The state's defense fell apart as textbook screeners admitted, in federal court, their desire to whitewash Mississippi history. When committee chair John Turnipseed complained about the lynching photograph on

FIGURE E.1

The unmarked graves of Ernest Green and Charlie Lang lie within a small
pen of wrought-iron fencing, just twenty yards beyond the northern bound-
ary of Shubuta's white cemetery. The exact locations of the unmarked
graves of Major and Andrew Clark and Maggie and Alma Howze are
unknown but likely nearby. Shubuta, Mississippi, September 2015.
Photograph by author.

page 178, Judge Orma R. Smith—a fellow white Mississippian—asked,
"But that happened, didn't it? Didn't Mississippi have more lynchings than
any other state?" Turnipseed replied, "Well, yes, but that happened so long
ago. Why dwell on it now?" The judge, who quickly shot back that this was
in fact the purpose of a *history* book, ruled in favor of the textbook authors.
Nevertheless, the battle to keep Mississippi's unrivaled record of atrocities
out of the classroom continues. In 2009, one day after I gave a talk at the
Hanging Bridge, a high school student told his teacher about the lynchings
that occurred there. "That never happened," the teacher shot back.[13]

Many who deny or discount white supremacy's bloody legacy prefer
heritage to history, but that path is no less rocky. Three decades after its

textbook fiasco, Mississippi's flag fight generated more heat than light. Mississippi legislators first endorsed the battle-flag-emblazoned banner in 1894, the same year that they elected the race-baiting James K. Vardaman their House speaker. Adopted in the wake of Mississippi's 1890 disenfranchisement convention and a thirty-three-day southern filibuster against a federal voting rights bill, the flag embodied Lost Cause nostalgia and unyielding defiance. A century later, as a referendum on a new flag design approached, the 1894 flag's defenders doled out denial and resentment in equal measure. Some complained that striking the battle flag emblem was just one more concession "to what the colored people want," while others decried the "assault on our Confederate heritage." Black Mississippians, of course, had their own understanding of their place in that history. "It is my *heritage*," a descendent of enslaved Mississippians argued at a public hearing, "to resist [the flag] with every fiber of my being."[14]

White Mississippians turned out in record numbers to keep the battle flag flying. The overall vote—two to one in opposition to the new design—closely mirrored the state's white-black population ratio. To demonstrate "the overwhelming influence of race" on the flag referendum, a pair of political scientists singled out Clarke County. Thirty-five percent of the county's residents were black, and 35 percent of the county's residents had voted to strike the Confederate emblem from the state flag. In Shubuta's black-majority voting precincts, the new flag carried the day by comfortable margins. By contrast, in the county's whitest precinct only four voters supported the new flag. If Clarke County was any indication, the analysts concluded gloomily, "Mississippi's white electorate may still be in a state of perpetual opposition… as the flag's designer intended in 1894." Symbols still matter in Clarke County, but their meaning and memory remain contested. The flag flies high, and it remains for many a point of pride. Yet to black freedom fighters across three generations, other symbols mattered more.[15]

Shubuta's Hanging Bridge, just a few years younger than the state flag and just as durable, represented a stain that neither nostalgia nor amnesia could blot out. For Mississippians, black and white, stories of racial violence tap a deep well. Discussion of these atrocities frequently provokes reflexive denial, born of an impulse, as the battle-flag-waving governor Ross Barnett used to say, to "Stand Up for Mississippi." For others, every new story adds another name to the list, as the NAACP's Roy Wilkins once put it, of "a lot of dead way back yonder." The lynchings and beatings in Shubuta affected people, places, and politics far beyond Clarke County, but attempts to confront Mississippi's record of racial violence dredge up fears and resentments that many would prefer to keep below the surface. Yet Mississippi's racial baggage has proven remarkably buoyant, and the legacy of the state's urge to submerge is apparent in the fallout from a steady stream of divisive—and sometimes deadly—racial controversies.[16]

In June 2011, when I was still deep in research for this book, white suburban teens attacked a black autoworker in a Jackson motel parking lot. As James Craig Anderson staggered away, eighteen-year-old Daryl Dedmon revved his Ford pickup, hopped the curb, and crushed Anderson under the wheels as he sped off. When Dedmon caught up with the other assailants at a nearby McDonald's, he reportedly bragged, "I ran that nigger over." The attack, caught on motel security cameras, furnished enough evidence for state prosecutors to secure a double life sentence for Dedmon and hate crime convictions against him and several accomplices. Unlike black victims in earlier generations, perpetrators faced swift trials and stiff sentences for their roles in the attack. State and federal officials cooperated to bring the attackers to justice. An interracial coalition organized vigils and marches. The Anderson family, with the help of civil rights lawyers, brought a civil lawsuit against the attackers. Anderson's same-sex partner of seventeen years, with whom he was raising a four-year-old son, could not legally participate. Despite the reminder that barriers to full citizenship remained encoded in Mississippi law, many hailed the vigorous prosecution as a sign of how far Mississippi had come.[17]

However, as journalists and investigators descended on the attackers' hometown of Brandon, a Jackson suburb eighty miles west of Shubuta, I heard echoes of the Hanging Bridge in the resentments and rationalizations of white locals. Despite evidence of racial harassment and bullying in the months leading up to the killing, local officials characterized the attack as "an isolated incident." When a dissenter complained that the authorities considered Dedmon "a good kid" who "just made one bad mistake," I could not help but think of Sheriff McNeal's rationalization of the 1942 double lynching: "We got some good people who get kind of wild." While relatively few Brandon residents had anything bad to say about the killer or his accomplices, rumors spread that their victim was a drug dealer. That urge to shift blame to the victim, and the implication that white males still enjoyed the prerogative to police and punish black crime without waiting on cops or courts, echoed earlier atrocities. Some rationalized the violence, while others vilified outsiders—from the media to the black district attorney—for playing the "race card" and sullying the town's good name. "We have colored people in our class," a white high school student told a reporter. "Brandon is one of the top places to live in the country. There is nothing bad about Brandon." When local police spotted the journalist speaking with students at the high school homecoming game, they escorted her to her car.[18]

One person who did not try to explain away his motive or play the victim was the killer himself. Daryl Dedmon admitted in a courtroom apology that he was "ignorant and full of hatred" when he ran over James Craig Anderson. A surprising number of classmates, neighbors, and local officials claimed not to have noticed, which suggested that Dedmon's racism was a tragic aberration that defied explanation. There was a more troubling possibility, one whose roots reached deep into the past and whose implications extended far beyond the Brandon town limits—or the shadow of a rusty Shubuta bridge. The 2011 killing revealed how much everyone involved remained trapped in a history that they often feel more than they know. Perhaps none of them, from activists who protested "an old-fashioned lynching" to apologists who fired back with charges of "reverse racism," had heard of Stanley Hayes, a black farmhand gunned down by a Brandon mob in 1899. Or Etoy Fletcher, a black World War II veteran abducted and beaten in 1946 after he attempted to register to vote at the Rankin County courthouse. Or the civil rights activists, including Jackson-based evangelist and community organizer John Perkins, jailed and tortured by the town's white policemen in 1970. Like Shubuta, Brandon had witnessed racial violence across generations. Unlike Shubuta, Brandon had reaped the rewards of Sunbelt suburbanization and white flight in the years since the civil rights movement. Just months before the 2011 killing, Brandon—85 percent white—cracked an annual list of America's best small towns. That shine, at least compared to Shubuta's crumbling main drag, makes it harder to see the past. But no town can escape its history for long.[19]

Shubuta seems but a shadow of the community once denounced by the black press as "the worst town in the worst state in the union." However, unlike so many places where the past lays buried, Shubuta's "monument to Jim Crow" still stands. When I began this project, you could drive out to the bridge. Today, if you turn onto East Street and follow the northerly bend in the road, you will encounter a padlocked gate just a few hundred yards from the river crossing. Flanked by "Road Closed" signs, with "No Trespassing" and "No Hunting" warnings hanging from it, the metal gate signifies the county's effective abandonment of the structure. At the time of the road closure, the bridge deck had decayed to the point that vehicles could not cross safely—a local road crew had removed the ramps years before to prevent anyone from trying. Since the county washed its hands of the bridge, a private citizen who owns land on either side of the river reinstalled ramps and laid a new deck so that all-terrain vehicles could cross the bridge safely. Like the road that leads out to the bridge, padlocked gates block access from either riverbank.

Except for the bridge's new deck, not much has changed since the last lynchings that took place there (fig. E.2). A rusted frame sits atop concrete piers. In the winter, the woods, water, and bridge blend in shades of grayish and reddish brown. The barren scene has changed little since the two autumn mornings, twenty-four years apart, when passersby spotted dangling corpses. In warmer months, the riverbanks are still choked with green, just as they were when a civil rights worker snapped a photograph of it in 1966. The skull-and-crossbones graffiti has faded, but the hateful spirit the bridge inspired has persisted. Over the barely perceptible "Danger" warning, someone sketched two swastikas—the preferred symbol of hate in the world handed down to us by the civil rights movement and its bitter-end enemies.[20]

FIGURE E.2

East Road now ends a few hundred yards short of the Hanging
Bridge. Shubuta, Mississippi, September 2015. Photograph by Andrew
Lichtenstein. Courtesy of Andrew Lichtenstein.

Before the gate blocked access to the bridge, a more expensive prop-
osition—demolition—went nowhere. For those who shared the sentiment of one local official, who argued that "people don't need to see
that," a padlocked barrier seemed sufficient to keep the historically
inclined at bay. Yet even if it eventually collapses into the river below, the
rusty bridge—like the deteriorating downtown just two miles away—
will not take its history with it when it goes (fig. E.3). That story was
made, and told, by people who passed down glimpses of a past that
continues to echo in our remembering and our forgetting. That this
story will not be buried is a testament to a freedom struggle that left its
mark on the tiniest hamlets and farthest reaches of the rural South. If
not for a gory landmark and the generations of violence that occurred
in its shadow, Shubuta's racial history might simply fade into a nameless pile of past wrongs. "Its only distinction" from other Mississippi

FIGURE E.3

The Hanging Bridge, from the banks of the Chickasawhay River. Shubuta, Mississippi, September 2015. Photograph by Andrew Lichtenstein. Courtesy of Andrew Lichtenstein.

towns, as a black journalist noted after a 1942 visit, was its "impressive lynch record." Yet to isolate this place is to miss a larger point—that the Hanging Bridge repeatedly fixed attention on Jim Crow's brutal excesses and unresolved legacies. That the landmark is largely forgotten, and intentionally obscured, reminds us that heritage is a poor substitute for history. And that retreat—from the past and its echoes in the present—does not bring redemption.[21]

NOTES

INTRODUCTION

1. John Cumbler, interview by author, 6 November 2009, Louisiville, Kentucky.
2. Jack Elliott, "Mississippi Bridge Survey and Inventory," 13 February 1986, filed in 023-SHB-6004, HPD (see list of abbreviations at beginning of bibliography).
3. Cumbler interview.
4. Greenberg, *The Devil Has Slippery Shoes*, 95–6; "Governor of Mississippi Tells NAACP to Go to Hell," *Baltimore Daily Herald*, 31 December 1918, n.p., clipping in box I:360, NAACP. Brief summaries of the 1918 Shubuta lynchings appear in K. Williams, *They Left Great Marks on Me*, 194–5; Finnegan, *A Deed So Accursed*, 114–6; Feimster, *Southern Horrors*, 172–3; Berg, *Popular Justice*, 110.
5. Walter Atkins, "Shubuta Bridge's Toll Stands at Six Lynch Victims, but Span Is Doomed," *Chicago Defender*, 7 November 1942, 1; Enoc P. Waters, "Two Lynched Boys Were Ace Scrap Iron Collectors in Mississippi Town," *Chicago Defender*, 6 March 1943, 13.
6. Craigen Kennedy, "Shubuta and Quitman, Mississippi," 30 November 1942, 1, box II: A859, NAACP.
7. Atkins, "Shubuta Bridge's Toll Stands at Six Lynch Victims," 1.
8. Hobert Kornegay, interview with Don Williams, 6 January 1999, CRDP; Victor Bernstein, "A Belligerent Program for Limited Objectives: An Editorial," *Baltimore Afro-American*, 19 September 1942, 17.
9. G. Yates, *Life and Death in a Small Southern Town*, 68.
10. Data from 1840, 1850, and 1860 United States Censuses taken from the Historical Census Browser, University of Virginia, Geospatial and Statistical Data Center: http://mapserver.lib.virginia.edu/, accessed 6 August 2015.
11. Sarah McCarty, "Historical Research-Assignment #15: Old Homes," 21 October 1936, n.p.; "Langsdale Plantation, House Stand as Majestic Remnant of Old South," Jackson *Clarion-Ledger*, 14 August 1966, n.p.; Rosalie Primm, "Antebellum Homes: The Lang Plantation," *Clarke County Tribune*, 25

September 1980, n.p.; all excerpts and clippings filed in 023-SHB-6002-NR, HPD; "Chapter IX: Reconstruction," typed draft, 1–2, folder "Reconstruction," box 10670, series 447, WPA.

12. Primm, "Antebellum Homes,"n.p.; Sarah McCarty, "Historical Research: Assignment #10," 22 July 1936, 2, folder "Clarke County, Negro," box 10670, series 447, WPA.

13. "Langsdale Plantation, House Stand," n.p.; Howell, *Mississippi Back Roads,* 245; J. Yates, *Mississippi to Madrid,* 16; Weems, *My Shubuta,* 103; "Allen V. Manning," in Baker and Baker, *WPA Oklahoma Slave Narratives,* 278–85.

14. Yates, *Life and Death in a Small Southern Town,* 73–4; Moore, *Cotton Kingdom,* 174.

15. Ellen Goodrich, "Mississippi: From a Teacher," *American Missionary* 12 (August 1868): 175; United States Bureau of Refugees, Freedmen, and Abandoned Lands, *Eighth Semi-Annual Report on Schools for Freedmen,* 44.

16. Fitzgerald, *The Union League Movement,* 52; untitled, *Hinds County Gazette,* 26 October 1870, 1.

17. Newton, *Ku Klux Klan in Mississippi,* 32–3; Lemann, *Redemption,* 71; Rable, *But There Was No Peace,* 144–62; "The Truth about Mississippi," *San Francisco Chronicle,* 26 August 1876, 2 [*Shubuta Times* quoted in *Chronicle* article].

18. "Reconstruction," *Mississippi Messenger,* 16 July 1915, 1.

19. "Echoes from the January 1 Emancipation Celebration," *Southwestern Christian Advocate,* 30 January 1890, 4; Enoc P. Waters, "Right to Vote in South Is Key to Real Emancipation, Believes Tougaloo Vet," *Chicago Defender,* 6 March 1943, 9.

20. Rowland, *Encyclopedia of Mississippi…Contemporary Biography,* 212–4.

21. Untitled news item, *Southwestern Christian Advocate,* 9 April 1891, 5. Blair L. M. Kelley has characterized the Jim Crow–era smoking car as "a lurid, public space in which the standard social order was confused and African American women and children were exposed to white men behaving in a rough and un-cultured manner….Increasing numbers of black passengers were prevented from using the first-class facilities, but no one sought to bar white men from colored compartments." See Kelley, *Right to Ride,* 25.

22. "A Murderer Lynched in Mississippi," *St. Louis Globe-Democrat,* 15 June 1883, 1; Tolnay and Beck, *A Festival of Violence,* 67; Finnegan, *A Deed So Accursed,* 22–31; Wells-Barnett, *Red Record.* For a recent critique of the "counting" and comparing of lynching across regions and states, see Trotti, "What Counts."

23. Elliott, "Mississippi Bridge Survey and Inventory."

24. Ibid.; House Committee on Rivers and Harbors, *Chickasahay River* [*sic*], *Miss.,* 6–7; Weems, *My Shubuta,* xvi–xvii.

25. Mae Ngai has argued that while "the construction of racial hierarchies has been, of course, an ongoing project in American history," this process is also

"historically specific." Certain historical moments "impelled major shifts in society's understanding and construction of race and its constitutive roles in national identify formation." See Ngai, *Impossible Subjects*, 7. Drawing on this framework of "historically specific" moments of racial change, historian Kimberley Phillips has more recently argued that "U.S. wars consistently have created these times." See Phillips, *War! What Is It Good For?*, 5.

CHAPTER ONE

1. Walter F. White, "An Example of Democracy in Mississippi," unedited typescript, 2–3, Shubuta folders, box I:C360, NAACP.
2. "Four Negroes Met Death by Hanging at Hands of Unknown Parties," [*Meridian Star*], n.d., n.p.; "Two of Shubuta Mob Victims Negro Girls," *New Orleans Item*, 22 December 1918, n.p.; "Four Negroes Lynched by Mob at Shubuta; Two Women," *Jackson Daily News*, 21 December 1918, n.p.; all clippings in Shubuta folders, box I:C360, NAACP.
3. "Lynch Four Negroes; Two of Them Women," *New York Times*, 21 December 1918, 7. The *Times* and some other sources list the brothers' surname as "Clarke" and the sisters' surname as "House."
4. "Four Negroes, Two of Them Women, Lynched in Mississippi," *Baltimore Daily Herald*, 23 December 1918, n.p.; W. T. Andrews to John R. Shillady, 14 January 1919; both in Shubuta folders, box I:C360, NAACP.
5. White, *A Man Called White*, 41.
6. "A Matter of Regret," *Laurel Leader*, 23 December 1918, 2; "Four Negroes Lynched by Mob at Shubuta," n.p., both in Shubuta folders, box I:C360, NAACP.
7. A. [Arista] Johnston, "A History of the Johnston Family," 26 September 1907, n.p., unpublished typescript available at http://www.angelfire.com/planet/tiner/johnston/A_Johnston.pdf, accessed 23 August 2009; Rowland, *Official and Statistical Register of Mississippi*, vol. 2, 1043; *Clarke County Land Roll, 1917–1918*, 34, CCCH.
8. Ad, *Threshermen's Review* 16 (January 1907): 62; "What the Foundries Are Doing," *Foundry* 43 (March 1915): 128; "Inventions of Interest to Lumbermen and Machinery Men," *Lumber World*, 15 July 1908, 28; *Lumber Trade Journal*, 15 October 1917, 53; Rowland, *Encyclopedia of Mississippi History*, 664; G. Yates, *Life and Death in a Small Southern Town*, 32.
9. Weems, *My Shubuta*, 6.
10. Biographical and professional information on Johnston gleaned from two decades of MCD, 1899–1918.
11. White, "An Example of Democracy in Mississippi," 2; Everett Levega Johnston, Clarke County, Mississippi, roll MS9, M-1509, WWI-SS.

12. White, "An Example of Democracy in Mississippi," 1.

13. "Mob Binds Deputy; Hangs 4 Negroes," *Gulfport Daily Herald*, 21 December 1918, 1; "Most Citizens of Shubuta Deplore the Fact That Law Was Not Permitted to Execute Four Negro Murderers," *Laurel Leader*, 23 December 1918, 1.

14. "Mob Binds Deputy," 1; "Bloodhounds Hunt Assassin," *Washington Herald*, 11 December 1918, 6; "Man Hiding in Barn Fatally Shoots Doctor," *Washington Times*, 11 December 1918, 15.

15. White, "An Example of Democracy in Mississippi," 2, 4.

16. "Four Negroes Met Death by Hanging," n.p.; "Mississippi News," *Macon Beacon*, 20 December 1918, 2.

17. "Mob Shackles Deputy; Hangs Four Negroes," unnamed New Orleans newspaper, 21 December 1918, n.p., Shubuta folders, box I:C360, NAACP; White, "An Example of Democracy in Mississippi," 2–3.

18. White, "An Example of Democracy in Mississippi," 3.

19. Patton, "How a Mississippi Town Was Revolutionized by Prohibition," 92; untitled, Jackson *New Mississippian*, 29 July 1884, 1; "Dry Again!" Jackson *New Mississippian*, 18 March 1889, n.p.; untitled, *Biloxi Herald*, 16 January 1897, 4; Yates, *Life and Death in a Small Southern Town*, 99–100.

20. "Most Citizens of Shubuta Deplore the Fact," 1.

21. Ibid., 1.

22. Walter F. White to John R. Shillady, 20 January 1919, Shubuta folders, box I:C360, NAACP; White, "An Example of Democracy in Mississippi," 3–4.

23. White, "An Example of Democracy in Mississippi," 3.

24. "Lynching of 4 Negroes in Miss. Brings Protest," *New York Call*, 17 December 1918, n.p.; "Governor of Mississippi Tells NAACP to Go to Hell," *Baltimore Daily Herald*, 31 December 1918, n.p.; "Folly of 'Butting In,'" *Houston Post*, n.d., n.p.; all clippings in Shubuta folders, box I:C360, NAACP.

25. McMillen, *Dark Journey*, 306. On Bilbo's progressive record as governor, see Morgan, *Redneck Liberal*, 37; "Influential Papers Condemn Lynching," *Southwestern Christian Advocate*, 2 January 1919, n.p., clipping in frame 656, reel 221, TNCF.

26. Sullivan, *Lift Every Voice*, 61–100.

27. Waldrep, *African Americans Confront Lynching*, 59–62.

28. Sullivan, *Lift Every Voice*, 1–24; Dyja, *Walter White*, 40.

29. White, *A Man Called White*, 11.

30. Janken, *Walter White: Mr. NAACP*, 10; White, *A Man Called White*, 21–2.

31. As historian Allyson Hobbs notes, fittingly in her lone mention of Walter White, "Passing reveals the bankruptcy of the race idea." See Hobbs, *A Chosen Exile*, 8–9.

32. Sullivan, *Lift Every Voice,* 63, 75; Waldrep, *African Americans Confront Lynching,* 68; White, *A Man Called White,* 40.

33. White, *A Man Called White,* 41.

34. Ibid., Walter White, "The Burning of Jim McIlherron," *The Crisis* 16 (May 1918): 16–20.

35. "11 Lynched Instead of 6 as First Reported in Georgia," *Philadelphia Tribune,* 7 September 1918, 8.

36. Dyja, *Walter White,* 51–2; Armstrong, *Mary Turner,* 192.

37. Sullivan, *Lift Every Voice,* 61–100.

38. White to Shillady, 17 January 1919, box I:C76, NAACP.

39. Walter White to E. T. Belsaw, 11 February 1919; E. T. Belsaw to Walter White, 31 January 1919; both in Shubuta folders, box I:C360, NAACP; Lamon, *Black Tennesseans,* 44–6; Lauterbach, *Beale Street Dynasty,* 1–3.

40. James Weldon Johnson to Robert R. Church, Jr., 27 December 1918; James Weldon Johnson to Bodeker's National Detective Agency, 27 December 1918; both in box I:C337, NAACP.

41. Walter White to John R. Shillady, 17 January 1919, box I:C76, NAACP; Janken, *Walter White: Mr. NAACP,* 42.

42. White to Shillady, 20 January 1919; Walter White to James Weldon Johnson, 20 January 1919, both in box I:C76, NAACP.

43. White to Shillady, 17 January 1919; White to Johnson, 20 January 1919.

44. Janken, *Walter White: Mr. NAACP,* 30; Dyja, *Walter White,* 46; "A Matter of Regret," *Laurel Leader,* 23 December 1918, 2.

45. Dyja, *Walter White,* 47.

46. White to Shillady, 20 January 1919.

47. White, "An Example of Democracy in Mississippi," 3.

48. Ibid., 2; "Shubuta," handwritten notes, 1 February 1919, Shubuta folders, box I:C360, NAACP.

49. White to Shillady, 20 January 1919.

50. "Mississippi Mobs Two Women and Two Men in Prison," *New York News,* 26 December 1918, n.p., clipping in Shubuta folders, box I:C360, NAACP.

51. "A Matter of Regret," 2; "Influential Papers Condemn Lynching," n.p. State officials increasingly embraced the argument that swift state-sponsored executions made lynching unnecessary. See Vandiver, *Lethal Punishment,* 26; Pfeifer, *Rough Justice,* 147.

52. "Our Black Brothers," *New York Call,* 23 December 1918, n.p., clipping in Shubuta folders, box I:C360, NAACP.

53. Smith, *Philosophy of Race Relations,* 12, copy in reel 14, CIC; "Mob Shackles Deputy Sheriff and Hangs 4 Negroes at Shubuta," *Laurel Leader,* 21 December 1918, 1.

54. White, "An Example of Democracy in Mississippi," 2.

55. "A Matter of Regret," 2.

56. Wells-Barnett and Harris, *Selected Works of Ida B. Wells Barnett*, 146; Yarborough, "Violence, Manhood, and Black Heroism," 228–9. On Wells's pioneering antilynching activism and fraught relationship with the later NAACP campaigns and the association's relatively moderate, male-dominated leadership, see Bay, *To Tell the Truth Freely*; Giddings, *A Sword among Lions*.

57. White, "An Example of Democracy in Mississippi," 2.

58. "Four Negroes, Two of Them Women," n.p.

59. White to Shillady, 20 January 1919; White, "An Example of Democracy in Mississippi," 2.

60. "Four Negroes, Two of Them Women," n.p.; "Shubuta Makes Christmas Gift," Baltimore *Afro-American*, 27 December 1918, 4; Feimster, *Southern Horrors*, 173.

61. "Jury Fails to Locate Guilty Mob Members," *Hattiesburg American*, 23 December 1918, 6; White, "An Example of Democracy in Mississippi," 3.

62. "Our Black Brothers," n.p.

63. White, "An Example of Democracy in Mississippi," 5; Walter White to W. H. P. Freeman, 7 February 1919, Shubuta folders, box I:C360, NAACP.

64. "The Shubuta Lynching and a Query," *Southwestern Christian Advocate*, n.d., n.p., clipping in Shubuta folders, box I:C360, NAACP; White, "An Example of Democracy in Mississippi," 1.

65. "Is This an Invitation to Negroes to Move?," *Southwestern Christian Advocate*, 26 December 1918, n.p., clipping in Shubuta folders, box I:C360, NAACP; White, "An Example of Democracy in Mississippi," 5; Janken, *Walter White: Mr. NAACP*, 42.

66. "The Shubuta Lynching and a Query," n.p.; White, "An Example of Democracy in Mississippi," 1; "Our Black Brothers," n.p.

67. "Mississippi Mobs Two Women and Two Men in Prison," n.p.; Lewis, *Biography of a Race*, 514; Dray, *At the Hands of Persons Unknown*, 219; Wood, *Lynching and Spectacle*, 179–80; "Is This an Invitation to Negroes to Move?," n.p.

68. Janken, *Walter White: Mr. NAACP*, 38–40; Mason, *Shubuta*, 35.

69. Walter White, "'Work or Fight' in the South," *New Republic,* 1 March 1919, 144–6; Shenk, *Work or Fight*, 41–3; "An Interview with J. R. S., W. F. W., and Bodeker at Hotel Tuwiler," Birmingham, Alabama, 1 February 1919, Shubuta folders, box I:C360, NAACP.

70. Walter F. White to Henry Muzzey, 14 February 1919; Henry Muzzey to Walter F. White, 24 February 1919; both in Shubuta folders, box I:C360; Walter F. White to Henry Muzzey, 27 February 1919, box I:C337, NAACP.

71. "The Shubuta Lynchings," *The Crisis* 18 (May 1919): 25; White, "An Example of Democracy in Mississippi," 5.

72. White, "An Example of Democracy in Mississippi," 4; "A Bald Pretext," *Shreveport Journal*, 26 December 1918, n.p., cliping in Shubuta folders, box I:C360, NAACP.

CHAPTER TWO

1. J. Yates, *Mississippi to Madrid*, 20.
2. Ibid., 20.
3. Sullivan, *Lift Every Voice*, 82; White, "An Example of Democracy in Mississippi," 4, typescript in Shubuta folders, box I:C360, NAACP.
4. "Safe for Democracy," *Mississippi Messenger*, 26 October 1917, 16.
5. "Our Black Brothers," *New York Call*, 23 December 1918, n.p., clipping in Shubuta folders, box I:C360, NAACP.
6. Bolton Smith, "A Philosophy of Race Relations," March 1919, 11–2, reel 14, CIC.
7. "Is This an Invitation to Negroes to Move?" *Southwestern Christian Advocate*, 26 December 1918, n.p., clipping in Shubuta folders, box I:C360, NAACP.
8. Seymour, *Woodrow Wilson and the World War*, 113; "Memorandum for N.A.A.C.P. Branches"; James W. Johnson to branch secretaries, 9 August 1917; both in folder 12, box I:C334, NAACP.
9. "100 Lynchings since the Beginning of World War," *St. Louis Argus*, 27 December 1918, n.p., clipping in Shubuta folders, box I:C360, NAACP.
10. "Our Black Brothers,"n.p.; J. Lyle Caston, "The Latest Lynching Horror," *St. Louis Post-Dispatch*, 24 December 1918, 14.
11. White, "An Example of Democracy in Mississippi," 4.
12. "Shubuta Makes Christmas Gift," Baltimore *Afro-American*, 27 December 1918, 4; "The Reward for Devotion," *St. Louis Argus*, 27 December 1918, n.p., clipping in Shubuta folders, box I:C360, NAACP; W. E. B. Du Bois, "Close Ranks," *The Crisis* 16 (July 1918): 111; "The Shubuta Lynchings," *The Crisis* 18 (May 1919): 25. On the "Close Ranks" editorial and the resulting controversy, see Du Bois, *Dusk of Dawn*, 252–5; Lewis, *Biography of a Race*, 555–7; Ellis, *Race, War, and Surveillance*, 163–82; Jordan, "The Damnable Dilemma," 1564–5; C. Williams, *Torchbearers of Democracy*, 63.
13. "The Reward for Devotion," n.p. On black veterans' reactions to racial violence, including the Shubuta lynchings, see K. Williams, *They Left Great Marks on Me*, 145–6.
14. C. Williams, *Torchbearers of Democracy*, 223–4, 241–5; Lentz-Smith, *Freedom Struggles*, 169–205; Wright, *Racial Violence in Kentucky*, 119–20; White, "An Example of Democracy in Mississippi," 4.
15. J. Yates, *Mississippi to Madrid*, 28; McMillen, *Dark Journey*, 306.
16. Zangrando, *The NAACP Crusade against Lynching*, 48.
17. NAACP, *Thirty Years of Lynching*, 33, 41. Scholars have since noted the shortcomings in the NAACP's 1919 lynching count, and subsequent inventories have confirmed that Mississippi, not Georgia, was indeed the South's leader in lynchings. Tolnay and Beck, *A Festival of Violence*, 260. Tolnay (with Bailey) has recently noted that while the Tolnay and Beck tally is an improvement

over the Tuskegee and NAACP inventories, "any inventory of victims must be considered incomplete and evolving." Bailey and Tolnay, *Lynched*, 5–6. On the practice, importance, and shortcomings of the lynching "count" for activists and scholars, see Trotti, "What Counts."

18. NAACP, *Thirty Years of Lynching*, 27.
19. Ibid., 28.
20. J. Yates, *Mississippi to Madrid*, 15–8.
21. Ibid., 17; Painter, *Exodusters*, 83, 207; Rolinson, *Grassroots Garveyism*, 198; Hahn, *Nation under Our Feet*, 333, 471; Kelley, *Race Rebels*, 25–6. Census data on the Yates family compiled from 1910 and 1920 US census data for Clarke County, Mississippi, and Seminole County, Oklahoma.
22. J. Yates, *Mississippi to Madrid*, 19–20.
23. Quoted in McMillen, *Dark Journey*, 43.
24. Mitchell, *A New History of Mississippi*, 264.
25. Cresswell, *Rednecks, Redeemers, and Race*, 196; "A Card from Mr. Johnston," *Clarke County Times*, 31 January 1903, 4.
26. Cresswell, *Rednecks, Redeemers, and Race*, 196–7; Chadbourn, *Lynching and the Law*, 113–4.
27. A. Johnston, "Mississippi Has No Such Law," New Orleans *Daily Picayune*, 5 August 1900, 8.
28. "Clarke's Official Vote on Thursday"; "Vardaman the Chief"; both articles in *Clarke County Times*, 29 August 1903, 1.
29. Holmes, *The White Chief*, vii–ix.
30. "War on 'Favorites,'" *Washington Post*, 26 July 1913, 1; "Revolt on Patterson," *Washington Post*, 27 July 1913, 1; Patler, *Jim Crow and the Wilson Administration*, 167–8; Yellin, *Racism in the Nation's Service*, 93, 140, 159.
31. Woodrow Wilson, "Lynching Is Unpatriotic," in Hart, *Selected Addresses and Public Papers*, 270.
32. "Shubuta Makes Christmas Gift," 4; Kennedy, *Over Here*, 68; McMillen, *Dark Journey*, 304–5.
33. Keith, *Rich Man's War, Poor Man's Fight*, 52, 121; McMillen, *Dark Journey*, 306.
34. "Wilson against Vardaman," *Mississippi Messenger*, 16 August 1918, 1; "The Vote in Clarke County," *Mississippi Messenger*, 23 August 1918, 6.
35. "What the Negro Will Demand," *Issue*, 21 November 1918, 2; "Japan to Raise the Race Question," *Issue*, 28 November 1918, 5.
36. J. Yates, *Mississippi to Madrid*, 22–3.
37. Frank Andrews to Theodore G. Bilbo, 26 June 1917, folder "Negro Migrants," letters from, [typescripts], 1916–8, box I:F86, NUL.
38. "Farmers' Institutes for Negroes," *Mississippi Messenger*, 10 November 1916, 8; Andrews to Bilbo, 26 June 1917.
39. Scott, *Negro Migration*, 22; "Is This an Invitation for Negroes to Move?," n.p.; "The Shubuta Lynching and a Query," n.p.; New Orleans *Southwestern*

Christian Advocate, n.d., n.p.; "Four Are Lynched, Suicide Discovered," *Chicago Defender*, 8 February 1919, n.p. all clippings in Shubuta folders, box I:C360, NAACP.

40. Executive Committee, Mississippi Welfare League, to J. R. Bingham, 15 February 1919, box I:C333, NAACP.

41. Lamon, *Black Tennesseans,* 251; Bolton Smith to John P. Shillady, 29 January 1919, 8–9, box I:C333, NAACP.

42. Executive Committee to Bingham; *Organization of the Mississippi Welfare League*, n.p.

43. *Organization of the Mississippi Welfare League*, n.p. For examples of national press coverage of the Mississippi Welfare League, see "League Proposed for State Uplift," *Christian Science Monitor*, 8 February 1919, 6.

44. *Organization of the Mississippi Welfare League*, n.p.; Executive Committee to Bingham; "National Conference on Lynching—May 6, 1919 (afternoon)," 2, box I:C334, NAACP.

45. Smith to Shillady, n.p.; Frederick Sullens to Moorfield Storey, 21 February 1919, box I:C333, NAACP.

46. "Convention to Consider Lynching," *Vardaman's Weekly*, 24 April 1919, 14; "A Stitch in Time Saves Nine," *Vardaman's Weekly*, 22 May 1919, 6.

47. "National Conference on Lynching: The Call," n.d.; "Suggestions Re: Anti-Lynching Conference," March 1919, 3, box I:C333, NAACP.

48. McWhirter, *Red Summer*, 34–6; "Address of Honorable Emmet O'Neal Delivered before the National Conference on Lynching," 5 May 1919, 8, box I:C334, NAACP.

49. "Address Delivered by James Weldon Johnson, National Conference on Lynching, Carnegie Hall," 5 May 1919, 6, Box I:C334, NAACP; Dray, *At the Hands of Persons Unknown*, 258.

50. Jack C. Wilson, "National Conference on Lynching—May 6, 1919 (afternoon)," n.p.; Jack C. Wilson, "National Conference on Lynching—May 6, 1919 (evening)," n.p.; both in box I:C334, NAACP.

51. Wilson, "National Conference on Lynching—May 6, 1919 (evening)," n.p.; Wilson, "National Conference on Lynching—May 6, 1919 (afternoon)," n.p.

52. "Address of Mr. William Pickens," 6 May 1919, 1–2, box I:C334, NAACP; "Negroes Radically Divided," *Brooklyn Daily Eagle*, 7 May 1919, n.p., clipping in box II:L248, NAACP.

53. William Pickens, "Lynching and Debt Slavery," in Rice, *Witnessing Lynching*, 211–2; Woodruff, *American Congo*, 112; Avery, *Up from Washington*, 114–5.

54. Pickens, "Lynching and Debt Slavery," 211–2.

55. "Negroes Radically Divided," n.p.; Wilson, "National Conference on Lynching—May 6, 1919 (afternoon)," n.p.; "National Conference on Lynching," typed resolution, box I:C334; "Address to the Nation," folder 12, box I:C205; both in NAACP.

56. Sullivan, *Lift Every Voice*, 84; "To Bring Negroes South"; "Negroes Should Remain in South"; both in *Mississippi Messenger*, 5 September 1919, 2.

57. Kerlin, *Voice of the Negro*, 133; "Exodus of Negroes from Chicago Following Riots," folder "Migration Study, Source Materials," box I:F87, NUL; "The South Must Repent!" *Cleveland Gazette*, 17 November 1919, 1.

58. Only four counties—George, Hancock, Issaquena, and Montgomery—had higher percentage drops in their black population ratio from 1910 to 1920. See US Department of Commerce, *Thirteenth Census of the United States*, vol. 2, 1044–59, and *Fourteenth Census of the United States*, vol. 2, 1347–8. For analysis of wartime population loss and outmigration in the region surrounding Clarke County, see untitled draft, 29–34, folder "Migration Study Draft (Early)," box I:F86, NUL.

59. NAACP, *Eleventh Annual Report*, 22.

60. "To Bring Negroes South," 2.

61. J. Yates, *Mississippi to Madrid*, 21.

62. Ibid., 22.

63. S. B. Johnson to the N.A.A.C.P., 14 July 1920; James W. Johnson to A. S. Burleson, 7 July 1920; Office of the Chief Inspector to Walter White, 25 August 1920; all in folder 8, box I:C360, NAACP; "Negro Postal Clerk Taken from Officer...," *Meridian Star*, 6 July 1920, 1.

64. "Plan Banquet to Celebrate Lynching," *Chicago Defender*, 2 October 1920, 7; "Will Echols, Murder Companion of Henry Lloyd, Taken from Quitman Jail...," *Meridian Star*, 13 September 1920, 1.

65. J. Yates, *Mississippi to Madrid*, 23–6.

66. Scott, *Negro Migration*, 77–8; Grossman, *Land of Hope*, 44; Lemann, *Promised Land*, 16–7; Wilkerson, *Warmth of Other Suns*, 163.

67. J. Yates, *Mississippi to Madrid*, 30–1.

68. Zangrando, *NAACP Crusade against Lynching*, 42–3.

69. Hall, *Revolt against Chivalry*, 64.

70. J. Yates, *Mississippi to Madrid*, 75; Frederickson, *The Dixiecrat Revolt*, 24; Weiss, *Farewell to the Party of Lincoln*, 83–9; John Temple Graves, "South Discusses a Two-Party Plan," *New York Times*, 6 November 1936, E10.

71. Theodore G. Bilbo to Mrs. L. W. Alford, 6 March 1939, folder 15, box 1057; Mrs. Bettie B. Kansler to Theodore G. Bilbo, 21 January 1938, folder 13, box 1053; both in TGB.

72. Lemak, *Southern Life, Northern City*, 58–61; J. Yates, *Mississippi to Madrid*, 79–80.

73. Carroll, *Abraham Lincoln Brigade*, 356; J. Yates, *Mississippi to Madrid*, 163–4; Carroll, Nash, and Small, *Good Fight Continues*, 128–9.

74. S. V. McRee to Walter White, 11 May 1935, box I:G106, NAACP.

CHAPTER THREE

1. James F. McRee, interviewed by author, 6 February 2009, Laurel, Mississippi; John W. T. Falkner, IV, "Unknown Subjects: Lynching of Charles Lang...and Ernest Green," 27 October 1942, 39–40, box 46, file 44–674, FBI.

2. McRee interview; Isaiah Shine, 24 January 1941, Electronic Army Serial Number Merged File, 1938–1946, AER.

3. McRee interview; Falkner, "Unknown Subjects," 47.

4. McRee interview.

5. On white racial anxiety and political backlash in the World War II South, see Burran, "Racial Violence in the South during World War II"; Daniel, "Going among Strangers"; Feldman, "Southern Disillusionment"; Finley, *Delaying the Dream*, 56–96.

6. Nelson, "Organized Labor and the Struggle for Black Equality in Mobile," 952–7, 967–8.

7. Sara Craigen Kennedy, "Pearl River County (Bilbo's Home), Mississippi," 23–5 November 1942, 1, box II:A859, NAACP.

8. Odum, *Race and Rumors of Race*, 73; Sparrow, *Warfare State*, 96–100.

9. Odum, *Race and Rumors of Race*, 73; Craigen Kennedy, "Pearl River County (Bilbo's Home), Mississippi," 1–2.

10. Enoc P. Waters, "Ignorance and War Hysteria Found Underlying Causes of 2 Lynchings," *Chicago Defender*, 13 March 1943, 13; Robert N. Ford, Mississippi State College, 4 March 1943, folder "Observational Reports...(1 of 5)," box 84, HWO; Craigen Kennedy, "Pearl River County (Bilbo's Home), Mississippi," 3.

11. Pearlie Goldman, University of Alabama, 30 January 1943, folder "Observational Reports...(1 of 5)," box 83, HWO; "From One Who Knows the Situation of the South" to Franklin D. Roosevelt, 22 October 1942, section 2, box 955, case file #144-41-5, Civil Rights Division, DOJ; Sara Craigen Kennedy, "Shubuta, Mississippi," 21 November 1942, 2, box II:A859, NAACP.

12. McRee interview; Victor Bernstein, "Mississippi Laments Lynchings—but Doing Something about Them Is Another Matter," *PM*, 28 October 1942, 3; Waters, "Ignorance and War Hysteria," 13.

13. Enoc P. Waters, "Two Lynched Boys Were Ace Scrap Iron Collectors in Mississippi Town," *Chicago Defender*, 6 March 1943, 13; Falkner, "Unknown Subjects," 17, 44.

14. Waters, "Ignorance and War Hysteria," 13.

15. Ibid.

16. Falkner, "Unknown Subjects," 32–4.

17. Ibid., 54.

18. Ibid., 32–3, 36–7, 54.

19. Ibid., 26–7, 32–3, 37.

20. Ibid., 32–4; US Department of Commerce, *US Census, 1940: Characteristics of the Population*, vol. 2, part 4, 255.
21. Falkner, "Unknown Subjects," 53, 37.
22. Ibid., 26–7, 34.
23. Ronald Earl Sherk, "Unknown Subjects: Lynching of Charles Lang...and Ernest Green," 13 November 1942, 2, box 46, file 44–674, FBI; Falkner, "Unknown Subjects," 43.
24. Sherk, "Unknown Subjects," 2; Falkner, "Unknown Subjects," 40. Dorothy Martin's testimony, and that of her father, corroborates that she had never seen Ernest Green; see Falkner, "Unknown Subjects," 34–5.
25. Falkner, "Unknown Subjects," 27–8.
26. J. Don Davis, "Here's the Real Story of Lynching of Children," Baltimore *Afro-American*, 31 October 1942, 2; McRee interview; Waters, "Two Lynched Boys Were Ace Scrap Iron Collectors," 13.
27. Falkner, "Unknown Subjects," 42, 44.
28. Ibid., 45.
29. J. A. Cimperman, "Memorandum for Mr. Mumford," 13 October 1942; Wendell Berge, "Memorandum for the Director, FBI," 13 October 1942; J. Edgar Hoover to SAC [special agent in charge], Jackson, 14 October 1942; all in box 46, file 44–674, FBI.
30. Waldrep, *African Americans Confront Lynching*, 85–7; Sitkoff, *New Deal for Blacks*, 66.
31. Sullivan, *Lift Every Voice*, 237–41; Zangrando, *NAACP Crusade against Lynching*, 162, 266.
32. Rotnem, "The Federal Civil Right 'Not to Be Lynched,'" 57; Capeci, *Lynching of Cleo Wright*; Plummer, *Rising Wind*, 93.
33. Hoover to SAC, Jackson.
34. "Governor Says to Push Probe," *Meridian Star*, 13 October 1942, 1; "Lynching Prober Working on Case, Johnson Reveals," *Jackson Daily News*, 15 October 1942, 10.
35. For a general survey of politics and society in wartime Mississippi, see Morgan, "At the Crossroads."
36. "Governor Says to Push Probe," *Meridian Star*, 13 October 1942, 3.
37. Falkner, "Unknown Subjects," 3. Mary Wesley, a Quitman native who migrated to Las Vegas, claims the town's leading lawmen aided and abetted the mob that gunned down her father, Alec Wesley, in 1941. The "Sheriff Faulkner" referred to in her account is most likely a reference to Fortner Dabbs. See Orleck, *Storming Caesar's Palace*, 22–5.
38. "Ozie Wilkerson Killed Tuesday Night," *Clarke County Tribune*, 2 January 1931, 1; "Dabbs Freed in Circuit Court," *Clarke County Tribune*, 18 March 1932, 1.

39. Parchman Penitentiary ledgers, inmate 5730, book N (1930–5), microfilm roll 13795, series 1567, MDOC; "G. F. Dabbs for Town Marshall," *Clarke County Tribune*, 15 April 1938, 1.
40. Falkner, "Unknown Subjects," 15–6.
41. Ibid., 15–6.
42. Ibid., 9.
43. Ibid., 30.
44. Sherk, "Unknown Subjects," 3; Falkner, "Unknown Subjects," 52.
45. Richard E. Nelson, "Unknown Subjects: Lynching of Charles Lang…and Ernest Green," 3 December 1942, 2, box 46, file 44–674, FBI; Falkner, "Unknown Subjects," 18, 29, 52.
46. Falkner, "Unknown Subjects," 41, 45, 8, 31.
47. Ibid., 25–6, 29.
48. Sherk, "Unknown Subjects," 1, 3.
49. Falkner, "Unknown Subjects," 46, 35, 39.
50. Ibid., 45–6.
51. Ibid., 45.
52. Ibid., 41, 51.
53. "An (Axis?) to Grind?," *Meridian Star*, 20 October 1942, 4.
54. Madison Jones to Walter White, 7 November 1942; Madison S. Jones, "Shubuta, Miss.," typescript, n.d.; both in box II:A411, NAACP; Victor Bernstein, "Deep South Fights, but Not for 4 Freedoms," Baltimore *Afro-American*, 19 September 1942, 17; Jane Dailey, "Sexual Politics of Race," 151.
55. Bernstein, "Deep South Fights," 17.
56. Victor Bernstein, "Folks in Dixie 'Lynch Town' Don't Care about FBI Probe," *Pittsburgh Courier*, 31 October 1942, 1; Falkner, "Unknown Subjects," 3.
57. Bernstein, "Mississippi Laments Lynchings," 2. The county sheriff, county attorney, and justice of the peace who presided over the boys' preliminary hearing all claimed that the boys were older than fourteen. See Falkner, "Unknown Subjects," 8, 18, 23 (and see 49 for confirmation of the boys' ages).
58. Bernstein, "Mississippi Laments Lynchings," 2.
59. Ibid.
60. Ibid.
61. Ibid.
62. "Two Negro Boys Lynched by Mob," *Clarke County Tribune*, 16 October 1942, 1; Bernstein, "Mississippi Laments Lynchings," 2.
63. Bernstein, "Mississippi Laments Lynchings," 2.
64. E. A. Jackson, "Mob Lynches 3rd Victim," Baltimore *Afro-American*, 24 October 1942, 1; "State Troops Placed on Guard after Negro Howard Wash Was Taken and Lynched," *Laurel Leader-Call*, 17 October 1942, 1.

65. Victor Rotnem and Frank Coleman, "Memorandum for Mr. Wendell Berge," 9 December 1942, section 6; Wendell Berge, "Memorandum for the Attorney General," 10 December 1942, section 1; both in box 956, case file #144-41-5, Civil Rights Division, DOJ. For an extended discussion of the Wash case, see Boyett, *Right to Revolt*, 21–31.
66. Bernstein, "Mississippi Laments Lynchings," 3.
67. "State Troops Placed on Guard," 1; "Police Officer Slain by Negro at Hazlehurst," *Jackson Daily News*, 18 October 1942, 1; "5 Negroes Moved to City Jail after Laurel Lynching," *Jackson Daily News*, 18 October 1942, 1.
68. "Biddle Orders Probe Lynchings in Mississippi," *Meridian Star*, 20 October 1942, 1; "Governor Says Duty Is Finished in Lynchings," *Jackson Daily News*, 21 October 1942, 1.
69. Bernstein, "Mississippi Laments Lynchings," 3.
70. Sara Craigen Kennedy, "Jackson, Mississippi," 2 December 1942, 3, box II:A859, NAACP; "Take Us Over, Yankees!," *Jackson Daily News*, 21 October 1942, 4; "Governor Is 'Shocked,'" *Jackson Daily News*, 19 October 1942, 6.
71. Craigen Kennedy, "Jackson, Mississippi," 3; "Take Us Over, Yankees!," 4; "Governor Is 'Shocked,'" 6.
72. Bernstein, "Mississippi Laments Lynchings," 2.
73. Ibid.
74. Ibid., 2–3.
75. Rotnem and Coleman, "Memorandum for Mr. Wendell Berge."
76. Toxey Hall to Wendell Berge, 2 November 1942, section 4, box 955, case file #144-41-5, Civil Rights Division, DOJ.
77. Falkner, "Unknown Subjects," 20-2.
78. McRee interview. The hospital doctor confirmed to FBI agents that Shine was received on 15 October 1942—three days after the lynching. See Falkner, "Unknown Subjects," 47–8.
79. Faulkner, "Unknown Subjects," 47–8.
80. Ibid., 48.
81. Ibid.

CHAPTER FOUR

1. Roy Wilkins, "Fury Spurs Foes of Lynching," *Amsterdam Star-News*, 24 October 1942, 1.
2. "Defiant Dixie in Poll Tax Rout, Lynches 2, Forms Vigilantes" and "Answer to the Poll Tax," both in *Amsterdam Star-News*, 17 October 1942, 1.
3. "Defiant Dixie in Poll Tax Rout" and "Answer to the Poll Tax," 1; Wilkins, "Fury Spurs Foes of Lynching," 1.

4. "An American Citizen" to Franklin D. Roosevelt, 30 October 1942, case file #144-41-5, section 3, box 955, Civil Rights Division, DOJ; "Jail Warden Censors Mob Victims' Picture," Baltimore *Afro-American*, 31 October 1942, 2; Leon Harris to Thurgood Marshall, 23 October 1942, box II:A411, NAACP.

5. Wilkins, "Fury Spurs Foes of Lynching," 1; "Defiant Dixie in Poll Tax Rout," 1, 19.

6. Wilkins, *Standing Fast*, 1–3, 14.

7. Ibid., 15–6.

8. Ibid., 41–4.

9. Sullivan, *Lift Every Voice*, 255–6; Egerton, *Speak Now Against the Day*, 214–7; Garfinkel, *When Negroes March*, 60–2, Anderson, *A. Philip Randolph*, 257–9; Janken, *Mr. NAACP*, 253–7; Bates, *Pullman Porters*, 157–60; Lucander, *Winning the War for Democracy*, 32–7.

10. Wilkins, *Standing Fast*, 178–9.

11. Ibid., 178–81; NAACP, *On Guard against Racial Discrimination*, n.p.

12. Rotnem, "The Federal Civil Right 'Not to Be Lynched,'" 57.

13. Hall, *Revolt against Chivalry*, 207–8. The NAACP was not alone in making the argument that lynching was changing. White antilynching activist Jessie Daniel Ames, while advocating a more narrow definition of lynching than other activists, followed the NAACP's lead with her 1942 pamphlet, *The Changing Character of Lynching*. On activists' disagreements regarding the precise definition of lynching in the 1940s, see Waldrep, *Many Faces of Judge Lynch*, 127–50. The decline in lynching has led to a relative dearth of scholarship on the latter years of lynching. See Brundage, "Conclusion: Reflections on Lynching Scholarship," 412; Carrigan, "No Ordinary Crime," 848.

14. NAACP, *Lynching Goes Underground*, 1–7. Kester had investigated and written for the NAACP before. See Dunbar, *Against the Grain*, 34, 82, 158.

15. NAACP, *Lynching Goes Underground*, 1–7; Zangrando, *NAACP Crusade against Lynching*, 163; Rushdy, *The End of American Lynching*, 98.

16. Anonymous to "The NAACP," 12 October 1942, box II:A411, NAACP.

17. Walter White appeared on the cover of the 28 January 1938 issue of *Time*; Roy Wilkins to Walter White, 8 September 1942, folder "Kennedy, Craigen, Study, 1942–43," box II:A859, NAACP.

18. Sara Craigen Kennedy to Walter White, 5 October 1942, box II:A859, NAACP.

19. Ibid.

20. Odette Harper to Walter White, 23 February 1943, 1; C. Freeland to Craigen Kennedy, 26 October 1942; "A Survey of Opinions Held by Mississippi and Alabama White People Regarding Negroes," 2–3; all in box II:A859, NAACP.

21. Walter F. White to Sara Craigen Kennedy, 18 November 1942; Sara Craigen Kennedy to Odette Harper, n.d.; Sara Craigen Kennedy to Odette Harper, 16 November 1942; all in box II:A859, NAACP.

22. Sara Craigen Kennedy, "Shubuta, Mississippi," 21 November 1942, 1, box II:A859, NAACP; Enoc P. Waters, "Ignorance and War Hysteria Found Underlying Causes of 2 Lynchings," *Chicago Defender*, 13 March 1943, 13.
23. Craigen Kennedy, "Shubuta, Mississippi," 1.
24. Ibid.
25. Ibid., 1–2.
26. Sara Craigen Kennedy, "Shubuta and Quitman, Mississippi," 30 November 1942, 1, box II:A859, NAACP.
27. Ibid.
28. Ibid.
29. Ibid., 1–2.
30. Ibid., 2–3.
31. Sara Craigen Kennedy, "Interview with Dr. H. M. Ivy," 20 November 1942, box II:A859, NAACP.
32. Sara Craigen Kennedy, "Jackson, Mississippi," 2 December 1942, 1, box II:A859, NAACP.
33. Sara Craigen Kennedy, "Pearl River County (Bilbo's Home), Mississippi," 23–5 November 1942, 1, box II:A859, NAACP.
34. S. Kennedy, *Southern Exposure*, 95. Alabama, Arkansas, Florida, Georgia, Mississippi, South Carolina, Tennessee, Texas, and Virginia required the poll tax, although South Carolina waived the requirement for the white primary. For a comprehensive study of the poll tax in these states, see Ogden, *The Poll Tax*.
35. "Defiant Dixie in Poll Tax Rout," 19; Congress, House, 77th Cong., 2nd sess., *Congressional Record* 88, 8078; "Rankin Attacks Edgar Brown as Vote Looms for Negroes in South," *Chicago Defender*, 24 October 1942, 8.
36. "Defiant Dixie in Poll Tax Rout," 1; "Two Negro Children Lynched," *Daily Worker*, 13 October 1942, 1; Eugene Gordon, "Davis, Marcantonio Demand U.S. Jail Mississippi Lynchers," *Daily Worker*, 14 October 1942, 1, 4.
37. "The Bitter Fruit," *Meridian Star*, 13 October 1942, 4.
38. Craigen Kennedy, "Pearl River County," 3; "Survey of Opinions," 21.
39. Craigen Kennedy, "Shubuta and Quitman, Mississippi," 2–3; Rev. J. H. Roseberry to Theodore G. Bilbo, 6 April 1944, folder 2, box 1076, TGB.
40. Robert De Vore, "Bilbo Touches Off Filibuster on Poll Tax Bill," *Washington Post*, 14 November 1942, 1; Theodore G. Bilbo to A. M. Jones, 23 November 1942, folder 1, box 1076; Pvt. Robert Roberts to Theodore G. Bilbo, 11 May 1944, folder 6, box 1076; Lester Etheridge to Theodore G. Bilbo, 24 October 1945, folder 10, box 1084; all in TGB; Craigen Kennedy, "Pearl River County," 3, box II:A859, NAACP.
41. "Biddle Orders Probe [of] Lynchings in Mississippi," *Meridian Star*, 20 October 1942, 1, 3.
42. "Seventy-One Mississippi Leaders Urge Action on Lynchings," NAACP press release, 14 November 1942, box II:A411, NAACP.

43. Buhite and Levy, *FDR's Fireside Chats*, 240–8.

44. Roy Wilkins to *Pittsburgh Courier* and Baltimore *Afro-American*, 19 October 1942, box II:A411, NAACP; "Chicago Negro Leaders Angry about Lynchings," *Chicago Tribune*, 14 October 1942, n.p., clipping in frame 634, reel 232, TNCF.

45. Albert Deutsch, "Kid-Lynchers," *PM*, 13 October 1942, 21; "Men of the 93rd Division" to Franklin Roosevelt, 7 November 1942, section 5; Lena Harris, Luna Lane, et al., to Franklin D. Roosevelt, 22 October 1942, section 2; Isaac Oden to Franklin Roosevelt, 14 November 1942, section 5; all in box 955, case file #144-41-5, Civil Rights Division, DOJ; Hilliard Lang, 16 December 1942, Electronic Army Serial Number Merged File, 1938–1946, AER; "Tan Yank Engineers Paved Way for Armies in Europe," Baltimore *Afro-American*, 14 April 1945, 7.

46. White, *Rope and Faggot*, 3; NAACP, *Annual Report for 1942*, 33–4.

47. Victor Bernstein, "Mississippi Laments Lynchings—but Doing Something about Them Is Another Matter," *PM*, 28 October 1942, 2.

48. Joint Legislative Committee, *Subversion in Racial Unrest*, 265.

49. Natchez Social and Civic Club to Francis Biddle, 8 November 1942, section 5; M. C. Atkins to Franklin D. Roosevelt, 19 October 1942, section 1; Rita Reese to Franklin D. Roosevelt, 22 October 1942, section 2; Lois L. Moses to Franklin D. Roosevelt, 21 October 1942, section 2; all in box 955, case file #144-41-5, Civil Rights Division, DOJ.

50. "Two Dixie Youngsters Lynched by Crackers," *People's Voice*, 17 October 1942, 2; "Soap Box," *People's Voice*, 25 April 1942, 5; Hamilton, *Adam Clayton Powell, Jr.*, 125.

51. Gordon, "Davis, Marcantonio Demand U.S. Jail Mississippi Lynchers," 1, 4. For more on New York's "Black Popular Front," see Biondi, *To Stand and Fight*, 6–10.

52. D. T. Carter, *Scottsboro*, 331–5; Goodman, *Stories of Scottsboro*, 244–5; Gilmore, *Defying Dixie*, 123–4.

53. Paul B. Johnson to Vito Marcantonio, 14 October 1942; Vito Marcantonio et al. to Arthur Spingarn, 19 October 1942; Vito Marcantonio et al. to Walter White, 19 October 1942; all in box II:A411, NAACP; "New Yorkers Up in Arms against Mobs," Baltimore *Afro-American*, 24 October 1942, 14; "Emergency Stop Lynching Committee Formed," 31 October 1942, *Norfolk Journal and Guide*, A13; "Mississippi's Lynching Spree Spurs Many Groups into Action," *People's Voice*, 24 October 1942, 1.

54. Miller, *Born along the Color Line*, 234; Eugene Gordon, "2,000 in Harlem Say: Act against Lynchers," *Daily Worker*, 26 October 1942, 1; "Antilynchers Rally Sunday: Great Mass Meeting to Be Held at Salem Church," *Amsterdam Star-News*, 24 October 1942, 15.

55. A. Philip Randolph to "Dear Reverend," 28 October 1942, frame 551, reel 20, APR; "Anti-Lynching Meeting Held in City Hall Park," *Amsterdam Star-News*,

14 November 1942, 2. On Randolph's leadership of, and eventual split with, the National Negro Congress, see Gellman, *Death Blow to Jim Crow*, 26–30, 155–9.

56. Roy Wilkins to Franklin D. Roosevelt, 16 October 1942, box II:A512, NAACP.

57. Adam Clayton Powell, "Mississippi Secedes from the Union," *People's Voice*, 24 October 1942, 24.

58. Rollins and Hines, *All Is Never Said*, 74–6, 89–92.

59. Waters, *American Diary*, 325–6; Enoc P. Waters, "War Bound to Improve Mississippi since State Cannot Be Any Worse," *Chicago Defender*, 6 March 1943, 7.

60. Waters, *American Diary*, 231, 326–7.

61. Ibid., 327, 350; Enoc P. Waters, "Waters Finds Rural Areas Lag behind Cities in Race Militancy," *Chicago Defender*, 15 May 1943, 13.

62. Enoc P. Waters, "Right to Vote in South Is Key to Real Emancipation, Believes Tougaloo Vet," *Chicago Defender*, 6 March 1943, 9.

63. Enoc P. Waters, "War Improving Mississippi Race Relations Slowly but Very Surely," *Chicago Defender*, 13 March 1943, 8; "Mississippi Approaches a Reign of Terror," *Jackson Advocate*, 24 October 1942, 8; "On the Shubuta Lynchings," *Jackson Advocate*, 17 October 1942, 8; Thompson, *Lynchings in Mississippi*, 127.

64. Waters, *American Diary*, 328–9.

65. Ibid., 330.

66. Ibid.

67. William Pickens to Roy Wilkins, 11 April 1940, Box II:C97, NAACP; "Two Negro Children Lynched at the Age of 14," *Weekly Echo*, 16 October 1942, 2; "3 Lynchings in One Week," *Weekly Echo*, 23 October 1942, 2.

68. Roy Young to William Pickens, 5 August 1940, box II:C97, NAACP; Waters, *American Diary*, 331.

69. Waters, *American Diary*, 331; Enoc P. Waters, "Two Lynched Boys Were Ace Scrap Iron Collectors in Mississippi Town," *Chicago Defender*, 6 March 1943, 13; Enoc P. Waters, "Ignorance and War Hysteria Found Underlying Causes of 2 Lynchings," *Chicago Defender*, 13 March 1943, 13.

70. Waters, "Two Lynched Boys Were Ace Scrap Iron Collectors," 13; Waters, "Ignorance and War Hysteria," 13.

71. Waters, "Ignorance and War Hysteria," 13; "Miss. Lyncher's Conscience Talks on His Death Bed," *Chicago Defender*, 10 July 1943, 2; McRee interview.

72. Waters, *American Diary*, 328–9. "As important as the responses of black institutions and black elites to white violence were," historian W. Fitzhugh Brundage argues, "the resistance of unorganized and seemingly powerless blacks is of equal significance, especially in a region and at a time when only a small minority of blacks were either members of reform groups or participants

in organized protest." See Brundage, "The Roar on the Other Side of Silence," 271.

73. Waters, "Waters Finds Rural Areas Lag," 15 May 1943, 13; Waters, "Ignorance and War Hysteria," 13.

74. Waters, "Waters Finds Rural Areas Lag," 13.

75. J. Don Davis, "Here's Real Story of Lynching of Children," Baltimore *Afro-American*, 31 October 1942, 2.

76. Ibid., 1; J. Don Davis, "Negroes Refuse to Inter Boys Killed by Mob," *Houston Informer*, 31 October 1942, n.p., clipping in frame 631, reel 232, TNCF; Walter Atkins, "Shubuta Bridge's Toll Stands at Six Lynch Victims, but Span Is Doomed," *Chicago Defender*, 7 November 1942, 1.

77. Atkins, "Shubuta Bridge's Toll Stands at Six Lynch Victims," 1; Rampersad, *Life of Langston Hughes*, vol. 2, 53–5; Hughes, *Collected Works*, vol. 2, 245.

78. E. Jackson, "Mob Lynches 3rd Victim," Baltimore *Afro-American*, 24 October 1942, 1; Langston Hughes, "Jim Crow's Last Stand," Baltimore *Afro-American*, 24 October 1942, 14.

79. Langston Hughes, "Here to Yonder," *Chicago Defender*, 21 November 1942, 14; Hughes, *Collected Poems*, 242–4.

80. C. P. Trussell, "House Democratic Revolt Demies Post to Marcantonio," *New York Times*, 20 January 1943, 1; Harry McAlpin, "Poll Taxers Riding High in New Congress Session," *Chicago Defender*, 30 January 1943, 9.

81. "Langston Hughes Wonders Why No Lynching Probes," *Chicago Defender*, 1 October 1955, 4.

82. Ibid.

CHAPTER FIVE

1. Caroline Buxton Thomas, interview by author, 24 August 2010, Shubuta, Mississippi.

2. Untitled newsletter, [ca. December 1965], frame 286, reel 65, SNCC; FDP key list mailing #5, 7 January 1966, 7, SCR-ID 2-165-6-29-5-1-1, MSSC.

3. Greenberg, *The Devil Has Slippery Shoes*, 95–96.

4. Yahya Ibn Shabazz (John Otis Sumrall), telephone interview by author, 8 February 2009; John Cumbler, interview by author, 6 November 2009, Louisville, Kentucky; Payne, *I've Got the Light of Freedom*, 36–40, 53; NAACP, *M Is for Mississippi and Murder*; Smead, *Blood Justice*.

5. Stern, "Right to Vote in Clarke County," 174–7. Medgar Evers biographer Michael Vinson Williams has emphasized the pivotal role of the state NAACP in early voter registration attempts across the state. See Williams, *Mississippi Martyr*, 149–52.

6. A. L. Hopkins, investigator report, 31 July 1961, SSC-ID 2-100-0-25-1-1-1, MSSC; Stern, "Right to Vote in Clarke County," 173.

7. Stern, "Right to Vote in Clarke County," 167–8.

8. Ibid. On the voting rights provisions of the Civil Rights Acts of 1957 and 1960, see Lawson, *Black Ballots*, 203–87. On the role of the Civil Rights Division in early voting rights cases in Mississippi, see Martin, *Count Them One by One*, 19–29.

9. A. L. Hopkins, "Investigation of NAACP Activities in Clarke and Lauderdale Counties," 9 January 1961, SSC-ID 2-100-0-10-1-1-1; Zack J. Van Landingham, "Subject: NAACP, Clarke County, Mississippi," 27 January 1960, SSC-ID 2-100-0-3-1-1-1; Zack J. Van Landingham to director, "Subject: NAACP, Clarke County, Mississippi," 2 March 1959, SSC-ID 2-100-0-2-1-1-1; all in MSSC. On the origins and mission of the Sovereignty Commission, see Katagiri, *Mississippi State Sovereignty Commission*, 3–139; Crespino, *In Search of Another Country*, 18–74.

10. Bolton, *Hardest Deal of All*, 53.

11. Ibid., 56; Office of School Building and Transportation, "Survey—Clarke County Public Schools—1955," 9–11, 20–1, 44, 56, box 2670, series 1653, school building surveys, MDED.

12. Hopkins, "Investigation of NAACP activities in Clarke and Lauderdale Counties," 9 January 1961, 2; "Accuse Miss. Educator of Backing Bias," *Chicago Defender*, 2 January 1954, 1; C. W. Falconer, "What We Must Not Do," 17 July 1958, clipping in SSC-ID 9-6-0-3-1-1-1; C. W. Falconer, untitled editorial, West Point *Daily Times-Leader*, 27 March 1959, clipping in SSC-ID 9-6-0-7-1-1-1; Zack J. Van Landingham to C. W. Falconer, 4 November 1958, SSC-ID 9-6-0-1-1-1-1; C. W. Falconer to Gov. J. P. Coleman, 25 October 1958, SSC-ID 9-6-0-2-1-1-1 and 9-6-0-2-2-1-1; all in MSSC. For a general discussion of black defenders of segregation in Mississippi and elsewhere, see Winner, "Doubtless Sincere."

13. Virgil Downing, "Civil Rights and NAACP Activity in Clarke County," 20 March 1961, SSC-ID 2-100-0-24-1-1-1, MSSC; Stern, "Right to Vote in Clarke County," 167–8; "File First Vote Suits in Mississippi," *Chicago Defender*, 8 July 1961, 1; "'Fill the Jails', King Tells 2,500," Baltimore *Afro-American*, 15 July 1961, 3. An important earlier visit to the state, a voter registration conference organized by the Southern Christian Leadership Conference's Ella Baker, convened in Clarksdale in May 1958. See Hamlin, *Crossroads at Clarksdale*, 53–5; Ransby, *Ella Baker*, 185–6.

14. Stern, "Right to Vote in Clarke County," 169.

15. Ibid., 169, 172–3.

16. "Clarke County Registrar Told to Stop Delays in Voter Registration," *Mississippi Free Press*, 16 February 1963, 1; "Justice Department Suit Hits Miss. Prosecutions," *Atlanta Daily World*, 22 March 1964, 1; Stern, "Right to Vote in Clarke County," 181–5.

17. Dittmer, *Local People*, 91–9, 118; Arsenault, *Freedom Riders*, 265–9.

18. Dittmer, *Local People*, 246; Huie, *Three Lives for Mississippi*, 73–4; Mickey Schwerner, "Field Report for Mickey and Rita Schwerner," 26 January 1964; Mickey Schwerner, "Weekly Report from Meridian Community Center," 2–7 February 1964; both in folder 14, box 1, SEDF; J. C. Killingsworth, MFDP chapter 59, interview transcript, 18, folder 165, box 7, KZSU.

19. Dittmer, *Local People*, 272–302; Dallek, *Flawed Giant*, 162–4; "Fourth District Caucus MFDP, Minutes," 2 August 1964, 3, section 7, reel 1, LCFDP.

20. A. L. Hopkins, "Clarke County," 6 November 1964, SSC-ID 10-22-0-16-1-1-1, MSSC; "Clarke County," 25 January 1965, frame 276; "Memo for Attorneys to Visit Clarke County," frame 274; both in reel 65, SNCC; "1964 Presidential and Congressional Election Results—Typed," box E-2; D. H. Donald, Jr., to Wert A. Yerger, 5 September 1964, folder "1963–64, County: Clarke," box F-3; both in MSGOP. A standard-bearer of the state GOP's "Lily-White" faction, Walker "had no interest in the black vote" and attempted to "outsegregate" his Democratic opponents. See Danielson, *After Freedom Summer*, 23–4.

21. Hopkins, "Clarke County," 1.

22. Branch, *At Canaan's Edge*, 84; Killingsworth, MFDP chapter 59, 2–3, 16.

23. "Demonstration Sponsored by COFO at Federal Building, Quitman, Mississippi, March 30, 1965," 5 April 1965, file 157–2835, FBI.

24. Killingsworth, MFDP chapter 59, 23 (part of the quotation is omitted from the transcript, but is on the taped recording); "Clark County" [*sic*], *Mississippi Freedom Democratic Party Newsletter*, no. 6, 28 July 1965, 5, segment 17, reel 1, LCFDP.

25. Killingsworth, MFDP chapter 59, 2, 15–7.

26. "Clarke County Project," December 1964; Ed Hollander to Bill Curtis, 5 January 1965; Greg Kaslo, "Semi-annual Project Report," 16 March 1965; all in part 2, reel 6, CORE; "Community Spotlight Shines on the Rufus & Katie McRee Hotel in Quitman, MS," February 2009, clipping in file 023-QTM-0026, HPD.

27. Shabazz (Sumrall) interview, 8 February 2009; Warner Buxton, MFDP chapter 51, interview transcript, 1, folder 150, box 6, KZSU; Yahya Ibn Shabazz, "Author Biography," http://www2.xlibris.com/bookstore/author.aspx?authorid=5561, accessed 13 September 2010.

28. Judith Wright, untitled, [March 1965]; John Sumrall, affidavit, 20 January 1964; both in segment 54, reel 2, LCFDP; W. C. Bester, affidavit, 7 January 1965; Robert Hand, affidavit, 7 January 1965; both in frames 281–2, reel 65, SNCC; Buxton, MFDP chapter 51, 5; FDP county reports, 6–19 November 1965, 3, SCR-ID 2-165-5-10-3-1-1; A. L. Hopkins, "Investigation of Activities in Clarkeco State Park near Quitman, Mississippi in Clarke County," 9 June 1965, 3, SCR-ID 2-82-0-63-3-1-1; both items in MSSC.

29. "M.F.D.P. Attempts to Picket Sheriff Clark," *Mississippi Freedom Democratic Party Newsletter*, no. 3, 24 April 1965, 1, 3; Killingsworth, MFDP chapter 59, 6–7; Dittmer, *Local People*, 344–5.

30. Killingsworth, MFDP chapter 59, 10; Nina Boal, MFDP chapter 50, interview transcript, 15–6, folder 25, box 1; Don Chapman, MFDP chapter 52, interview transcript, 13–4, folder 27, box 1; both in KZSU. For registration estimates, see "Voter Registration Figures," 21 August 1965, 1–2; "Miss. Voter Registration—A September Break-down," n.d., 1; both in folder 4, box 4, RHM. Statewide, nearly a quarter-million African Americans registered in the first two years following the president's signing of the Voting Rights Act in August 1965. Parker, *Black Votes Count*, 30.
31. "Memo for Attorneys to Visit Clarke County."
32. Untitled newsletter, [ca. December 1965]; Newman, *Divine Agitators*, 177.
33. Buxton, MFDP chapter 51, 15.
34. Greenberg, *The Devil Has Slippery Shoes*, 96.
35. Dittmer, *Local People*, 370; Sanders, "'To Be Free of Fear'"; D. C. Carter, *Music Has Gone out of the Movement*, 31–50.
36. *Friends of Children of Mississippi*, 6 April 1968, n.p., folder 6, box 4, CDGM-NY.
37. Ibid., n.p.; Greenberg, *The Devil Has Slippery Shoes*, 95–6.
38. *Friends of Children of Mississippi*, n.p.; Greenberg, *The Devil Has Slippery Shoes*, 95–6, 626.
39. Carter, *Music Has Gone out of the Movement*, 31–4; Andrew Kopkind, "Bureaucracy's Long Arm: Too Heady a Start in Mississippi?" *New Republic*, 21 August 1965, 21; John C. Stennis to Mrs. L. P. Newsome, 23 August 1965, folder 6, box 4, series 1, JCS; Dittmer, *Local People*, 369–71.
40. "Copies of Letters Some of Our Community People Wrote to Washington," *Child Development of Mississippi Newsletter*, no. 5, n.d., 7, in folder 3, box 1, CDGM-NY.
41. Jimana Sumrall to John Mudd, 6 October 1965; "Problems Connected with Quitman Headstart Center," 11 October 1965; both in F283—Quitman, reel 4; Mamie H. Jones to Sargent Shriver, 29 January 1966, F291—Shubuta and Quitman, reel 5; all in CDGM.
42. Carter, *Music Has Gone out of the Movement*, 31–49; Sanders, "'To Be Free of Fear,'" 178–80. Student registration and employee rosters located in F290—Shubuta, reel 5, CDGM.
43. Mary Emmons, "Shubuta Center," 1, 1 February 1965, F289—Shubuta, reel 5, CDGM.
44. Carrie Davis, "Shubuta Center," 2 December 1965; Garlee Johnson, "Shubuta Center," 6 January 1966, both in F289—Shubuta; "Community Preparedness Form," 10 January 1966, F290—Shubuta; Polly Greenberg, "Shubuta Lodge Hall," 24 March 1966, F289—Shubuta; all in reel 5, CDGM.
45. Allie H. Jones, "Shubuta," n.d., 2, F289—Shubuta; untitled and handwritten questionnaire responses from Dorothy Lee Carpenter, Lucile Smith, and Frankie M. Terrell, n.d.; all in F287—Shubuta–Mt. Zion, reel 5, CDGM.

46. John Cumbler to Judith Kwiat, July [n.d.] 1966, handwritten personal correspondence in possession of author. Françoise Hamlin has argued that War on Poverty programs in Mississippi "diversified the movement landscape with [their] focus on economic equality." In Clarksdale, the focus of her study and a non-CDGM town, she notes that programs supported by the Office of Economic Opportunity like Head Start often elevated black "elites" over the less educated and politically connected but nonetheless put federal money and "muscle" behind community development and economic opportunity. See Hamlin, *Crossroads at Clarksdale*, 209–43. On the role of antipoverty programs in civic engagement and black political empowerment, see Ashmore, *Carry It On*, 132–3, 163–77.

47. Gail Falk, "Child Development Group in Mississippi Fights for Its Life against Politicians," *Southern Courier*, 13–4 August 1966, 4; Andrew Kopkind, "How Do You Fight It?" *New Republic*, 3 September 1966, 7.

48. Falk, "Child Development Group in Mississippi," 4; Emmons, "Shubuta Center," 1; "Memo Re: Personnel in Shubuta, Quitman Area," n.d., F282-Quitman, reel 4, CDGM.

49. Cumbler to Kwiat, July; Falk, "Child Development Group in Mississippi," 4.

50. T. George Silicott and William K. Wolfe, typescript, "Investigation and Explanation of a Head Start Program in Mississippi," n.d., 2–4, folder "Reports of Investigations...1966, 2 of 2," box 18, subject files 1965–9, CAP Office, Records of the Director, OEO; Hamlin, *Crossroads at Clarksdale*, 225–6.

51. Dittmer, *Local People*, 389; Goudsouzian, *Down to the Crossroads*, 47.

52. Branch, *At Canaan's Edge*, 476–8; Dittmer, *Local People*, 391–4; Frank Hunt, "It Won't Be the Same...," Baltimore *Afro-American*, 18 June 1966, 1–2.

53. Goudsouzian, *Down to the Crossroads*, 70–1; Roy Reed, "Marchers Detour for Voting Drive," *New York Times*, 12 June 1966, 82.

54. Carter, *Music Has Gone out of the Movement*, 110; Dittmer, *Local People*, 396; Tuck, *We Ain't What We Ought to Be*, 328; Goudsouzian, *Down to the Crossroads*, 142–3.

55. Dittmer, *Local People*, 397; Goudsouzian, *Down to the Crossroads*, 141–4, 149–52; Joseph, *Waiting 'Til the Midnight Hour*, 132–46; Jeffries, *Bloody Lowndes*, 185–92.

56. Shabazz (Sumrall) interview, 8 February 2009; Goudsouzian, *Down to the Crossroads*, 144, 164; Ladner, "What 'Black Power' Means," 12–3.

57. Ladner, "What 'Black Power' Means," 8; Shabazz (Sumrall) interview, 8 February 2009; Cumbler to Kwiat, July. For more on the role of armed self-defense in the civil rights and Black Power era, see Tyson, *Radio Free Dixie*; Hill, *Deacons for Defense*; Umoja, *We Will Shoot Back*; Cobb, *This Nonviolent Stuff'll Get You Killed*.

58. Greenberg, *Devil Has Slippery Shoes*, 633; Dupont, *Mississippi Praying*, 166; A. L. Hopkins, "Investigation of Integrated Audience at the Commencement

Exercises...," 9 June 1966, 2, SCR-ID 2-100-0-37-2-1-1, MSSC; Shabazz (Sumrall) interview, 8 February 2009; Goudsouzian, *Down to the Crossroads*, 144, 164; Ladner, "What 'Black Power' Means," 15.

59. Umoja, *We Will Shoot Back*, 149.

60. John Cumbler to Judith Kwiat, June [n.d.] 1966, personal correspondence in possession of author.

61. Ibid.

62. Umoja, *We Will Shoot Back*, 130–44, 159–76. On a more prolonged and successful boycott in a smaller Mississippi town, see Crosby, *A Little Taste of Freedom*, 128–47.

63. Cumbler to Kwiat, June; Gail Falk, "Shubuta March Ends in Scuffle and Arrests," *Southern Courier*, 13–4 August 1966, 1.

64. Cumbler to Kwiat, July; Dan Givelber, memo re: "State v. Sumrall," 12 July 1966, in "Sumrall, John, MS v.," reel 112, LCCR.

65. Cunningham, "Shades of Civil Rights Violence"; Crespino, *In Search of Another Country*, 110–5.

66. Cunningham, "Shades of Anti-Civil Rights Violence," 183; House Committee on Un-American Activities, *The Present-Day Ku Klux Klan Movement*, 153; "Racial Situation, Clarke County," 4 August 1966, 3-4, file 157-6512, FBI.

67. Mary Emmons, "Masonic Hall Center, Shubuta," 5 August 1966, F289—Shubuta, reel 5, CDGM; Arrest affidavits in SCR-ID 2-100-0-63-1-1-1 through 2-100-0-66-1-1-1, MSSC; Cumbler to Kwiat, July.

68. L. E. Cole, investigator report, 20 September 1966, 3, SCR-ID 2-100-0-57-3-1-1; Shubuta Community Planning and Improvement Committee to Shubuta Board of Alderman, 20 July 1966, SCR-ID 2-100-0-54-5-1-1; Shubuta Head Start Committee to Board of Alderman, SCR-ID 2-100-0-54-3-1-1; all in MSSC.

69. Terry Keeter, "Russell Considers Shubuta CR Case," *Meridian Star*, 22 October 1966, 5; George S. Busby to "Gentlemen," 3 August 1966, filed in "Killingsworth v. Riley," reel 113, LCCR; "Shubuta," 5 August 1966, F289—Shubuta, reel 5, CDGM.

70. "Chicago Whites 'Stone' King, Battle Policeman," *Meridian Star*, 6 August 1966, 1, 5; Gail Falk, telephone interview by author, 3 July 2012; Falk, "Shubuta March Ends in Scuffle and Arrests," 1; "Racial—Shubuta," 17 August 1966," folder 9, box 19, CAM.

71. Falk, "Shubuta March Ends in Scuffle and Arrests," 1.

72. David R. Underhill, "March's Leaders Argue, Non-Violence or Arms?," *Southern Courier*, 25–6 June 1966, 6; J. M. Curtis, "Civil Rights March, Shubuta, Mississippi," 6 August 1966; "G. S. Busby—H. A. Green," 6 August 1966; both in folder 9, box 19, CAM; Falk, "Shubuta March Ends in Scuffle and Arrests," 1.

73. John Otis Sumrall, typed statement, 8 August 1966, filed in "Killingsworth v. Riley," reel 113, LCCR; Falk, "Shubuta March Ends in Scuffle and Arrests," 1.

74. Sumrall, typed statement; Peter Houghteling, written statement, 9 August 1966; Joseph M. Morse, typed affidavit, 9 August 1966; Fred C. Mittleman, statement, n.d. [August 1966]; Eleanor Gail Falk, typed statement, 8 August 1966; all filed in "Killingsworth v. Riley," reel 113, LCCR.

75. Mittleman, statement; Falk, "Shubuta March Ends in Scuffle and Arrests," 1.

76. "Burnin' the Beatles," *Meridian Star*, 7 August 1966, 1; Michael Grossman, memo re: Shubuta Demonstrations, 13 August 1966, filed in "Killingsworth v. Riley," reel 113, LCCR.

77. Gail Falk, "Shubuta Firings as of Wednesday, Aug. 10...," filed in "Killingsworth v. Riley," reel 113, LCCR.

78. Cole, investigator report, 5; Mamie McFarland, "Statement," 19 September 1966; SCR-ID 2-100-0-54-1-1-1; Houston Nelson, "Statement," 22 September 1966, SCR-ID 2-100-0-70-1-1-1; both in MSSC.

79. Special agents Robert E. Lee and Donald R. Hamrick, "Demonstration March, August 20, 1966, Shubuta...," 30 August 1966, 6, file 157–6579, FBI; J. C. Killingsworth, typed statement "Re: Shubuta on August 20, 1966," 1–3; Joe Gelb and Jack Joyce, "Shubuta March," 1, joint statement; both filed in "Killingsworth v. Riley," reel 113, LCCR; "Shubuta Detail," folder 9, box 19, CAM; H. C. Slay, "Negro March at Shubuta, Mississippi, on August 20, 1966," folder 6, box 147, PBJ.

80. Gelb and Joyce, "Shubuta March," 2; Slay, "Negro March at Shubuta"; Keeter, "Russell Considers Shubuta CR Case," 5.

81. Gelb and Joyce, "Shubuta March," 3; Walter Pickett, typed statement, n.d. [August 1966]; Ann Miller, written statement, n.d. [August 1966]; both in "Killingsworth v. Riley," reel 113, LCCR.

82. Terry Keeter, "Black Power Theme Echoes Here Today in Shubuta Trial," *Meridian Star*, 20 October 1966, 1; Greenberg, *The Devil Has Slippery Shoes*, 629; Killingsworth, "Re: Shubuta on August 20, 1966," 4; Pickett, typed statement.

83. Patricia James, "A Reporter's Story," *Southern Courier*, 27–8 August 1966, 1.

84. Gelb and Joyce, "Shubuta March," 3–5.

85. Yahya Ibn Shabazz (John Otis Sumrall), telephone interview by author, 1 October 2009; Joe Willie Kirksey, written statement, n.d. [August 1966], "Killingsworth v. Riley," reel 113, LCCR; Gelb and Joyce, "Shubuta March," 4; Lee and Hamrick, "Demonstration March," 5.

86. Warner Buxton, "Statement re State v. Sumrall, et al.," n.d., filed in "Sumrall, John, et al., MS v.," reel 113, LCCR.

87. Ibid.; Jimana Sumrall, "Statement re State v. Sumrall, et al.," n.d.; Randall M. Sumrall, "Statement re State v. Sumrall, et al.," n.d.; both in "Sumrall, John, et al., MS v.," reel 113, LCCR; special agent Donald R. Hamrick, "Altercation at Quitman, Mississippi," 27 August 1966, 7–10, file 157–6580, FBI.

88. Kevin W. Cary to Denison Ray, 20 August 1966; John Milton Brown, "Statement re State v. Sumrall, et al.," n.d.; Solomon Marshall, "Statement re State v. Sumrall, et al.," n.d.; all filed in "Sumrall, John, et al., MS v.," reel 113, LCCR.

89. Hamrick, "Altercation at Quitman, Mississippi," 9; Kenneth C. Howard, memo re: "Altercation at Quitman, Mississippi," 20 August 1966, file 157–6580, FBI; Cary to Ray, 20 August; Richard Wylie, memo re: "Summary of Facts," 30 August 1966, 2; Solomon Marshall, "Statement re State v. Sumrall, et al.," n.d.; both in "Sumrall, John, et al., MS v.," reel 113, LCCR.

CHAPTER SIX

1. Gail Falk, "Shubuta after August Marches: Black-Out, Pressure, and Fear," *Southern Courier*, 1–2 October 1966, 2.

2. Shubuta Planning and Improvement Committee to Shubuta Mayor et al., 25 July 1966; Shubuta Head-Start Committee to Shubuta Mayor et al., n.d.; both in folder "CDGM—Gen. Corr.—Folder 3 of 5," box 17, subject files, 1965–9, CAP Office, Office of the Director, OEO.

3. Dan Givelber, memo re: "State v. Sumrall," 12 July 1966, 4, filed in "Sumrall, John, MS v.," reel 112, LCCR; Mayor [Edgar Harris] to Selective Service, 16 September 1966, SCR-ID 2-100-0-56-1-1-1, MSSC.

4. "Negroes Dismissed in Mississippi Town," *New York Times*, 21 August 1966, 74; "Claim of 'Brutality' in Shubuta March Contradicted by DA," *Meridian Star*, 21 August 1966, 1; H. C. Slay, "Negro March at Shubuta, Mississippi, on August 20, 1966," folder 6, box 147, PBJ.

5. "State to Seek Injunction for Clarke County," *Meridian Star*, 26 August 1966, 2; C. A. Marx to Herman Glazier, 22 August 1966, SCR-ID 2-100-0-38-1-1-1, MSSC; "Shubuta Mayor Protests: Racial Agitation Backed by Government Funds?" *Meridian Star*, 30 August 1966, 1; "Poverty Unit's Link to Boycott Studied," *New York Times*, 30 August 1966, 30.

6. Grayson S. Taketa, memo re: Killingsworth v. Riley, 4 September 1966, filed in "Killingsworth v. Riley," reel 113, LCCR; George S. Busby, affidavits against Minnie Lee House and Rachel Smith, 5 September 1966, SCR-ID 2-100-0-60-1-1-1 and 2-100-0-61-1-1-1; L. E. Cole, investigator report, 20 September 1966, 6, SCR-ID 2-100-0-57-6-1-1; all in MSSC. Nine total affidavits were sworn out and signed by Busby against Allie Jones and persons on her property in her first year as the local Head Start committee chairwoman.

7. Houston Nelson, "Statement," 22 September 1966, SCR-ID 2-100-0-70-1-1-1; Mamie McFarland, "Statement," 19 September 1966, and Lester McFarland, 19 September 1966, SCR-ID 2-100-0-54-1-1-1 and 2-100-0-54-2-1-1; Cole, investigator report, 20 September 1966, 4; Mamie Heard, "Statement," SCR-ID 2-100-0-55-1-1-1 and SSC 2-100-0-55-2-1-1, all items in MSSC.

8. Cole, investigator report, 20 September 1966, 4–7.

9. Ibid., 2, 5, 7.

10. Falk, "Shubuta after August Marches: Black-Out, Pressure, and Fear," *Southern Courier*, 1–2 October 1966, 2; Cole, investigator report, 23 September 1966, 2, SCR ID 2-100-0-69-2-1-1, MSSC.

11. Ruth Heard, "Shubuta Centers," 29 September 1966, F291—Shubuta and Quitman, reel 5, CDGM; L. E. Cole, investigator report, 23 September 1966, 1, MSSC.

12. Shirley Scheibla, "Head Start for What? The Story of the Child Development Group of Mississippi," *Barron's National Business and Financial Weekly*, 26 September 1966, 5, 20–1. Scheibla later included the Shubuta anecdote and allegations in her 1968 book *Poverty Is Where the Money Is.*

13. Congress, House, 89th Cong., 2nd sess., *Congressional Record* 122 (27 September 1966): 23122; "Thinks Stennis Will Stage Fight," Baltimore *Afro-American*, 1 October 1966, 16.

14. Gail Falk, "OEO Decides: No Money for CDGM," *Southern Courier*, 8–9 October 1966, 2; D. C. Carter, *Music Has Gone out of the Movement*, 121–4.

15. Patricia James, "People Speak at CDGM Meeting," *Southern Courier*, 20–1 August 1966, 1; Peter D. Mickelson to Bob Moore, 19 September 1966, folder "CDGM—Gen. Corr.—Folder 2 of 5," box 17, subject files, 1965–9, CAP Office, Office of the Director, OEO.

16. Untitled flier, 3 October 1966, folder "CDGM—Gen. Corr.—Folder 5 of 5," box 17, subject files, 1965–9, CAP Office, Office of the Director, OEO; Gail Falk to "Family," 8 October 1966, correspondence in author's possession.

17. "Cutoff of 'Obnoxious Group' Draws Cheers of Governor," Memphis *Commercial Appeal*, 11 October 1966, 1.

18. Falk, "OEO Decides," 2.

19. Greenberg, *The Devil Has Slippery Shoes*, 633–4.

20. James B. McCartney and Peter D. Mickelson to Sargent Shriver, 28 September 1966, folder "CDGM—Gen. Corr.—Folder 2 of 5," box 17, subject files, 1965–9, CAP Office, Office of the Director, OEO; Owen Brooks, "Statement," n.d., segment 71, reel 3, LCFDP. Citizens' Council membership and activity was on the wane by the mid-1960s in Mississippi—its state of origin—where an estimated 80,000 had joined the organization at its height in the late 1950s. See Crespino, *In Search of Another Country*, 38.

21. Falk to "Family."

22. Gail Falk, "A Center for St. Mary," *Southern Courier*, 13–4 August 1966, 4; Greenberg, *The Devil Has Slippery Shoes*, 632.

23. Citizens' Board of Inquiry, "Final Report on the Child Development Group of Mississippi," 20, folder "CDGM—Citizens' Crusade against Poverty," box 17, subject files, 1965–9, CAP Office, Office of the Director, OEO; Falk, "OEO Decides," 2.

24. William Chapman, "Miss. Poverty War Rages On," *Washington Post*, 10 July 1967, A1; Patricia M. Derian, weekly report, 29 November–3 December 1966, 5–7, folder 3, box 1, PDP.

25. Lynn Kirk to Jule Sugarman, 1 December 1966, folder "CDGM—Gen. Corr.—Folder 5 of 5," box 17, subject files, 1965–9, CAP Office, Office of the Director, OEO.

26. Greenberg, *The Devil Has Slippery Shoes*, 626, 630, 632.

27. Derian, weekly report, 29 November–3 December, 5–7.

28. Patricia M. Derian, report for 5–6 December 1966, 1–2, folder 3, box 1, PDP; Gail Falk, "Head Start in Mississippi: 'New People Are Running Things Now,'" *Southern Courier*, 18–9 February 1967, 4; Greenberg, *The Devil Has Slippery Shoes*, 627–8.

29. Gail Falk, "People in Quitman Say They Don't Want MAP," *Southern Courier*, 17–8 December 1966, 6; Derian, report for 5–6 December, 2.

30. Secelia Etheredge, typescript—dictated phone report, 13 January 1967, folder 4, box 1, PDP.

31. Greenberg, *The Devil Has Slippery Shoes*, 631–2.

32. Chester Higgins, "Headstart Agency Takes Toys from Miss. Kids," *Jet*, 2 February 1967, 19–26; Chapman, "Miss. Poverty War Rages On," A3.

33. Yahya Ibn Shabazz (John Otis Sumrall), telephone interview with author, 8 February 2009.

34. Cole, investigator report, 20 September 1966, 5.

35. Ibid., 5; A. L. Hopkins, investigator report, 21 October 1966, 1–3, SCR-ID 2-100-0-71-1-1-1 through 2-100-0-71-3-1-1, MSSC; "Suit Demands Negroes Be Put on Draft Boards," *New York Times*, 16 November 1966, 2; Barbara Ann Flowers and Mertis Rubin, "CR Workers Defy Draft in Jackson, Montgomery," *Southern Courier*, 13–4 May 1967, 1; "Mississippi Suit Attacks Draft Bias," *Southern Patriot* 25 (January 1967): 8; D. C. Carter, *Music Has Gone out of the Movement*, 137.

36. "Mississippi Suit Attacks Draft Bias," 8.

37. "McComb Soldier's Death in Vietnam Sparks Protest," *Mississippi Freedom Democratic Party Newsletter*, no. 6, 28 July 1965, 3–4, segment 17, reel 1, LCFDP; Phillips, *War! What Is It Good For?*, 242; Dittmer, *Local People*, 365–6; Lucks, *Selma to Saigon*, 98–9. On grassroots protest in McComb, see Payne, *I've Got the Light of Freedom*, 103–31.

38. Warner Buxton, MFDP chapter 51, typed transcript, 8, folder 150, box 6, KZSU; Patricia James, "Views on Viet Nam War," *Southern Courier*, 28–9 January 1967, 2; James, "People Speak at CDGM Meeting," 1.

39. Gail Falk, "Pickets, Praise Greet McNamara in Jackson," *Southern Courier*, 4–5 March 1967, 6; Killingsworth and fellow demonstrators depicted in photograph, SCR-ID 99-185-0-5-1-1-1ph, MSSC.

40. Shabazz (Sumrall) interview, 8 February 2009; Paul Lauter, Richard Flacks, and Florence Howe, "The Draft: Reform or Resistance?," *Liberation* 11 (January 1967): 34.

41. James Bevel, "A Movement to End Mass Murder," 2, in "We Won't Go: A Conference on Draft Resistance," typescript of compiled speeches, n.d., folder "Involvement w/Conference," box 1, ASL.

42. "John Otis Sumrall: 'We Won't Go Conference,'" 4 December 1966, 2, folder "Lynds: Alice: Book, We Won't Go," box 13, ASL; Lauter, Flacks, and Howe, "The Draft," 34.

43. "John Otis Sumrall: 'We Won't Go Conference,'" 4–5. Black servicemen confirmed the widespread practice of segregated bars, brothels, and clubs in Vietnam. See Phillips, *War! What Is It Good For?*, 221–2.

44. Arnold Rosenweig, "Rights Leaders Rap SNCC Narcotics Raid as Bogus," *Chicago Daily Defender*, 5 December 1966, 1, 3, 8; "SNCC Aide Released on Bail," *Chicago Daily Defender*, 6 December 1966, 1, 3; "We Won't Go Conference," 4 December 1966, audiorecording, reel 4, ASL.

45. "John Otis Sumrall: 'We Won't Go Conference,'" 6–7.

46. John Otis Sumrall to Alice Lynd, 14 October 1967, folder "Lynds: Alice: Book, We Won't Go," box 13, ASL.

47. John Sumrall and Sears Buckley, Jr., "Two Week Report on Smith County CDGM Program," 27 March–8 April 1967; John Sumrall and Sears Buckley, Jr., "Report on Smith County CDGM Program," 14 March 1967; John Sumrall and Sears Buckley, Jr., to Margree Miller, "Work in Smith County," n.d. [February 1967]; John Sumrall and Sears Buckley, Jr., "Report on Smith County CDGM Program," 4 March 1967; all in reel 15, Community Program, Papers of Marvin Hoffman, CDGM.

48. John Sumrall press conference footage, 10 May 1967, items 3435–8, reel F2484, WLBT.

49. "Negro Says He Won't Take 'Step,'" Jackson *Clarion-Ledger*, 9 May 1967, n.p., clipping in SCR-ID 2-100-0-58-1-1-1, MSSC; press release, 24 May 1967, folder 95, box 17, series 16, GVM.

50. William Vaughn, "Parents, 10 Children Know Poverty: When Family Is Hungry: 'We Watch Television,'" *Norfolk Journal and Guide*, 15 July 1967, 7.

51. Ibid.

52. Higgins, "Headstart Agency Takes Toys," 28.

53. Chapman, "Miss. Poverty War Rages On," A3; US Senate, *Hunger and Malnutrition in America*, 41; Falk, "Head Start in Mississippi," 4; Higgins, "Headstart Agency Takes Toys," 26.

54. US Senate, *Examining the War on Poverty*, 582–4.

55. Ibid., 655; Dittmer, *Local People*, 382–3; Joseph A. Loftus, "Johnson Asked to Rush Food Aid," *New York Times*, 30 April 1967, 51.

56. Wheeler et al., *Hungry Children*, 1–3, 5–6.

57. "MD Finds Children Starving," *Charlotte Observer*, 16 June 1967, 1A; Nan Robertson, "Severe Hunger Found in Mississippi," *New York Times*, 17 June 1967, 14; "Shame!, Shame!, Shame!" Baltimore *Afro-American*, 1 July 1967, 4. Laurie B. Green has argued that "the crusade against hunger and malnutrition" represented a "deepening and broadening" of the southern freedom struggle in the wake of the Civil Rights Act of 1964 and Voting Rights Act of 1965. See Green, "Saving Babies in Memphis," 135.

58. Dittmer, *Local People*, 384; A. L. Gray to John C. Stennis, 18 October 1967, folder 9, box 113, series 32, JCS; Kenneth Sooker to SAC [special agent in charge] Jackson, 15 July 1967, file 157–6512, FBI; US Senate, *Hunger and Malnutrition in America*, 219–33, 241.

59. Cliff Langford, "$500 Reward," *Bolivar Commercial*, 13 July 1967, n.p., clipping in SCR-ID 99-85-0-88-1-1-1, MSSC; Mississippi Republican Party, *Genocide…Are They Deliberately Starving Negroes in Mississippi?* (Jackson, 1967); Clarke Reed, memo to "Key Leaders and Regular Contributors," 15 August 1967; both in box F-7, series V, MSGOP; Stennis, "A Bill to Authorize the Secretary of Agriculture and the Surgeon General…," 1, folder 10; Stennis to H. L. Broun, 30 August 1967, folder 9; both in box 113, series 32, JCS.

60. Freedom Information Service, "Davis Backs Down—Sumrall Firm," *Mississippi Newsletter*, 7 July 1967, 2; Mertis Rubin, "Sumrall Gets 5 Years on U.S. Draft Charge," *Southern Courier*, 22–3 July 1967, 1; Freedom Information Service, "Sumrall," *Mississippi Newsletter*, 21 July 1967, 1.

61. Rubin, "Sumrall Gets 5 Years," 1; Freedom Information Service, "Davis Backs Down," 1.

62. Freedom Information Service, "Bus Lines Shut Down by Boycott," *Mississippi Newsletter*, 21 July 1967, 1; Boyett, *Right to Revolt*, 170–1; Mertis Rubin, "Old Demands, New Protest," *Southern Courier*, 22–3 July 1967, 5; Gail Falk, "Judge Permits March—about a Year Later," *Southern Courier*, 8–9 July 1967, 1.

63. Falk, "Judge Permits March," 1; A. L. Hopkins, investigative report, 31 July 1967, 1–2, SCR-ID 2-100-0-72-1-1-1 and 2-100-0-72-2-1-1, MSSC.

64. Chapman, "Miss. Poverty War Rages On," A1; Jimana Sumrall, "To the Editor," *Southern Courier*, 9–10 September 1967, 2.

65. Shabazz (Sumrall) interview, 8 February 2009; John Otis Sumrall to Alice Lynd, 14 October 1967; John Otis Sumrall to Alice Lynd, handwritten post-card, n.d.; both in folder "Lynds: Alice: Book, We Won't Go," box 13, ASL.

66. John C. Diamante, "996 Youths Turn in Draft Cards at Protest Rally in Washington," *Southern Courier*, 4–5 November 1967, 4.

67. Carl Bernstein, "Hershey Is Burned in Effigy," *Washington Post*, 20 April 1967, A1; Roy Wilkins, "Negro Youth Must Find Something Better Than…," *Los Angeles Times*, 15 May 1967, A5; Biondi, *Black Revolution on Campus*, 35–6.

68. "Curfew Imposed by Governor in Orangeburg, S.C.," *New York Times*, 10 February 1968, 23; Biondi, *Black Revolution on Campus*, 32–3; Cram and Richardson, *Scarred Justice*.

69. Dittmer, *Local People*, 413–4.

70. Spofford, *Lynch Street*, 35; *The Jacksonian*, n.p.

71. Spofford, *Lynch Street*, 30–1, 38; Rogers, *Black Campus Movement*, 101–3.

72. Jon Nordheimer, "Thousands in Mississippi Mourn Student Who Was Slain in Jackson," *New York Times*, 23 May 1970, 1; "Students Tell Congressional Delegation Police Only Shooters," *Tupelo Daily Journal*, 21 May 1970, n.p., clipping in GGM.

73. Testimony of Warner Buxton, Jackson, Mississippi, 12–3 August 1970, 513–4, part 1, reel 25, PCCU; Spofford, *Lynch Street*, 153.
74. "Goals and Objectives," typescript, 1–7, GGM.
75. Warner Buxton, "Jackson State College: Community or Genocide?," GGM.
76. "Buxton Attends Fund Raiser," *Blue and White Flash* 32 (October 1970): 1, 4; "Kent State and Jackson State Students Speak at YLS Midyear Meeting," *Law Notes for the Young Lawyer* 7.3 (1971), 1; testimony of Buxton, 508–10, 512–3; Dallek, *Flawed Giant*, 413–5; D. C. Carter, *Music Has Gone out of the Movement*, 165–234.
77. Testimony of Buxton, 515–6, 525–6, 519.
78. Ibid., 529, 525, 519; "Anarchy Must Be Stopped," *Jackson Daily News*, n.d., n.p., clipping in GGM.
79. "What J-State Students Think about Conditions," *Mississippi Press Forum*, May–June 1970, 3; "The State's Poverty-Systematic," *Mississippi Press Forum*, May–June 1970, 6.

EPILOGUE

1. Caroline Buxton Thomas, handwritten statement, n.d., in author's possession.
2. Population and economic characteristics available at factfinder.census.gov; accessed 31 October 2015.
3. *Friends of Children of Mississippi*, 6 April 1968, n.p., folder 6, box 4, CDGM-NY.
4. Untitled booklet (n.p., n.d.), folder 4, box 4; Friends of Children of Mississippi, grant proposal (pt. 2), 1971, n.p., folder 5, box 5; *Friends of Children of Mississippi*, 6 April 1968, n.p., folder 6, box 4; all in CDGM-NY.
5. "Report to County Staff of the Friends of Children of Mississippi Headstart Program on Black Awareness," 2–3 December 1968, 41, folder 6, box 4, CDGM-NY.
6. Robin D. G. Kelley has conceptualized "freedom dreams" as a broad set of hopeful "visions fashioned mainly by…marginalized black activists" informed by international events, radical politics, and questions of sexuality, oppression, and violence. Over three generations, African Americans in Clarke County reflected this broader conception of "freedom." See Kelley, *Freedom Dreams*, xii. Hasan Kwame Jeffries contends that the struggle for "freedom rights" in the rural Deep South reflected a broader conceptualization of civil and human rights that extended beyond electoral politics and institutional access. See Jeffries, *Bloody Lowndes*, 4. The term has had an immediate impact on the field, as evidenced by the title of Danielle L. McGuire and John Dittmer's recent collection of emerging civil rights scholarship—*Freedom Rights*.
7. "Cutters Organize in Mississippi," *Gulfcoast Pulpwood News*, March–April 1971, 1, 3; Edgar C. Fortenberry to W. Webb Burke, "Gulfcoast Pulpwood Association, and Southern Conference Education Fund, Inc.," 5 January 1972, 1–3, SCR-ID

10-96-0-13-1-1-1 through 10-96-0-13-3-1-1, MSSC; Wayne Greenhaw, "Big Profits and Little Pay in South's Backwoods: Woodcutters Organize (Part II)," *Southern Changes* 3:2 (1981): 16; Wayne Greenhaw, "Woodcutters Organize: Echoes of Change in the South's Backwoods," *Southern Changes* 3:1 (1980): 16.

8. Walton, *Shubuta*, 48. For a sampling of the literature and local histories that the town has inspired, see Howell, *Have You Been to Shubuta?*; Mason, *Shubuta*; G. Yates, *Life and Death in a Small Southern Town*.

9. Weems, *My Shubuta*, 6.

10. Ibid., 95.

11. "The Shubuta (Miss.) Monument," *Confederate Veteran* 18 (February 1910): 66.

12. Loewen and Sallis, *Mississippi: Conflict and Change*; Johnson, "Guardians of Historical Knowledge," 244, 274.

13. Loewen, *Teaching What Really Happened*, 5–6.

14. Nash and Taggart, *Mississippi Politics*, 280–1; Bolton, *William F. Winter*, 260–7.

15. Leib and Webster, "Black, White or Green," 317–9.

16. Cram and Richardson, *Scarred Justice*.

17. Kim Severson, "Weighing Race and Hate in a Mississippi Killing," *New York Times*, 22 August 2011, A1; Michael Deibert, "What James Craig Anderson's Murder Means to America," *Huffington Post*, 9 August 2011, http://www.huffingtonpost.com/michael-deibert/what-james-craig-anderson_1_b_922733.html, accessed 31 October 2015.

18. Scott Bronstein and Drew Griffin, "Teen Murderer Carried 'Backpack of Hatred,'" *CNN.com*, 24 October 2011, http://www.cnn.com/2011/10/22/us/mississippi-hate-crime-teens/, accessed 31 October 2015; Lacey McLaughlin, "Divided We Fall: The Killing of James Craig Anderson," *Jackson Free Press*, 5 October 2011, http://www.jacksonfreepress.com/news/2011/oct/05/divided-we-fall-the-killing-of-james-craig/, accessed 31 October 2015.

19. Kim Severson, "White Teenager Who Drove Over and Killed a Black Man Is Sentenced to Life," *New York Times*, 22 March 2012, A15; "A Mississippi Negro Shot: Mob Kills Him for Attacking a White Farmer's Daughter," *New York Times*, 27 July 1899, 3; Dittmer, *Local People*, 6; Balmer, *Mine Eyes Have Seen the Glory*, 182–3. For recent work on racial violence and community memory, see Ifill, *On the Courthouse Lawn*; Armstrong, *Mary Turner*.

20. Walter Atkins, "Shubuta Bridge's Toll Stands at Six Lynch Victims, but Span Is Doomed," *Chicago Defender*, 7 November 1942, 1; Enoc P. Waters, "Two Lynched Boys Were Ace Scrap Iron Collectors in Mississippi Town," *Chicago Defender*, 6 March 1943, 13.

21. Waters, "Two Lynched Boys Were Ace Scrap Iron Collectors," 13.

BIBLIOGRAPHY

MANUSCRIPT COLLECTIONS

CHAPEL HILL, NC

Southern Historical Collection, Louis Round Wilson Library, University of
North Carolina
CIC   Commission on Interracial Cooperation Papers
HWO   Howard Washington Odum Papers

COLLEGE PARK, MD

National Archives and Records Administration
AER   World War II Army Enlistment Records
DOJ   Records of the Department of Justice
FBI   Records of the Federal Bureau of Investigation
OEO   Records of the Community Services Administration

HATTIESBURG, MS

McCain Library and Archives, University of Southern Mississippi
CAM   Charles A. Marx Papers
PBJ   Paul B. Johnson Papers
TGB   Theodore G. Bilbo Papers

JACKSON, MS

H. T. Sampson Library, Jackson State University
GGM   Phillip Gibbs and James Green Memorial Collection

Mississippi Department of Archives and History
HPD   Historic Preservation Division
MDOC   Department of Corrections—Penitentiary Records
MDED   Department of Education Records
MSSC   Mississippi State Sovereignty Commission Records
WLBT   WLBT Newsfilm Collection
WPA   Historical Records Survey, Works Progress Administration
             Records

Tougaloo College Archives
CRDP   Civil Rights Documentation Project

MADISON, WI

Wisconsin Historical Society
CORE   Congress of Racial Equality Papers
MFDP   Mississippi Freedom Democratic Party Papers
RHM   R. Hunter Morey Papers
SEDF   Scholarship, Education and Defense Fund for Racial Equality
             Records

MONTGOMERY, ALABAMA

Alabama Department of Archives and History
MCD   Mobile City Directories

NEW ORLEANS, LA

Amistad Research Center, Tulane University
CDGM   Child Development Group of Mississippi Papers
LCFDP   FDP—Lauderdale County (MS) Records

NEW YORK, NY

Schomburg Center for Research in Black Culture
CDGM-NY   Child Development Group of Mississippi Collection

PALO ALTO, CA

University Archives, Stanford University
KZSU   KZSU Project South Interviews

QUITMAN, MS
Clarke County Courthouse
CCCH   Land Roll Records

STARKVILLE, MS
Congressional and Political Research Center, Mitchell Memorial Library, Mississippi State University
GVM   G. V. "Sonny" Montgomery Papers
JCS   John C. Stennis Collection
Special Collections, Mitchell Memorial Library, Mississippi State University
MSGOP   Mississippi Republican Party Records
PDP   Patricia Derian Papers

SWARTHMORE, PA
Swarthmore College Peace Collection
ASL   Alice Nyles Lynd and Staughton Lynd Papers

WASHINGTON, DC
Library of Congress
NAACP   National Association for the Advancement of Colored People Papers
NUL   Records of the National Urban League

SELECTED MANUSCRIPTS ON MICROFILM
APR   A. Philip Randolph Papers
LCCR   Lawyers' Committee for Civil Rights under the Law, Southern Civil Rights Litigation Records for the 1960s, Collection on Legal Change
PCCU   Records of the President's Commission on Campus Unrest
SNCC   Student Nonviolent Coordinating Committee Papers
TNCF   Tuskegee News Clippings File
WWI-SS   World War I Selective Service System Draft Registration Cards

SELECTED PERIODICALS

Afro-American [Baltimore]
American Missionary
Amsterdam Star-News [Harlem, NY]

Atlanta Daily World
Baltimore Daily Herald
Biloxi [MS] *Herald*
Bolivar Commercial [Cleveland, MS]
Brooklyn Daily Eagle
Charlotte Observer
Chicago Defender
Chicago Tribune
Christian Science Monitor
Clarion-Ledger [Jackson, MS]
Clarke County Times [Enterprise, MS]
Clarke County Tribune [Quitman, MS]
Cleveland Gazette
Commercial Appeal [Memphis, TN]
Confederate Veteran
Crisis
Daily Picayune [New Orleans]
Daily Times-Leader [West Point, MS]
Daily Worker
Foundry
Gulfcoast Pulpwood News
Gulfport [MS] *Daily Herald*
Hattiesburg [MS] *American*
Hinds County Gazette [Raymond, MS]
Houston Informer
Houston Post
Issue [Jackson, MS]
Jackson Advocate
Jackson Daily News
Jackson Free Press
Jet
Laurel [MS] *Leader-Call*
Liberation
Los Angeles Times
Lumber Trade Journal
Lumber World
Macon [MS] *Beacon*

Meridian [MS] *Star*
Mississippi Free Press
Mississippi Messenger [Shubuta, MS]
Mississippi Newsletter
Mississippi Press Forum
New Mississippian [Jackson, MS]
New Orleans Item
New Republic
New York Call
New York News
New York Times
Norfolk Journal and Guide
People's Voice [Harlem, NY]
Philadelphia Tribune
Pittsburgh Courier
PM
San Francisco Chronicle
Southern Changes
Southern Courier
Southern Patriot
Southwestern Christian Advocate [New Orleans]
St. Louis Argus
St. Louis Globe-Democrat
St. Louis Post-Dispatch
Threshermen's Review
Time
Tupelo Daily Journal
Vardaman's Weekly [Jackson, MS]
Washington Herald
Washington Post
Washington Times
Weekly Echo [Meridian, MS]

GOVERNMENT DOCUMENTS

Joint Legislative Committee. Louisiana State Legislature. *Subversion in Racial Unrest: An Outline of a Strategic Weapon to Destroy the Governments of*

Louisiana and the United States. Baton Rouge: Louisiana State Legislature, 1957.

United States. Bureau of Refugees, Freedmen, and Abandoned Lands. *Eighth Semi-Annual Report on Schools for Freedmen.* Washington, DC: Government Printing Office, 1869.

United States. Congress. House. Committee on Un-American Activities. *The Present-Day Ku Klux Klan Movement.* Washington, DC: Government Printing Office, 1967.

United States. Congress. House. Committee on Rivers and Harbors. *Chickasahay River [sic], Miss.* Washington, DC: Government Printing Office, 1916.

United States. Congress. Senate. Subcommittee on Employment, Manpower, and Poverty. *Examining the War on Poverty.* Hearing. 10 April 1967. 90th Cong. 1st sess. Washington, DC: Government Printing Office, 1967.

United States. Congress. Senate. Subcommittee on Employment, Manpower, and Poverty. *Hunger and Malnutrition in America.* Hearing. 11–12 July 1967. 90th Cong. 1st sess. Washington, DC: Government Printing Office, 1967.

United States. Department of Commerce. *Fourteenth Census of the United States.* Washington, DC: Government Printing Office, 1922.

United States. Department of Commerce. *Sixteenth Census of the United States.* Washington, DC: Government Printing Office, 1943.

United States. Department of Commerce. *Thirteenth Census of the United States.* Washington, DC: Government Printing Office, 1913.

BOOKS, ARTICLES, AND PAMPHLETS

Ames, Jessie Daniel. *The Changing Character of Lynching: Review of Lynching, 1933–41.* Atlanta: Commission on Interracial Cooperation, 1942.

Anderson, Jervis. *A. Philip Randolph: A Biographical Portrait.* New York: Harcourt Brace Jovanovich, 1972.

Armstrong, Julie Buckner. *Mary Turner and the Memory of Lynching.* Athens: University of Georgia Press, 2011.

Arsenault, Raymond. *Freedom Riders: 1961 and the Struggle for Racial Justice.* New York: Oxford University Press, 2006.

Ashmore, Susan Youngblood. *Carry It On: The War on Poverty and the Civil Rights Movement in Alabama, 1964–1972.* Athens: University of Georgia Press, 2008.

Avery, Sheldon. *Up from Washington: William Pickens and the Negro Struggle for Equality, 1900–1954.* Plainsboro, NJ: Associated University Presses, 1989.

Bailey, Amy Kate, and Stewart E. Tolnay. *Lynched: The Victims of Southern Mob Violence.* Chapel Hill: University of North Carolina Press, 2015.

Baker, T. Lindsay, and Julie P. Baker, eds. *The WPA Oklahoma Slave Narratives.* Norman: University of Oklahoma Press, 1996.

Balmer, Randall. *Mine Eyes Have Seen the Glory: A Journey into the Evangelical Subculture in America,* 4th ed. New York: Oxford University Press, 2006.

Bates, Beth Tompkins. *Pullman Porters and the Rise of Protest Politics in Black America, 1925–1945.* Chapel Hill: University of North Carolina Press, 2001.

Bay, Mia. *To Tell the Truth Freely: The Life of Ida B. Wells.* New York: Hill and Wang, 2010.

Berg, Manfred. *Popular Justice: A History of Lynching in America.* Lanham, MD: Ivan R. Dee, 2011.

Biondi, Martha. *The Black Revolution on Campus.* Berkeley: University of California Press, 2012.

Biondi, Martha. *To Stand and Fight: The Struggle for Civil Rights in Postwar New York City.* Cambridge, MA: Harvard University Press, 2003.

Bolton, Charles. *The Hardest Deal of All: The Battle over School Integration in Mississippi, 1870–1980.* Jackson: University Press of Mississippi, 2005.

Bolton, Charles. *William F. Winter and the New Mississippi: A Biography.* Jackson: University Press of Mississippi, 2013.

Boyett, Patricia Michelle. *Right to Revolt: The Crusade for Racial Justice in Mississippi's Central Piney Woods.* Jackson: University Press of Mississippi, 2015.

Branch, Taylor. *At Canaan's Edge: America in the King Years, 1965–1968.* New York: Simon and Schuster, 2006.

Brundage, W. Fitzhugh. "Conclusion: Reflections on Lynching Scholarship." *American Nineteenth Century History* 6.3 (2005): 401–14.

Brundage, W. Fitzhugh. "The Roar on the Other Side of Silence: Black Resistance and White Violence in the American South, 1880–1940." In *Under Sentence of Death: Lynching in the South,* edited by W. Fitzhugh Brundage, 271–91. Chapel Hill: University of North Carolina Press, 1997.

Buhite, Russell D., and David W. Levy, eds. *FDR's Fireside Chats*. Norman: University of Oklahoma Press, 1992.

Burran, James Albert, III. "Racial Violence in the South during World War II." PhD diss., University of Tennessee, 1977.

Capeci, Jr., Dominic J. *The Lynching of Cleo Wright*. Lexington: University of Kentucky Press, 1998.

Carrigan, William D. "'No Ordinary Crime': Reflections on the Future of the History of Mob Violence." *Journal of American History* 101 (December 2014): 847–9.

Carroll, Peter. *The Odyssey of the Abraham Lincoln Brigade: Americans in the Spanish Civil War*. Palo Alto, CA: Stanford University Press, 1994.

Carroll, Peter, Michael Nash, and Melvin Small, eds. *The Good Fight Continues: World War II Letters from the Abraham Lincoln Brigade*. New York: New York University Press, 2006.

Carter, Dan T. *Scottsboro: A Tragedy of the American South*. Baton Rouge: Louisiana State University Press, 1969.

Carter, David C. *The Music Has Gone out of the Movement: Civil Rights and the Johnson Administration, 1965–1968*. Chapel Hill: University of North Carolina Press, 2009.

Chadbourn, James Marmon. *Lynching and the Law*. Chapel Hill: University of North Carolina Press, 1933.

Cobb, Charles. *This Nonviolent Stuff'll Get You Killed: How Guns Made the Civil Rights Movement Possible*. New York: Basic, 2014.

Cram, Bestor, and Judy Richardson, dirs. *Scarred Justice: The Orangeburg Massacre, 1968*. Independent Television Service / National Black Programming Consortium, 2010.

Crespino, Joseph. *In Search of Another Country: Mississippi and the Conservative Counterrevolution*. Princeton, NJ: Princeton University Press, 2007.

Cresswell, Stephen. *Rednecks, Redeemers, and Race: Mississippi after Reconstruction, 1877–1917*. Jackson: University Press of Mississippi, 2006.

Crosby, Emilye. *A Little Taste of Freedom: The Black Freedom Struggle in Claiborne County, Mississippi*. Chapel Hill: University of North Carolina Press, 2001.

Cunningham, David. "Shades of Civil Rights Violence: Reconsidering the Ku Klux Klan in Mississippi." In *The Civil Rights Movement in Mississippi*, edited by Ted Ownby, 180–203. Jackson: University Press of Mississippi, 2013.

Dailey, Jane. "The Sexual Politics of Race in World War II America." In *Fog of War: The Second World War and the Civil Rights Movement*, edited by Kevin M. Kruse and Stephen G. N. Tuck, 145–70. New York: Oxford University Press, 2012.

Dallek, Robert. *Flawed Giant: Lyndon Johnson and His Times, 1961–1973*. New York: Oxford University Press, 1998.

Daniel, Pete. "Going among Strangers: Southern Reactions to World War II." *Journal of American History* 77 (December 1990): 886–911.

Danielson, Chris. *After Freedom Summer: How Race Realigned Mississippi Politics*. Gainesville: University Press of Florida, 2011.

Dittmer, John. *Local People: The Struggle for Civil Rights in Mississippi*. Urbana: University of Illinois Press, 1994.

Dray, Phillip. *At the Hands of Persons Unknown: The Lynching of Black America*. New York: Random House, 2002.

Du Bois, W. E. B. *Dusk of Dawn: An Essay toward an Autobiography of a Race Concept*. New York: Harcourt, 1940.

Dunbar, Anthony P. *Against the Grain: Southern Radicals and Prophets, 1929–1959*. Charlottesville: University of Virginia Press, 1981.

Dupont, Carolyn Renee. *Mississippi Praying: Southern White Evangelicals and the Civil Rights Movement*. New York: New York University Press, 2013.

Dyja, Thomas. *Walter White: The Dilemma of Black Identity in America*. Lanham, MD: Ivan R. Dee, 2008.

Egerton, John. *Speak Now against the Day: The Generation before the Civil Rights Movement in the South*. Chapel Hill: University of North Carolina, 1995.

Ellis, Mark. *Race, War, and Surveillance: African Americans and the United States Government during World War I*. Bloomington: Indiana University Press, 1993.

Feimster, Crystal. *Southern Horrors: Women and the Politics of Rape and Lynching*. Cambridge, MA: Harvard University Press, 2009.

Feldman, Glenn. "Southern Disillusionment with the Democratic Party: Cultural Conformity and 'the Great Melding' of Racial and Economic Conservatism in Alabama during World War II." *Journal of American Studies* 43.2 (2009): 199–230.

Finley, Keith M. *Delaying the Dream: Southern Senators and the Fight against Civil Rights, 1938–1965*. Baton Rouge: Louisiana State University Press, 2008.

Finnegan, Terence. *A Deed So Accursed: Lynching in Mississippi and South Carolina, 1881–1940.* Charlottesville: University of Virginia Press, 2013.

Fitzgerald, Michael W. *The Union League Movement in the Deep South: Politics and Agricultural Change during Reconstruction.* Baton Rouge: Louisiana State University Press, 1989.

Frederickson, Kari. *The Dixiecrat Revolt and the End of the Solid South, 1932–1968.* Chapel Hill: University of North Carolina Press, 2001.

Garfinkel, Harold. *When Negroes March: The March on Washington Movement in the Organizational Politics for FEPC,* rev. ed. New York: Antheneum, 1969.

Gellman, Erik S. *Death Blow to Jim Crow: The National Negro Congress and the Rise of Militant Civil Rights.* Chapel Hill: University of North Carolina Press, 2012.

Giddings, Paula J. *A Sword among Lions: Ida B. Wells and the Campaign against Lynching.* New York: HarperCollins, 2008.

Gilmore, Glenda Elizabeth. *Defying Dixie: The Radical Roots of Civil Rights, 1919–1950.* New York: Norton, 2008.

Goodman, James. *Stories of Scottsboro.* New York: Random House, 1995.

Goudsouzian, Aram. *Down to the Crossroads: Civil Rights, Black Power, and the Meredith March against Fear.* New York: Farrar, Straus, and Giroux, 2014.

Green, Laurie B. "Saving Babies in Memphis: The Politics of Race, Hunger, and Health during the War on Poverty." In *The War on Poverty: A New Grassroots History, 1964–1980,* edited by Annelise Orleck and Lisa Gayle Hazirjian, 133–58. Athens: University of Georgia Press, 2011.

Greenberg, Polly. *The Devil Has Slippery Shoes: A Biased Biography of the Child Development Group of Mississippi.* Washington, DC: Youth Policy Institute, 1990.

Grossman, James R. *Land of Hope: Chicago, Black Southerners, and the Great Migration.* Chicago: University of Chicago Press, 1989.

Hahn, Steven. *A Nation under Our Feet: Black Political Struggles in the Rural South from Slavery to the Great Migration.* Cambridge, MA: Belknap Press of Harvard University Press, 2003.

Hall, Jacquelyn Dowd. *Revolt against Chivalry: Jessie Daniel Ames and the Women's Campaign against Lynching.* New York: Columbia University Press, 1979.

Hamilton, Charles V. *Adam Clayton Power, Jr.: The Political Biography of an American Dilemma*. New York: Simon and Schuster, 1991.

Hamlin, Françoise. *Crossroads at Clarksdale: The Black Freedom Struggle in the Mississippi Delta after World War II*. Chapel Hill: University of North Carolina Press, 2012.

Hart, Albert Bushnell, ed. *Selected Addresses and Public Papers of Woodrow Wilson*. New York: Boni and Liveright, 1918.

Hill, Lance. *The Deacons for Defense: Armed Resistance and the Civil Rights Movement*. Chapel Hill: University of North Carolina Press, 2004.

Hobbs, Allyson. *A Chosen Exile: A History of Racial Passing in American Life*. Cambridge, MA: Harvard University Press, 2014.

Holmes, William F. *The White Chief: James Kimble Vardaman*. Baton Rouge: Louisiana State University Press, 1970.

Howell, Elmo. *Have You Been to Shubuta?* Memphis, TN: Langford, 1996.

Howell, Elmo. *Mississippi Back Roads: Notes on Literature and History*. N.p.: n.p., 1998.

Hughes, Langston. *The Collected Works of Langston Hughes: The Poems, 1941–1950*, vol. 2, edited by Arnold Rampersad. Columbia: University of Missouri Press, 2001.

Hughes, Langston. *Collected Poems of Langston Hughes*, edited by Arnold Rampersad. New York: Vintage, 1994.

Huie, William Bradford. *Three Lives for Mississippi*. Jackson: University Press of Mississippi, 2000.

Ifill, Sherrilyn. *On the Courthouse Lawn: Confronting the Legacy of Lynching in the Twenty-first Century*. Boston: Beacon Press, 2007.

The Jacksonian. Jackson, MS: Jackson State University, 1971.

Janken, Kenneth Robert. *Walter White, Mr. NAACP*. Chapel Hill: University of North Carolina Press, 2006.

Jeffries, Hasan Kwame. *Bloody Lowndes: Civil Rights and Black Power in Alabama's Black Belt*. New York: New York University Press, 2009.

Johnson, Kevin Boland. "Guardians of Historical Knowledge: Textbook Politics, Conservative Activism, and School Reform in Mississippi, 1928–1982." PhD diss., Mississippi State University, 2014.

Jordan, William. "'The Damnable Dilemma': African American Accomodation and Protest during World War I.," *Journal of American History* 81 (March 1995): 1562–83.

Joseph, Peniel E. *Waiting 'Til the Midnight Hour: A Narrative History of Black Power in America*. New York: Henry Holt, 2006.

Katagiri, Yasuhiro. *The Mississippi State Sovereignty Commission: Civil Rights and States' Rights*. Jackson: University Press of Mississippi, 2001.

Keith, Jeanette. *Rich Man's War, Poor Man's Fight: Race, Class, and Power in the Rural South during the First World War*. Chapel Hill: University of North Carolina Press, 2004.

Kelley, Blair L. M. *Right to Ride: Streetcar Boycotts and African American Citizenship in the Era of Plessy v. Ferguson*. Chapel Hill: University of North Carolina Press, 2010.

Kelley, Robin D. G. *Race Rebels: Culture, Politics, and the Black Working Class* New York: Free Press, 1994.

Kelley, Robin D. G. *Freedom Dreams: The Black Radical Imagination*. Boston: Beacon Press, 2002.

Kennedy, David M. *Over Here: The First World War and American Society*. New York: Oxford University Press, 1980.

Kennedy, Stetson. *Southern Exposure*. New York: Doubleday, 1946.

Kerlin, Robert Thomas, ed. *The Voice of the Negro, 1919*. New York: E. P. Dutton, 1920.

Ladner, Joyce. "What 'Black Power' Means to Negroes in Mississippi." *Trans-action* 5 (November 1967): 7–15.

Lamon, Lester C. *Black Tennesseans, 1900–1930*. Knoxville: University of Tennessee Press, 1977.

Lauterbach, Preston. *Beale Street Dynasty: Sex, Song, and the Struggle for the Soul of Memphis*. New York: W. W. Norton, 2015.

Lawson, Steven F. *Black Ballots: Voting Rights in the South, 1944–1969*. New York: Columbia University Press, 1976.

Leib, Jonathan I., and Gerald R. Webster. "Black, White or Green: The Confederate Battle Emblem and the 2001 Mississippi State Flag Referendum." *Southeastern Geographer* 52.3 (2012): 299–326.

Lemak, Jennifer A. *Southern Life, Northern City: The History of Albany's Rapp Road Community*. Albany: State University of New York Press, 2008.

Lemann, Nicholas. *The Promised Land: The Great Black Migration and How It Changed America*. New York: Vintage, 1991.

Lemann, Nicholas. *Redemption: The Last Battle of the Civil War*. New York: Farrar, Straus and Giroux, 2006.

Lentz-Smith, Adrianne. *Freedom Struggles: African Americans and World War I.* Cambridge, MA: Harvard University Press, 2009.

Lewis, David Levering. *W. E. B. Du Bois, 1868–1919: Biography of a Race.* New York: Holt, 1993.

Loewen, James W. *Teaching What Really Happened: How to Avoid the Tyranny of Textbooks and Get Students Excited about Doing History.* New York: Teachers College Press, 2009.

Loewen, James W., and Charles Sallis. *Mississippi: Conflict and Change.* New York: Pantheon, 1974.

Lucander, David. *Winning the War for Democracy: The March on Washington Movement, 1941–1946.* Urbana: University of Illinois Press, 2014.

Lucks, Daniel S. *Selma to Saigon: The Civil Rights Movement and the Vietnam War.* Lexington: University Press of Kentucky, 2014.

Lynd, Alice, ed. *We Won't Go: Personal Accounts of War Objectors.* Boston: Beacon Press, 1967.

Martin, Gordon A. *Count Them One by One: Black Mississippians Fighting for the Right to Vote.* Jackson: University Press of Mississippi, 2010.

Mason, Jerry D. *Shubuta: Home of the Red Artesian Water.* N.p.: n.p., 2002.

McGuire, Danielle L., and John Dittmer, eds. *Freedom Rights: New Perspectives on the Civil Rights Movement.* Lexington: University Press of Kentucky, 2011.

McMillen, Neil. *Dark Journey: Black Mississippians in the Age of Jim Crow.* Urbana: University of Illinois Press, 1989.

McWhirter, Cameron. *Red Summer: The Summer of 1919 and the Awakening of Black America.* New York: Henry Holt, 2011.

Miller, Eben. *Born along the Color Line: The 1933 Amenia Conference and the Rise of a National Civil Rights Movement.* New York: Oxford University Press, 2012.

Mississippi Welfare League. *Organization of the Mississippi Welfare League.* Jackson, MS: Hederman Brothers, [1919].

Mitchell, Dennis J. *A New History of Mississippi.* Jackson: University Press of Mississippi, 2014.

Moore, John Hebron. *The Emergence of the Cotton Kingdom in the Old Southwest: Mississippi, 1770–1860.* Baton Rouge: Louisiana State University Press, 1988.

Morgan, Chester M. "At the Crossroads: World War II, Delta Agriculture, and Modernization in Mississippi." *Journal of Mississippi History* 57 (Winter 1995): 353–71.

Morgan, Chester M. *Redneck Liberal: Theodore G. Bilbo and the New Deal.* Baton Rouge: Louisiana State University Press, 1985.

Nash, Jere, and Andy Taggart, eds. *Mississippi Politics: The Struggle for Power, 1976–2008*, 2nd ed. Jackson: University Press of Mississippi, 2009.

National Association for the Advancement of Colored People (NAACP). *Eleventh Annual Report.* New York: NAACP, 1921.

National Association for the Advancement of Colored People (NAACP). *Lynching Goes Underground: A Report on a New Technique.* New York: NAACP, 1940.

National Association for the Advancement of Colored People (NAACP). *M Is for Mississippi and Murder.* New York: NAACP, 1955.

National Association for the Advancement of Colored People (NAACP). *On Guard against Racial Discrimination.* New York: NAACP, 1942.

National Association for the Advancement of Colored People (NAACP). *Thirty-third Annual Report.* New York: NAACP, 1942.

National Association for the Advancement of Colored People (NAACP). *Thirty Years of Lynching in the United States, 1889–1918.* New York: NAACP, 1919.

Nelson, Bruce. "Organized Labor and the Struggle for Black Equality in Mobile during World War II." *Journal of American History* 80 (December 1993): 952–88.

Newman, Mark. *Divine Agitators: The Delta Ministry and Civil Rights in Mississippi.* Athens: University of Georgia Press, 2004.

Newton, Michael. *The Ku Klux Klan in Mississippi: A History.* Jefferson, NC: McFarland, 2010.

Ngai, Mae M. *Impossible Subjects: Illegal Aliens and the Making of Modern America.* Princeton, NJ: Princeton University Press, 2004.

Odum, Howard W. *Race and Rumors of Race: Challenge to American Crisis.* Chapel Hill: University of North Carolina Press, 1943.

Ogden, Frederic D. *The Poll Tax in the South.* Tuscaloosa: University of Alabama Press, 1958.

Orleck, Annelise. *Storming Caesar's Palace: How Black Mothers Fought Their Own War on Poverty.* Boston: Beacon Press, 2005.

Painter, Nell Irvin. *Exodusters: Black Migration to Kansas after Reconstruction.* New York: Knopf, 1977.

Parker, Frank R. *Black Votes Count: Political Empowerment in Mississippi since 1965.* Chapel Hill: University of North Carolina Press, 1990.

Patler, Nicholas. *Jim Crow and the Wilson Administration: Protesting Federal Segregation in the Early Twentieth Century.* Boulder: University of Colorado Press, 2004.

Patton, W. H. "How a Mississippi Town Was Revolutionized by Prohibition." In *The Prohibition Question: Viewed from the Economic and Moral Standpoint,* 2nd ed, 92. Baltimore: Manufacturer's Record, 1922.

Payne, Charles M. *I've Got the Light of Freedom: The Organizing Tradition and the Mississippi Freedom Struggle.* Berkeley: University of California Press, 1995.

Pfeifer, Michael J. *Rough Justice: Lynching and American Society, 1874–1947.* Urbana: University of Illinois Press, 2004.

Phillips, Kimberley L. *War! What Is It Good For? Black Freedom Struggles and the U.S. Military.* Chapel Hill: University of North Carolina Press, 2012.

Plummer, Brenda Gayle. *Rising Wind: Black Americans and U. S. Foreign Affairs, 1935–1960.* Chapel Hill: University of North Carolina Press, 1996.

Rable, George C. *But There Was No Peace: The Role of Violence in the Politics of Reconstruction.* Athens: University of Georgia Press, 1984.

Rampersad, Arnold. *The Life of Langston Hughes,* volume 2: *1914–1967, I Dream a World.* New York: Oxford University Press, 1988.

Ransby, Barbara. *Ella Baker and the Black Freedom Movement: A Radical Democratic Vision.* Chapel Hill: University of North Carolina Press, 2003.

Rice, Anne P., ed. *Witnessing Lynching: American Writers Respond.* New Brunswick, NJ: Rutgers University Press, 2003.

Rogers, Ibram H. *The Black Campus Movement: Black Students and the Racial Reconstitution of Higher Education, 1965–1972.* New York: Palgrave Macmillan, 2012.

Rolinson, Mary G. *Grassroots Garveyism: The Universal Negro Improvement Association in the Rural South, 1920–1927.* Chapel Hill: University of North Carolina Press, 2007.

Rollins, Judith, and Odette Harper Hines. *All Is Never Said: The Narrative of Odette Harper Hines.* Philadelphia: Temple University Press, 1995.

Rotnem, Victor W. "The Federal Civil Right 'Not to Be Lynched.'" *Washington University Law Quarterly* 28 (February 1943): 57–73.

Rowland, Dunbar. *Encyclopedia of Mississippi History: Comprising Sketches of Counties, Towns, Events, Institutions, and Persons*, vol. 2. Madison, WI, 1907.

Rowland, Dunbar. *Encyclopedia of Mississippi History: Comprising Sketches of Counties, Towns, Events, Institutions, and Persons*, vol. 3, *Contemporary Biography*. Atlanta, 1907.

Rowland, Dunbar. *The Official and Statistical Register of Mississippi*. Jackson: Mississippi Department of Archives and History, 1908.

Rushdy, Ashraf H. A. *The End of American Lynching*. New Brunswick, NJ: Rutgers University Press, 2012.

Sanders, Crystal. "'To Be Free of Fear': Black Women's Fight for Freedom through the Child Development Group of Mississippi." PhD diss., Northwestern University, 2011.

Scheibla, Shirley. *Poverty Is Where The Money Is*. New Rochelle, NY: Arlington House, 1968.

Scott, Emmett J. *Negro Migration during the War*. New York: Oxford University Press, 1920.

Seymour, Charles. *Woodrow Wilson and the World War: A Chronicle of Our Own Times*. New Haven, CT: Yale University Press, 1921.

Shenk, Gerald. *Work or Fight! Race, Gender, and the Draft in World War One*. New York: Palgrave Macmillan, 2005.

Sitkoff, Harvard. *A New Deal for Blacks: The Emergence of Civil Rights as a National Issue*. New York: Oxford University Press, 1978.

Smead, Howard. *Blood Justice: The Lynching of Mack Charles Parker*. New York: Oxford University Press, 1986.

Smith, Bolton. *A Philosophy of Race Relations*. Memphis: n.p., 1919.

Sparrow, James T. *Warfare State: World War II Americans and the Age of Big Government*. New York: Oxford University Press, 2011.

Spofford, Tim. *Lynch Street: The May 1970 Slayings at Jackson State College*. Kent, OH: Kent State University Press, 1988.

Stern, Gerald M. "Judge William Harold Cox and the Right to Vote in Clarke County, Mississippi." In *Southern Justice*, edited by Leon Friedman, 165–86. New York: Pantheon, 1965.

Sullivan, Patricia. *Lift Every Voice: The NAACP and the Making of the Civil Rights Movement*. New York: New Press, 2009.

Thompson, Julius E. *Lynchings in Mississippi: A History, 1865–1965*. Jefferson, NC: McFarland, 2007.

Tolnay, Stewart E., and E. M. Beck. *A Festival of Violence: An Analysis of Southern Lynchings, 1882–1930*. Urbana: University of Illinois Press, 1995.

Trotti, Michael. "What Counts: Recent Trends in Racial Violence in the Postbellum South." *Journal of American History* 100.3 (2013): 375–400.

Tuck, Stephen G. N. *We Ain't What We Ought to Be: The Black Freedom Struggle from Emancipation to Obama*. Cambridge, MA: Harvard University Press, 2010.

Tyson, Timothy B. *Radio Free Dixie: Robert F. Williams and the Roots of Black Power*. Chapel Hill: University of North Carolina Press, 1999.

Umoja, Akinyele Omowale. *We Will Shoot Back: Armed Resistance in the Mississippi Freedom Movement*. New York: New York University Press, 2013.

Vandiver, Margaret. *Lethal Punishment: Lynchings and Legal Executions in the South*. New Brunswick, NJ: Rutgers University Press, 2005.

Waldrep, Christopher. *African Americans Confront Lynching: Strategies of Resistance from the Civil War to the Civil Rights Era*. Lanham, MD: Rowman and Littlefield, 2008.

Waldrep, Christopher. *The Many Faces of Judge Lynch: Extralegal Violence and Punishment in America*. New York: Palgrave Macmillan, 2004.

Walton, Frank L. *Shubuta: A Brief Story about Shubuta on the Banks of the Chickasaway*. Shubuta, MS: Shubuta Memorial Association, 1947.

Waters, Enoch P. *American Diary: A Personal History of the Black Press*. Chicago: Path Press, 1987.

Weems, Robert C. *My Shubuta: Boyhood Recollections of a Great Small Southern Town*. Ann Arbor, MI: Sheridan, 2004.

Weiss, Nancy Joan. *Farewell to the Party of Lincoln: Black Politics in the Age of FDR*. Princeton, NJ: Princeton University Press, 1983.

Wells-Barnett, Ida B. *The Red Record: Tabulated Statistics and Alleged Causes of Lynchings in the United States, 1892–1893–1894*. Chicago: n.p., 1895.

Wells-Barnett, Ida B. *Selected Works of Ida B. Wells-Barnett*, edited by Trudier Harris. New York: Oxford University Press, 1991.

Wheeler, Raymond M., et al. *Hungry Children: Special Report*. Atlanta: Southern Regional Council, 1967.

White, Walter F. *A Man Called White: The Autobiography of Walter White*. New York: Viking, 1948.

White, Walter F. *Rope and Faggot: A Biography of Judge Lynch*. New York: Knopf, 1929.

Wilkerson, Isabel. *The Warmth of Other Suns: The Epic Story of America's Great Migration*. New York: Vintage, 2010.

Wilkins, Roy. *Standing Fast: The Autobiography of Roy Wilkins*. New York: Penguin, 1984.

Williams, Chad L. *Torchbearers of Democracy: African American Soldiers in the World War I Era*. Chapel Hill: University of North Carolina Press, 2010.

Williams, Kidada E. *They Left Great Marks on Me: African American Testimonies of Racial Violence from Emancipation to World War I*. New York: New York University Press, 2012.

Williams, Michael Vinson. *Medgar Evers: Mississippi Martyr*. Fayetteville: University of Arkansas Press, 2011.

Winner, Lauren F. "Doubtless Sincere: New Characters in the Civil Rights Cast." In *The Role of Ideas in the Civil Rights South*, edited by Ted Ownby, 157–70. Jackson: University Press of Mississippi, 2002.

Wood, Amy Louise. *Lynching and Spectacle: Witnessing Racial Violence in America, 1890–1940*. Chapel Hill: University of North Carolina Press, 2009.

Woodruff, Nan Elizabeth. *American Congo: The Black Freedom Struggle in the Delta*. Cambridge, MA: Harvard University Press, 2003.

Wright, George C. *Racial Violence in Kentucky, 1865–1940: Lynchings, Mob Rule, and "Legal Lynchings."* Baton Rouge: Louisiana State University Press, 1990.

Yarborough, Richard. "Violence, Manhood, and Black Heroism: The Wilmington Riot in Two Turn-of-the-Century African American Novels." In *Democracy Betrayed: The Wilmington Race Riot of 1898 and Its Legacy*, edited by David S. Cecelski and Timothy B. Tyson, 225–62. Chapel Hill: University of North Carolina Press, 1998.

Yates, Gayle Graham. *Life and Death in a Small Southern Town: Memories of Shubuta, Mississippi*. Baton Rouge: Louisiana State University Press, 2004.

Yates, James. *From Mississippi to Madrid: Memoir of a Black American in the Abraham Lincoln Brigade*. Greensboro, NC: Open Hand, 1989.

Yellin, Eric S. *Racism in the Nation's Service: Government Workers and the Color Line in Woodrow Wilson's America*. Chapel Hill: University of North Carolina Press, 2013.

Zangrando, Robert L. *The NAACP Crusade against Lynching, 1909–1950*. Philadelphia: Temple University Press, 1980.

INDEX

Figures and notes are indicated by f and n following the page number.